INDIAN PARLIAMENTARY DEMOCRACY

VOLUME 1

U.N. GUPTA

ATLANTIC
PUBLISHERS & DISTRIBUTORS

Published by
ATLANTIC PUBLISHERS AND DISTRIBUTORS
B-2, Vishal Enclave, Opp. Rajouri Garden, New Delhi-27
Phones : 5413460, 5429987, 5466842

Sales Office
4215/1, Ansari Road, Darya Ganj, New Delhi-02
Phones : 3273880, 3285873, 3280451
Fax : 91-11-3285873
web : www.atlanticbooks.com
e-mail : info@atlanticbooks.com

ISBN 81-269-0191-8 (Vol. I)
ISBN 81-269-0192-6 (Vol. II)
ISBN 81-269-0193-4 (Set)

Typeset at
APD Computer Graphics, Delhi
Printed in India at
Nice Printing Press, Delhi

DEDICATED TO

Those who
By their lives or valour saved
Indian democracy from terrorist
attack of 13 December 2001
on Parliament

PREFACE

A study of the parliamentary democracy under the Constitution of India of the first fifty-two years of its existence in the year 2002 is essentially a commentary on the interaction of various constitutional institutions, national politics and the maturing of political awakening of the masses. While the people are getting better educated about their political rights and are vitally controlling the choice of their representatives for Parliament, the political leaders are becoming unsteady and less and less sure of their hold over the people and politics. Latter find that politics is a costly profession and power is a slippery proposition. Often, formation of a Government is also a process set in motion for disintegration of the ruling party or a coalition itself and the running of the Government becomes much like riding a wild horse. However, there is no alternative to an elected government at the Union in India and whichever party forms the Government, the people have to endure it for its term unless it is earlier changed for losing majority in the House of People. After first fifty-two years of functioning, the republican, secular and democratic Constitution of India, contemporarily appears to be in a state of stagnation and it is constantly inviting suggestions for its remodeling, but nevertheless it appears to be functioning with a slow graded stability.

Present Book *Indian Parliamentary Democracy* defines and critically analyses the principles of Constitution which come under stress in operating the Indian parliamentary democracy, along with those default settings which keep the parliamentary democracy operational despite the political pressures, failures and chaos. For the latter, one has only to see the parliamentary proceedings on the television and/or count the days of the year when business was earnestly transacted in Parliament over the last decade. One can hesitate only a little in expressing the opinion that Indian Parliament has lost that glory with which it had started functioning in 1950. Its eroded glory is to be found in the proxy legislation by way of judicial activism, enlarged interpretation of the powers of President, judiciary and the constitutional functionaries, like, the Election Commission of India. There is also direct usurpation of powers of legislation by 'guidelines' by Supreme Court under Article 141 of the Constitution on matters requiring legislation or the supervising of the executive directly by the Judges by way of public interest litigation. Yet the supervision of the executive essentially remains or constitutes one of the functions of Parliament. Differing from the approach to the Constitution in the era of Prime Minister Nehru, it clearly appears that the Constitution is being run by every authority except Parliament for keeping democracy a real working proposition in India.

There was direct conflict between rule of law and the politics of patriotism in pre-Independence era leading to civil disobedience of sovereign power of the British rulers. After Independence the politics of patriotism was replaced by politics for reconstruction, industrialization and socio-economic uplift of the country and the people. Now, the politics and the Constitution appear to be games for wielding political power. The parameters of democratic politics are set by the auto-limitation of internal sovereignty of the government as envisaged in the Constitution of India. Initially, this politics got converted into concept of one-party rule as the only viable or good politics for the country. The Constitution was or is maintained as a highly flexible document when the ruling party had or has two-third majority in the House of People. The Constitution is quite flexible also when the issues at stake are popular politics.

The dividing line between politics and the Constitution had been thin or non-existent and during the first forty years of freedom the Constitution had been frequently amended when the politics always maintained upper hand over the Constitution and law. Accordingly, in order to have a proper grasp the efficiency of the working of Indian parliamentary democratic system, it is necessary to study the political milieu which the captains of parliamentary system, the MPs and MLAs, at any particular point of time had either generated or had to face. The constitutional values in India have been markedly dependent on aggressive welfare politics during the fifty year of freedom. A functional study of evolution and legal status of Indian political parties and their political approach to the constitutional values has been, accordingly, felt to be necessary in this Book.

There was direct conflict between rule of law and the politics of patriotism in pre-Independence era leading to civil disobedience of sovereign power of the British rulers. After Independence the politics of patriotism was replaced by politics for reconstruction, industrialization and socio-economic uplift of the country and the people. Now at the time of golden jubilee of Independence the politics and the Constitution appear to be games for wielding political power the parameters of democratic politics are set by the auto-limitation of internal sovereignty of the government as envisaged in the Constitution of India. Initially, this politics got converted into concept of one-party rule as the only viable or good politics for the country.

Parliament and the State Legislatures are the constitutional venues where the Constitution, law and politics battle or co-operate with one another to provide stable or shaky government. The results of the parliamentary democracy vary according as the ruling party concentrates on politics for its own survival, plays a power game against other political parties including personal enrichment, or else the ruling party functions for the good of the country and the people who elected it to power. The half century of the Indian parliamentary democracy is a binder of all that politics can provide, that is, the quest for social and political equality or a corrupted despotic rule existing for the satisfaction of personal ego of rulers and Ministers. The Constitution has been developed and interpreted by the ruling parties accordingly leading to frequent amendments of the Constitution which changed or attempted to change basic principles and laid stress on federal units by way of imposition of President's Rule in States. A study of these aspects has been particularly made in the Book.

In the years since 1980s, leaders of the winning parties in general elections have been very much conscious of their electoral success, particularly when the Party has obtained clear majority in the House of People. Most of the newly elected Members including Ministers now often enter the Parliament with the idea that they can make, abrogate or amend any law, and even the Constitution can be amended, according to their dictates if these happen to come in their way. Those political leaders who are deficient in education, idealism and morality intake, and such persons have often been in majority in all political parties, have found Ministership and parliamentary system an easy means of personal enrichment. The economic reforms towards graded liberalization under a licensing system since early 1990s, have given a new content and meaning to Ministership under parliamentary form of government, that is, decisions taken for amassing wealth for personal gain or enrichment of party, in preparation for next elections.

Law and Constitution have been under pressure from practical difficulty faced in organizing national level political parties with financial solvency and capacity in order to contest 545 Lok Sabha seats. The vice was not in the Party or the Finance Minister but with the Ministers, particularly after the move for liberalization since 1991, who saw vast enrichment potential of their office with kick-back money liberally provided by foreign companies and Indian business as pay-off. The resulting corruption has led to development of a secondary 'politics of defection' from parties for a rewarding political career as a Minister. A patriot, altruistic, selfless, honest, free from hunger for power and dedicated to national cause type of politician is now an endangered species on verge of extinction in India. The Constitution as a living organism has to some extent reacted to these challenges by providing, though now found imperfect, an in-built system for purity in political life and in captains who operate the constitutional system. Rather, the people have risen to the occasion and by selectively casting their votes they have made politics as an uncertain profession. Since mid-1980s, as a consequence, the office of Speakers under the Tenth Schedule of the Constitution enacted in 1985, along with the role of Election Commission, have assumed new constitutional significance. Due emphasis has been given to the above aspects and the innovated powers of Speaker in this Study.

The strength of parliamentary democracy at all times depends on the direction and control received by the Executive from the Council of Ministers representing the people in the public administration. This naturally involves the ways in which parliamentary proceedings are conducted and the Members of Parliament or the State Legislatures are able to exert pressure on the Council of Ministers. This requires a functional study, made in the Book, of the Committee system, the discussion, the question-hours in the two Houses, the information elicited from the administrative agencies for critical scrutiny and the intelligent constructive role of elected Members of the Houses during the course of the proceedings. A study of the constitutional lay-out for this process has been pursued in this Book.

The potential value of subservient politician to the business houses and to the criminals, has led to gross manipulation of elections to Parliament and State Legislatures which muddles the purity of constitutional values and the democratic process. Consistently with this retrogressive development in the Indian constitutional system, the dependence on constitutionally provided Election Commission of India for free and fair elections has increased. Fortunately, in the last twenty years the Election Commission has had a history of success and it has tamed the political parties for providing free and fair elections. A detailed study, therefore, is necessary and has been made in this work of the election process and the role of Election Commission of India for inculcating and maintaining decency in politics and society in its endeavour for free and fair elections.

My impressions of the panorama of constitutional events of the first fifty-five years of Independence since 1947 which I have witnessed as a student or teacher of law, since 1958, and particularly while discussing constitutional problems of the time and sharing the concerns of people with my LL.M. students, in Seminars or lectures given at the (U.G.C.) Academic Staff College in University of Allahabad, are contained in this work. A sociological approach to the working of the Constitution, that is relating the politicians role and social and judicial reactions while operating the Constitution, has been motivated or inspired by the studies of British Constitution made particularly by Laski or Ivor Jennings among others. After all any Constitution which endures time, social changes and follies of its captains, has to be a living piece of organism vitally influencing and in turn being influenced by the society for which it provides a social mechanism for survival, development and progress.

The Book gives an analytical glimpse of parliamentary democracy in function, its travails and achievement by the beginning of twentieth century alongwith the analysis of constitutional provisions, judicial interpretations and the developed conventions. As such it is sincerely hoped that the readers will find this Book, meant both for general intelligentsia and experts, to be much more than an anatomical study of the constitutional provisions and it will particularly attract the attention of politicians who adorn the Houses of Parliament or State Legislatures, political parties, lawyers, journalists and scholars of law, constitutional history or political science.

For the ready convenience of scholars, legislators and foreign readers, various relevant statutory provisions and rules which are not commonly available have been included in the book as appendices. Further, the Index at the end has been made detailed and exhaustive so that the readers have easy access to wide ranging subject matter of the book. The paragraphs of each Chapter have also been numbered in order to make smooth for the readers the ever increasing number of precedents and the practices, which are relevant also for several chapters of the book at the same time.

I am highly conscious of my feelings bordering gratefulness for the much and often needed moral support intelligently given to me and valuable time saved for me without any grudge for writing this Book by my wife, Shashi Gupta.

U.N. GUPTA

Contents

VOLUME 2

Table of Case-Law Cited

Case	*Page No.*
A.C. Jose *versus* Sivan Pillai (1984)	341
A.K. Roy *versus* Union of India (1982)	267
Ankul Chandra Pradhan *versus* Union of India (1997)	348
Associated Cement Co. Ltd. *versus* PN Sharma (1965)	187
B. Nayak *versus* Election Commission (1965)	188
B.G. Tilak *versus* Emperor (1897)	100
B.R. Kapur *versus* State of T.N.	365
Barium Chemicals Ltd. *versus* Co. Law Bd. (1967)	267
Besant *versus* Advocate General (1919)	100
Common Cause (ARS) *versus* Union of India (1996)	178, 342, 383, 384
D.S. Mehta *versus* Raghraj Singh (1954)	188
Damayanti *versus* Union of India (1971)	38
Danby's Case (1679)	47, 60, 152
Digvijay Mote *versus* Union of India (1993)	345
Dr. Ramesh Yashwant *versus* Prabhakar Kunte (1996)	110
Election Commission *versus* AIADMK (1994)	374
Election Commission *versus* Dr. S. Swamy (1996)	329
Election Commission *versus* SBI Staff Assn. (1995)	330, 338

Table of Abbreviations

A.C.	Appeal Cases (England)
Act of 1935	Government of India Act of 1935
All. E.R.	All England Reports
A.I.R.	All India Reporter
Bom. L.R.	Bombay Law Reports
C.A.D.	Constituent Assembly Debates
C.L.R.	Commonwealth Law Reports
Cranch	Cranch's Reports (U.S. Supreme Court)
Cr. P.C.	Criminal Procedure Code
Ed./ed.	Edition
Et seq.	And those that follow
F.n./f.n.	Foot note
GOI Act	(British) Government of India Act
Hansard	Hansard's Parliamentary Debates
I.L.R.	Indian Law Reports
Infra	Pages below
L.R.	Law Reports (England)
Kier & Lawson	Cases on Constitutional Law, Ed. 3
Moo. P.C.	Moore's Privy Council Cases
Op. Cit.	Cited above
P./p.	At page
Q.B.	Queen's Bench Division (England)
Quia timet	Operating from a prior time
St. Tr./S.T.	State Trials (England)
SCC	Supreme Court Cases (India)
SCR	Supreme Court Reports (India)
Supra	pages above
U.S.	United States of America
U.S. (in foot note)	United States Reporter (Supreme Court)
UPLBEC	UP Local Bodies and Educational Cases (India)
Wheaton	Wheaton's Reports (U.S. Supreme Court)

1

What Parliamentary Democracy Means in India

1.01. To the contemporary generation of people in India at the beginning of twenty-first century the system of government for the people by their elected representatives appears to be a natural political phenomena. The freedom for India was achieved by a mass democratic movement based on non-violence with due regard to the rule of law imposed by an alien rule. It can be said that people of India want this democratic system which is enshrined in the Constitution of India to be everlasting and successful. In the year 1999 A.D. election to the thirteenth Parliament was held which demonstrated the vitality of Indian Constitution and political maturity of the masses, the capacity to sustain parliamentary system of democracy.

1.01A. It is only in desperation caused at times by the attendant evils which follow the failure of human elements who operate the system of government that people of India desire for alternative forms or systems of government. The presidential and parliamentary forms of government are the two methods by which the government by elected representatives are being made functional in the polities of the world. A question is often raised whether Indian polity would have fared better with presidential form of democracy. At the time of Independence in 1947 after due deliberations the choice was made in the Constituent Assembly of India in favour of a republican federal democratic polity with parliamentary system of constitution both for the Union and the constituent States.

1.01B. The political concepts were searched, examined and adopted for the Constitution of India by the Constituent Assembly for their idealistic content and these were modulated by the practical experience gained by the Indian leaders politically led by Mahatma Gandhi during the British rule in India. The course of the efforts, since the Independence in 1947, has been to develop Indian polity with a separate or distinctive national identity. It has not to be forgotten that the modern concepts of nation-state and the slogans of freedom from alien rule, liberties of people and the affirmative participation of State in the socio-economic development of a country are largely the creation of western rationalist political thinking developed since the middle of eighteenth century. All these ideas and principles which had been tested in the Constitutions of various States of the world have been the foundation on which the Constitution of India was framed. The Constitution of India is a synthesis of modernism, utilitarianism and welfare state concepts, without compromising with traditional Indian values under a democratic elected form of Government.

1. THE DEMOCRATIC TRADITIONS IN INDIAN CONSTITUTION

1.02. The Constitution of India framed by the Constituent Assembly in 1947-49 was based on the democratic pattern as developed in England and popularly referred to as Westminster Model. However, the federal structure, the supremacy of the written constitution and judicial review of the exercise of constitutional authority and functions were inducted from British experiences in working of federalist system in Australia and Canada, and, which already existed for British India under the Government of India Act, 1935.

1.03. The framers of Constitution of India had a notion of constitutional guarantees of the liberties of the people for which the war of independence had taken place and a new state of United States of America had been formed in 1783 out of the British Empire. During the struggle for Indian Independence, the due process of law system for guarantee of liberties of people in the U.S.A. had considerably appealed to the leaders most of whom were lawyers. The result was that the Charter of Liberties of People was incorporated as Fundamental Rights in Part III of the Constitution after defining the Territories of India in Part I and the Citizens of India in Part II and before the governmental system was provided for in Part IV onwards by the Constitution.

1.04. The democratic set up in India, therefore, is an integrated part of wider constitutional theory adopted to lay down and maintain a typical or indigenous polity contemplated and developed for India after long arduous discussions in and outside the Constituent Assembly. Till 1947, liberty meant freedom from foreign rule and after Independence it meant freedom against government arbitrariness, or positive assertions against social and economic inequalities. At the same time the democratic Indian polity involving government functions was to be flexible and prime mover for achievement of social and cultural regeneration and uplift along with general economic up-gradation of all sections of people. All this was visualised to be achieved in a basic system of equality functioning under the rule of law. Accordingly, on the score of political organisation the ancient Indian system of rule by experienced and old intelligentsia was cautiously given up in favour of popular government through universal adult franchise. The Indian framers of the Constitution had noted and accepted as genuine the caution that the ruling minority whether it is foreign or national cannot be taken for granted. This distrust is rooted in the proposition that power always corrupts and prompts its holder to remain in power by fair or fowl means. For this a system of check and balance as adopted in the Constitution of U.S.A. has been incorporated in India also.

1.05. *The Pre-Conditions for Parliamentary Democracy*: For enduring success, the constitutional government of the country by elected representatives of people requires certain pre-conditions and ground work. Objectively examined, the results of the 13th general elections of October 1999 point towards maturity of the Indian polity as against search for alternatives for parliamentary democracy. But, let us subjectively or academically also examine the inner contents and requirements for the legal bases of Indian democratic polity for a sustained perspective.

1.06. First, democracy is not compatible with *individual lust for power* since by theory the ministerial office in parliamentary form of government depends on elections and the power game ultimately operates through party support only. The ministerial office is not permanent in character, it is not even for a fixed term. Several Prime Ministers in India, *viz.*, Morarji Desai, Charan Singh, V.P. Singh, Chandra Shekhar, Atal Bihari Vajpayee or H.D. Deve Gowda had short-lived tenures; two of them, Charan Singh and Atal Bihari Vajpayee[1] resigned even before proving their initial majority in the House of People of Indian Parliament.

1.07. Secondly, the democracy presumes the supremacy of the Constitution and that in effect all political parties have more or less same national interest paramount in their minds. They might vary in the matter of approaches as to how to achieve them and how much to achieve. In India the birth of nation was by peaceful means and all the different political parties had joined the Indian National Congress as common platform for the struggle for freedom against alien rule, except for Communist Party. All the succeeding political parties after Independence were nationalist in outlook first and with this basic thinking they had developed their party programmes or priorities. Even the Communist Party later adopted non-violent strategy for coming into power, they formed Governments in Kerala (1957), West

[1] In May 1996. But, Shri Atal Bihari Vajpayee again became Prime Minister after twelfth general election in March 1998 and led a 19 party coalition government. He became Prime Minister for the third time in October 1999 after 13th general election heading the pre-election alliance of sixteen political parties.

Bengal (1967) and joined United Front Government at the Union in 1997.

1.07A. On the common national outlook there have been various leading instances.

(i) The Union, United Front Ministry in 1996 followed more or less the same policies on economic reforms started in 1991 towards liberalisation economy and foreign affairs as the Congress Party Ministry had earlier pursued.

(ii) Again, the BJP led Ministry of 1998 followed the same notable foreign policy in regard to nuclear options as that of United Front Ministry which had always opposed the ideology of BJP. When charged for towing the earlier policy line, the Prime Minister observed or revealed that the earlier Government consulted him in his capacity as leader of opposition on vital matters of policies and he had himself decided on the policy by taking into account the views of the leader of Opposition, as Member of the Standing Parliamentary Committee on External Affairs. Therefore, it was not necessary that the new government should not continue the Indian nuclear policy in the formulation of which its leaders were earlier consulted and were taken into confidence.

(iii) Subsequently, when in May 1998 the BJP Government conducted nuclear tests at Pokharan, many opposition leaders including former Prime Ministers HD Deve Gowda and IK Gujral who in the past and the present were hostile to BJP expressed their feelings of national pride over the bold step. The nuclear test had evoked sharp recrimination from world nuclear, developed and rich powers.

(iv) In November 1999, the Congress declared that it will support the B.J.P. led coalition Government on its economic policies when directed towards liberalisation, a policy matter which had been initiated by the Congress Ministry in 1991 and which was part of Congress Party manifesto for election to thirteenth Lok Sabha (House of People).

1.07B. In India and in England all the political parties make promises of providing increased material benefits to the masses. The regional or sectarian interests pursued by the regional parties are supposed to give way to national interest. It is found in India that when there is a coalition government the problems of the States get better attention due to constant pressure of regional constituent parties whose support is vital for keeping the coalition intact.

1.08. Thirdly, in parliamentary form of government there is a spirit of toleration for different policies adopted within the constitutional framework by other political parties and these are only shelved by the ruling party; other political parties are not suppressed for holding contrary views or policies. As Ivor Jennings has observed,[2] a "true democrat has a suspicion that he may not always be right. He is therefore tolerant of other people's opinions". The spirit of *intoleration* is marked in those countries where there are political parties based on religion and religion based politics is recognised and the State religion is intolerant of others, However, India is a secular state which believes in religious tolerance and equality of people of all religions before law and the State.

1.08A. All political parties in India are compulsorily required to register themselves with the Election Commission and the declaration submitted by the political parties for this purpose has to state that the party believes in secularism and the constitutional principles. Religious fanaticism and 'fundamentalism' are contrary to Indian constitutional thought. Therefore, whatever be the name of a political party, approach to the voters in the name of religion is prohibited and so is also asking people not to vote for candidates of other religion. Thus, the religious intolerance has been kept out of Indian constitutional process.

1.09. Fourthly, the minorities, ethnic or political, have to be respected and their interests have to be protected by the majority communities since the minorities do not have effective say in

---

[2] Ivor Jennings, *The British Constitution*, p. 30.

the Parliament. In Indian political scene gradually minority communities of religious nature have consolidated themselves in distinct vote banks and thus they have been able to influence the policies of political parties in their favour. Constitutionally the minorities have protected rights of educational, linguistic and cultural nature.[3] Historically also, India has been the haven of various ancient religious sects of non-Hindustani origin, like. Christians, Parsi or Jew.

1.09A. The political intolerance of communist fundamentalism to the capitalist system and its cult of revolution for establishment of workers' State, has been well known since the Soviet Revolution of 1917. Moreover, the Marxist politics in theory does not accept peace with other political systems. However, the Constitution of India has shown hostility to violence but not to peaceful politics even by the communists. The Communist Party of India (CPI) which was under the influence of Soviet Russia, accepted the Indian political and constitutional moderation as part of general Soviet revisionist approach towards counties which were becoming free from imperial or colonial system since the end of Second World War. Subsequently, the CPI (M) faction of Communist Party of India in mid-sixties, follower of Maoist Marxism, also accepted Indian constitutional polity of mutual tolerance.

1.10. Fifthiy, those who are *not in power* should not become restive in the power game and should not adopt unconstitutional, destructive or provocative means in order to come into power. The democracy is based on the principle of constant education by political parties of the masses for conversion to their socio-economic and political points of view. The evolutionary processes of natural selection by people and survival of the fittest political party in the long run are seen to apply for political parties of India also.[4] The slow but sure growth of

---

[3] *Constitution of India*, Articles 29 and 30.

[4] The study of Indian political parties in Indian constitutional set up is pursued in Third Chapter of the Book.

Bhartiya Janata Party or Communist Parties are examples of political parties coming to the threshold of political power gradually, showing that patience and appreciation by people of the causes pursued by the political parties pay dividends ultimately under the process established by the Constitution of India.

1.11. Sixthly, all political parties have to understand that they represent the people or electorate in the legislatures, whose interests they have to grasp, achieve or protect and that the political party by itself is not the end of democracy. The political parties are indispensable for success of democracy under the Constitution of India and these occupy distinct and unique place in polity created. The people of India depend on political parties for their welfare and the political parties ultimately wield the power of the State in the public administration. The regional political parties in India which also contest and win seats in the House of People of Union Parliament have since 1996 altered their general approach towards the political problems and these do work for national interest and actively participate in debates in Parliament to settle the national issues as well.

1.12. Seventhly, it is noted that since 1970s the democracy in India has gradually become very much susceptible to the vice of corrupt practices at the time of election, the misuse of public funds to support political party, purchasing votes of opposition party at crucial moments or for personal enrichment of the political leaders. As such, self-restraint on the part of politicians against corruption and corrupt practices is part of the democratic game. Every political party has to set a working balance between basic principles and the extent to which it will go to appease the voters or a section of people particularly when the appeasement is against public interest or morals, law or national interest. These are also the contents of political morality essential to the democratic principle. In the Indian politics of 1990s this has been a live problem which has endangered or placed a question mark on the survival of democracy in the country. Various measures including amendment of the Constitution and the enactments have been made in India to keep pace with vice and menace of corrupt politics.

1.12A. The constitutional and legal framework in India recognises that democracy in absence of political morality, is a very incoherent, brittle and week political system. Many times it was felt in India that there is no individuals' morality in the form of everlasting loyalty to one political party for a politician, one time political foes become partners in future. It was found that those who were targets of political vendetta or committed excess during Emergency of 1975 befriended the oppressors when the former came into power after 12th and 13th general elections. It is interesting to note that explaining this particular phenomenon in India, in June 2000 the news media reported the statement of Defence Minister alongwith the story that:

> " 'Every saint has a past and every sinner a future' Defence Minister George Fernandes now says as an explanation for being in the same boat today as some of the perpetrators of the Emergency excesses."
>
> "Asked about his feelings on being in the same government with those who had been part of Indira Gandhi's authoritarian regime, Fernandes on Saturday said the democratic system made room for people to realise their mistakes and reform themselves. The reference was to the presence of close associates of Indira Gandhi like Jagmohan, KC Pant and Sanjay Gandhi's widow Maneka Gandhi, in important positions in the National Democratic Alliance coalition (cabinet)."[5]

---

[5] The Times of India News Service: *The Times of India*, Lucknow ed. Dated 25th June 2000, under the heading "Fernandes defends dynamites, co-existence with Jagmohan"; latter was holding a high profile civil post as vice-chairman of Delhi Development, and had faithfully executed superior policy decisions and orders resulting in demolition of residential colonies etc, an activity which was regarded as highly atrocious.

1.13. It is a political reality that the small parliamentary democracies are always in the danger of take over by military or militant groups in case there is maladministration or lack of patience and toleration on the part of power seekers. This happens particularly in circumstances when sufficient time is not given to the constitutional government to achieve its policies or when the ruling party has proved its incapacity to keep up its promises to people or to rule but due to safe majority in Parliament it is not providing alternative forum to take up administration. The democracy in such situation does not provide any alternative principle. In new democracies the impatience of opposition political parties is often fatal for the ruling party and coups take place.

1.13A. However, in India the stability of governments of States and the strong executive organisation has had favourable impact for the democracy. Any viable unconstitutional take over of the Government must have an existing organisation of vast magnitude and this disturbing development cannot be kept a secret for long. Therefore a civil war type situation is inevitable in case the Constitutional government is to be ousted unconstitutionally.

1.13B. Reference in this context may be made to Soviet Russia which was biggest federal state at one time till it went for voluntary dissolution in 1990. The voluntary dissolution of Soviet Russia had taken place primarily due to corruption in one party system of Communist Party and insolvency of the State which forced it to change over to private liberal economy and also to multiparty democracy. Of course if Soviet Russia had been true democracy with multiple party system capable of providing alternate governments, that is, a system for providing remedies against misuse of powers by the Communist Party and the government. Also the Soviet Constitution lacked flexibility in federal relationship with federal units. The situation would have obviously been different if these constitutional pre-conditions had been present in Soviet Constitution and there might not have been disintegration of the State.

1.14. Theoretically, the government by the people for themselves is a sophisticated modern version of the tribal system of organisation which existed before the era of hereditary kingship. The tribes elected the physically most competent member as the leader of the group. This tribal chief was to protect and maintain the properties and common interests of the tribes against the marauders and also against internal division. Under the State system of political organisation the Parliament represents the tribe or the whole population by proxy of elected representatives, while the President in presidential form of democracy and the Council of Ministers in parliamentary form of government perform the functions of the chieftain of the tribe.

2. THE GENESIS OF DEMOCRATIC SYSTEM FOR INDIA

1.15. Any constitutional system which has withstood natural selection and ravages of time is likely to have inner vitality and strength against changing values, political, social and economic, in the society. Else, it must have capacity to change with times, that is, it does not suffer from an in-built rigidity. Both elements are necessary for survival of a constitution.

1.15A. A rule by consensus was the essence of the ancient or indigenous Indian *panchayat* system that is a rule by elected (five) elders of the community, alongwith the political theory that the King was bound by *dharma*, a superior rule of righteousness, like his subjects. Naturally the Indian political thinkers had little hesitation in accepting British parliamentary system fortified by the concept of rule of law as nearest to ancient *panchayat* political tradition. With the growth of population, elected Parliament is a contemporary replacement of the institution of *panchayat*. Also, in India a limited democracy was brought in by the British rulers in stages through various Acts enacted by British Parliament and the independent India had a vast bundle of the legacy of British parliamentary practices and traditions, many of which were incorporated in the Constitution of India as well.

1.16. *Great Britain*: English people had in the course of three or four centuries up to the middle of eighteenth century by reason of their peculiar geographical and ethnic position in the continent of Europe, evolved the political concept of representative government. Before the era of exploration and industrialisation, England had meagre natural resources and was accessible by sea routes being an island away from Europe. From the point of view of European imperial dynasties of 10th to 14th centuries England was a useless territory not regarded as a territory worthy of occupation except for preventing and punishing sea adventurers and pirates. On the other hand, English people had to import royal blooded kings from heirs of European royal families. In this process, only those members of European royal families who were not likely to inherit the Crown in Europe reluctantly accepted the offer of Kingship of England and even after appointment they were interested in participating in the wars of succession in Europe. But the people of England had by their political wisdom imposed certain basic terms and conditions on the imported Kings for the purpose of safeguarding their established rights with which they had become accustomed. They also refused to be drawn into or made part of European rivalries and intrigues in which such new Kings were interested. One of the political instrumentality evolved in this process was *Curia Regis*, a Council of local wise men, on whose advise the King was required to rule over the people of England. This *Curia Regis* later developed into the Privy Council and the present Parliament. The House of Commons of the Parliament was elected body and the Cabinet carried out the administration on behalf of the King with responsibility to the Parliament.

1.17. The Magna Carta of 1216, Petition of Rights of 1628, Bill of Rights of 1688 and Act of Succession of 170 now consolidate the terms which are, what is now called, a *social contract* between any King and the people. When Charles I, the second Stuart King disregarded the established freedoms of people with impunity and arrogance, the Long Parliament dethroned him and alongwith under Cromwell a Commonwealth was created which beheaded Charles I in 1649. But the Commonwealth constitutionally failed leading to restoration of kingship in 1651. Hobbs who was contemporary political philosopher had taught the people that men by nature are brutish and lawless, kings are essential in order to keep them in order and for preventing the rule of jungle in human society. However, the next new king Charles II honoured the established rights of people and the superior authority of Parliament and laws laid down by it.

1.17A. The relationship between the King and the people through the Parliament was defined to be a *Social Contract* by Locke and Montesquieu, the political philosophers of late seventeenth and early next century. Under this social contract the King was to function in internal matters effecting British people only on the advice of Parliament and the Cabinet. When James II the son of Charles II resisted the authority of Parliament in 1688, he had to flee the country and Parliament passed enactment which was later known as Bill of Rights of 1688 which contain most of the Fundamental Rights under Part III of the Constitution of India, 1950. This Glorious Revolution of 1688 of England is the groundwork for the organisation of (i) Cabinet, (ii) Party system in House of Commons and (iii) ministerial responsibility for the acts of government.

1.17B. The total achievement of Glorious Revolution was that the future kings remained titular only. The Kings could not raise money on British territory which only Parliament could do. At the same time the residuary powers of the King known as Royal Prerogatives, however, allowed King to exploit colonies and foreign lands. But there was no prerogative power on British Isles. It was confined to foreign affairs and foreign lands. Subsequently, however, since the Statute of Westminster of 1931, this part of prerogative power has also come to an end. Now if any territory of British Empire is to cease to be a British possession, an Act of Parliament is necessary. For example, The Indian Independence Act, 1947, was passed by the British

Parliament by which India became independent of British Empire.

1.17C. The status of British Parliament in relation to Cabinet, Ministers and the Crown is largely regulated by the Conventions of the Constitution.[6] These conventions are unwritten in character and are composed of traditions and practices which have been consistently followed particularly since Glorious Revolution of 1688. Limitaion developed on Convention is that once put into the form of enactment the law prevails and the Convention ceases to the extent of inconsistency.

1.18. After the bad experiences of failure of Commonwealth in 1649, British people have reconciled with the institution of monarchy as against a republican form of Constitution. Till 1949, the King was also the head of the British Commonwealth. When India declared itself a Republic in 1949 and wished to continue to remain a member of the Commonwealth without owing any allegiance to the British Crown, the name of the British Commonwealth was changed to Commonwealth of Nations by an Act and the King or Queen ceased to be the Head of this body.

1.19. Constitution for Democratic Process in British India. In British India since the Regulating Act of 1773, British Parliament had been providing for the administrative set up including the Governors, the Governor General, or organisation of Courts. However, when after the First War of Independence of 1857, the East India Company was deprived of its Charter, the British Parliament became a sort of perpetual Constituent Assembly for British India. The India Councils Act of 1861 and there after the periodic Government of India Acts till 1935 laid down various powers of Indian legislative and executive authorities for administration of British India keeping the British Parliament as a sovereign authority for Indian Dominion. The Privy Council in

---

[6] An extended analysis of the basic status of the Cabinet in England is further pursued in Chapter II, *infra*.

Emperor *versus* Burah[7] held that it was possible for Parliament to establish sovereign legislatures for Dominion by delegation of power which could alter or amend the laws in force which were enacted by British Parliament, but, of course not the law by which the sovereign power was delegated to the legislature. The legality of the amendment of Sections 81 and 82 of Criminal Procedure Code basically enacted by British Parliament made by Governor General in Council was in question in this case. But the point emphasised here is only that British Parliament was competent to delegate partly its sovereign powers with reference to the Dominion but subject to the sanctity of this enabling law.

1.20. On August 15, 1947 India became independent nation as a political fact which was recognised by the international community also. But the Constituent Assembly was a creation of British Government and was sanctioned by the Indian Independence Act 1947, and was constituted by elections held under the Government of India Act 1935 and Cabinet Mission Plan of 1946. It became the first Federal Legislature of independent India by virtue of Indian Independence Act of 1947. The Constitution of India had commenced from January 26, 1950, and, by Article 395 of the Constitution, the Government of India Act 1935, Indian Independence Act 1947 and the Adaptation Laws were repealed alongwith. Further, Article 372 of the Constitution of India saved all the existing laws evolved and developed in British India in so far as these were not inconsistent with the Constitution of India and these continued as the law of the land.

1.21. As imperial power England was not interested either in democracy or development of British India. There was no kind of obligation to provide a welfare government for the dominion either. There had been no treaty of peace behind the establishment of British rule on Indian sub-continent. The effort

---

[7] (1879) L.R. 3 A. C. 889; also Queen *versus* Mears, (1874) 14 R.L.R.106.

of the imperial power had been to maintain its rule since India was regarded to be the jewel of the Crown. The pressure of the demand for representation in legislature by the Indian leaders since 1880s was saddled with communal franchise leading to vertical divisions of the Indian society. For the form of government set up, the Government of India Act 1935 had provided a federal structure. Section 18 of this Act provided for Federal Legislature and Section 60 for Provincial Legislature. The First Schedule regulated the composition and membership of Federal and Fifth Schedule of the Provincial Legislatures, going into details of the religion and communal composition and demarcation of the Constituencies. The Indian leaders and the intelligentsia were very much disturbed by this kind of democratic establishment and desired for democracy on British pattern of representation at least. Further the voting rights were not based on adult or universal franchise but were restricted to rich or land owning Indians. Therefore, the pattern of democratic representation in Federal Parliament and State Legislature under the Constitution of India was envisaged to be radically different from the pattern prescribed during the British period and the features for universal franchise and common platform for all communities were incorporated in it.

3. PARTY SYSTEM FOR DEMOCRACY

1.22. By the beginning of twenty first century the democracy world over has become a way of political life in contrast with autocracy. Latter generally means a state in which an individual or a limited group or aristocracy rules the state and the people have to tolerate the ruler or the ruling class. Now this kind of system is regarded to be a temporary phase which has to give way to a popular rule which exists for the people as a whole fulfilling the aspirations of the nations. The autocracy is now in disrepute. Theoretically with reference to the state, as Rousseau had stated democracy implies that sovereignty of the state is in the people or masses. The political system of democracy is geared for making the administration a true self-rule by the people both in the matters of policy decisions and their implementation. Accordingly the task of democracy has been to devise the best method for ascertaining the wishes of the people.

1.23. The British method of organising Parliament as representative of the people for reaching a consensus on national issues and priorities for state action has since the end of Second World War become the general meaning of democracy. Of course, what will be the character of the chief executive body differs from State to State. At the same, it has now become a general practice, including that in the new Russia of 1991, that elections to the Parliament be on Party lines. It is believed that the discussions in Parliament bring out all aspects of a matter, favourable and unfavourable, to the attention of the members before they vote for the Bill or adopt a resolution approving the policy of the government, *e.g.*, foreign policy. When the government gets a measure adopted after strong criticism of members or opposition parties it gets credit for the success or discredit for the failure in the matter which effect its prospects in the next elections to the Parliament. The latter aspect makes the democracy or parliamentary form of government a viable proposition.

1.24. *Party System in Great Britain*: In England since eighteenth century there have been generally two main political parties, which probably centred around the community discussions as to who should succeed James II, after he had fled the country on the eve of Glorious Revolution. Later, of the two groups, Whigs represented trading class and Tories took the cause of landed aristocracy in Parliament. Subsequently, in nineteenth century Whigs became protagonists of natural rights, individual freedom and improvement of working conditions in industrial establishments and changed into Liberal Party by the end of nineteenth century. The Liberal Party also became attracted to the socialist movement in early twentieth century. On the other hand, the Tory Party was more attached to King's causes, interests of landed aristocracy, empire building in national interest and in exploiting of New World. Subsequently, Tories became Conservative Party by the twentieth century and took pride in British monarchy, traditions and capitalism.

1.24A. With the industrialisation and induction of socialism as a political philosophy the Trade Union movement also gradually developed in England. The Labour Party came into existence in the last quarter of nineteenth century by making claims for the representations for the trade unions in Parliament. After the First World War the Labour Party organised itself constituency-wise. It has had the support of various organised working class groups and has better non-parliamentary organisational base in which its policies are discussed and laid down. Since 1924 it has practically become second alternative Party to the Conservative Party in England. Now, after a long gap of about fifteen years it has again formed the Government in 1997.

1.25. For the efficient functioning of parliamentary government, in England it has been found that the segment of electorate uncommitted to any political party or mobile public opinion is very much important. It keeps the parties attentive to their aims and influences the results of the next election. The ruling party or the government has to keep itself in tune with the demands of the time or the general trends in the society. It has to justify itself for all of its actions and the opposition party is always criticising or censoring its actions including the personal life pattern of the Ministers. The result is that by the time next election takes place generally all parties forming the government become unpopular if they fail to keep up their promises at the time of elections. In such situation if any Party wins again in the election and again comes into power it is regarded to be highly creditable performance. However, the opposition party if it wins is not bound by the criticisms it had made earlier and can pursue the projects of the previous governments by making amendments. This is possible because the national interest is regarded to be paramount and the political parties profess to give cleaner administration and claim to be nearer to the popular aspirations and their supporters.

1.25A. It is not a secret in British politics that only those take part in active politics who aspire to become ministers one day. However, the principle of individual *ministerial responsibility* which is very vigilantly and strictly enforced is a powerful balancing proposition between the minister, his party obligations, duty to the government and his own social image. No politician can afford to commit mistakes in any of the above relationships. If he does commit mistake it is at the cost of his career. Further there are some statutory limits on Party activities, particularly for maintaining purity or sanctity of the election process, *viz.*, the Corrupt and Illegal Practices Act of 1885.

1.26. *Political Parties in United States*: Following the pattern of the two or multiple party system of democracy of England, the U.S.A. has also developed two political parties, namely, Democratic Party and Republican Party. These are alternatives right since 1783 out of which the people choose their President or Members of the House of Representatives of their Congress. There has not been much difference in political base of the two political parties except for difference of approach on matters of contemporary interest at any time. Republicans were initially for least interference by the Federal Government in the affairs of States which were Colonies of England while Democrats wanted more centralised administration which could reach the people directly for the good of people. Then the two had differing views on slavery in mid nineteenth century. In the last century the two Parties differed on the New Deal situation of 1936.

1.26A. The American Parties have much in common on ideological plane. They have similar perception of foreign relationships, of capitalistic economic system and of good administration. As no international wars have been fought on the U.S. soil and as no disasters have fallen on the country as such, except for the recession of 1930s, there has been no need for radical change in political thinking. There has been no pressure for new political thinking from the side of electorate, that is people, either.

1.26B. The people of the country are rich since even unskilled labourer is materially well off, 'they are not inspired by the heated winds of philosophic doctrine or transcendent ideology', they can browse and feel pity for the people of Asia and Africa lacking wealth and medicare. Of course, there are many who are parasites on their society in the U.S.A. as are in every country. United States is an under- populated country and it somewhat sucks the whole world for its demands for manpower by the lure of jobs and high wages through a strict immigration policy. The electorate of United States is well informed, makes judgements on success or failure of the political parties, and changes its selection of political parties at the time of election. Under such circumstances the two political parties fix their policies by steeling when necessary the future policies and the election strategies of the other party and even commit thefts and house breaking. At the time of elections the two political parties even solicit the same person to contest election on their party symbol.

1.26C. In the U.S.A. under the presidential form of democracy, there are lot of administrative offices for political appointment which the election winning party gives to its supporters and therefore, it is not necessary for the parties to give party tickets to their supporters at the time of election. They can be accommodated differently with the spoils of politics. Clean personal integrity on corruption, acquisition of property and sex fronts are essential basic qualifications for election of American politicians. A suppressed or subsequent discovery of past or present lapse easily spoils the political career and he is not tolerated on the elective post. Since both President and members of the Congress are elected for a fixed term, these have to maintain a clean image during their tenure also. In 1998, President Bill Clinton came under severe scrutiny for sex scandals despite his popularity as political strong man. The political figures are assiduously watched by vigilant investigative media, people and the other political parties and their performances are taken into account by the people at the time of next elections. At the primaries also the tainted politicians get weeded out.

1.26D. In the U.S.A., the electoral process is also under law for maintaining fairness and purity. Of course the federal law is of limited application and does not apply to election in States. The Federal Corrupt Practices Act of 1925 along with the Hatch Acts of 1939 and 1940 regulate various aspects of transactions connected with elections including the funding of the Party and the candidates. The party organisation and the process for the nomination of candidates are also under legal regulations.

1.27. *Political Party Movement in India*: Coming to the Indian scene after making a review of Party systems in England and the U.S.A., it is not difficult to understand the problems which the politics has generated or tried to tackle in India. In 1885 Indian National Congress was established as a platform for discussion by the British citizens with the noble purpose of knowing the trend of Indian thinking, the grave problems which were then troubling the people and also the aspirations which the people had and which they wanted to achieve. This was to help the British in providing a better administration in British India so that a situation which had led to First War of Independence in 1857 may not arise again.

1.27A. Obviously, the Indian National Congress was like the present lower house of Parliament in giving out the state of conditions in the Dominion. However, from the second decade of twentieth century after the dissatisfaction created by the Minto Morley Reforms of 1907-8, the Congress became a political party and it found its justification in educating the British of the Indian discontents. The debates within Indian National Congress at its conferences were as to whether a soft-line or a hard-line was to be adopted against the British on the political issues of the time. Mahatma Gandhi in the later part of second decade had transformed the Congress as a joint front of Indian nationalists against the British.

1.27B. Under the communal franchise system created and enforced by the Minto Morley Reforms of 1907-8, the British fortified their counter-Congress stand by helping the formation of religious and communal political parties. By 1935, a full political scene had evolved in India with a plethora of sectional parties and movements particularly, Muslim League, Hindu Mahasabha, Ram Rajya Parishad, Depressed Class League, or Sikh Federation. These sectional political parties were divisive in nature and were retarding forces against the freedom movement platform working under the aegis of Indian National Congress. Ultimately, in 1946 and 1947 the British played Hindu versus Muslim divide card politics and partitioned India on June 3, 1947 between Hindu and Muslim areas on the result of the communal franchise basis elections held under Government of India Act of 1935.

1.27C. Thus, when India became independent in 1947, *besides* Indian National Congress which had functioned as a platform for freedom struggle for the whole country, there were a number of political parties on the political scene which had not taken part in freedom struggle but had taken part in the elections held under the Government of India Act of 1935. The attitude of these political parties had been to safeguard the interests of their faction in the constitutional changes likely to take place. They had no territorial or constituency development or social uplift programmes as such, which mark the regular or mature political systems.

1.28. Political Party System under the Constitution of India: The Indian system since 1950 for popular government is of a completely different pattern since it operates under several constraints of the Constitution. The Preamble to the Constitution promises the ideal of political liberty to all citizens of India. Article 15(1) provides that 'State shall not discriminate against any citizen on grounds only of religion, race caste, sex, place of birth or any of them'. This provision is taken to imply that communal or religious franchise under which the total number of constituencies were divided earlier was unconstitutional[8]. Any demand or any law for providing for election on the basis of separate electorate for members of different religious communities or denominations offends Article 15, the right to equality available to all citizens of India. Further, Freedom of religion has been made a personal matter for the people and the State cannot be used to promote or propagate any particular religion though it may take measures which deal all religions with equality. The Preamble to the Constitution after amendment in 1976 also declares India to be a secular democratic republic. Therefore, the Constitution has made a radical departure from the democratic process of British period. Only those political parties can exist which believe in Constitution, its principles and constituencies formed on territorial basis. As will be discussed ahead the Representation of People Act, 1951, has made it mandatory that the political parties register themselves and the candidates for the election take oath of allegiance to the Constitution.

1.29. The party system for parliamentary democracy in India is now significantly recognised by various statutory provisions and the Tenth Schedule to the Constitution of India engrafted in 1985. The Tenth Schedule regulates in detail the situations arising from splits and defections taking place from one political party to another obviously of members elected on the tickets of particular political party. This anti-defection Tenth Schedule also provides for loss of membership of Parliament or State Legislative Assembly under some conditions or joining of a political party by an independently elected member. The Representation of the Peoples (Amendment) Act of 1988 also gives statutory recognition to political party system when it provides for registration of political parties with the Election Commission. Under paragraph 7 of the Election Symbols

---

[8] Nain Sukh Das *versus* State of U.P., A.I.R., 1953, S.C. 184.

(Reservation and Allotment) Order 1968, on the basis of the successes in last election to the House of People or State Legislatures, a Party may be designated as 'National Party' or 'State Party' or 'Unrecognised Party'. Further, the Model Code of Conduct, laid down and enforced by the Election Commission of India under Article 324 (1) of the Constitution, significantly regulates the election expenses by political parties and candidates for parliamentary or State Assembly elections. For corrupt practices as laid down in Representation of People Act 1951, a political Party may be de-recognised by the Election Commission and thereafter it will be unable to contest elections.

1.30. *Non-Party Candidates*: In India, individuals as independent candidates, that is without affiliation to any political party, contest election to the House of People or State Legislatures in large numbers and get elected by the force of their own personality or contribution to the cause of local people. Here it means that for Indian democratic system political parties are one of the method for getting elected but it is not necessary that a political aspirant must join a political party for his participation in Parliamentary process. On practical basis it can be said that an independent cannot become a member of the Upper House on account of the indirect election procedure. Generally, it has been found that when a party member is not given a party nomination for the election, for his face saving or else because of his confidence of direct public support irrespective of party affiliation, such politicians contest the election as independent Candidate. In 1996, for eleventh House of People general elections when Indian National Congress adopted the policy of not giving party nominations to those who had been implicated in various corruption scams, a good number of important party members left Congress and either formed their own new party or contested the election as independent candidates.

1.30A. Independents have noticeable weight in a 'Hung Parliament' when a coalition government is to be formed. In the tenth (1991), eleventh (1996) and twelfth (1998) House of People they have enjoyed considerable respect and attention of the ruling party or the coalitions. The independents are subject to anti-defection disabilities of Tenth Schedule of the Constitution and cannot join any party but they can join the government as Ministers.

1.31. Is Party System Indispensable? Election to Parliament on political party basis as against single party polity or encouragement to independents seeking parliamentary seat, has its own virtues which deserve assessment.

1.31A. First, it makes the selection of Prime Minister by President or of Chief Minister by the Governor in Indian Federation clear and easy after a general election. The President has the simple task of asking the leader of the elected members of the political party having the largest representation in the House of People to become Prime Minister and form the Council of Ministers. There is no need of any tedious exercise for ascertaining who is on which side by the President when any party has clear majority or when a number of political parties form a coalition before the election. The situation is obviously different when the independents are in such numbers that these can influence or tilt the majority. This happens when no single party has clear majority. The party system, therefore, helps cabinet system of government by reducing the process of determining who should be the Prime Minister.

1.31B. Secondly, (a) the political parties woo the voters by competitively claiming to be more nationalist and devoted to public welfare when their ideology is similar. This brings forth in public view the state of the nation since there is severe criticism of the ruling party by other contestants. If there is single party system as it is in communist states this critical assessment of the state of nation does not take place periodically. The heatedly contested elections help in reassessment or modification in various policies of the state which is ultimately good for the country in the long run. Of course when there is one party rule as it was during 1950 to 1977 in India, or as in communist states, like Soviet Russia or Communist China the pace of development appears to be well set and defined but there is dependence on few who monopolise the ruling party and which is not good for the country after two or three elections. After Stalin who or after Nehru–who? Such questions arise which undermine the future confidence of the people and make democracy shaky; this happened in India between 1965 and 1970 after demise of Prime Minister Nehru in 1964.

(b) Further, the manifesto of parties before elections try to be competitive on social, national economy, community uplift and constituency development or improvement aspects and try to reach the people. When there is a coalition government—the United Front Ministries (1996-98) were thirteen political party coalition while the BJP led Government of March 1998 was a 19 party coalition—the emphasis on common programme for masses and community come to the fore again and again for stability of the coalition and objectivity in the performances of the Government. The party manifesto gets clouded in a coalition government in favour of the national agenda or the minimum or common agreed programme. For instance,

(i) The United Front Coalition Government of 1996 which had CPI(M) as one of its constituents continued with the Congress economic reform ideology and the process for liberalisation involving liquidation of public sector, since it depended on its outside support in the House of People.

(ii) The BJP led coalition of March 1998, did not make any attempt to achieve Hindu fundamentalist elements of BJP election manifesto and at the outset of thirteenth general election of October 1999, as leader of National Democratic Alliance (NDA), BJP shelved its party manifesto and its fundamentalist programmes for next five years while it adopted the NDA manifesto for the general election.

1.31B. Thirdly, in order to get votes the political parties in parliamentary system have to reach remotest corners of the country and have to convey their ideals and objectives to the masses. They have also to explain the shortcomings and failures of the existing government. This involves constant contact with people and educating them orally about the political manifesto of the party as well as the rights and interests of the people so that the latter get excited and desire for better living prospects or for receiving what they had been denied so far due to their ignorance. As a matter of fact the thirteen general elections to the Parliament and ten or so elections of State Assemblies of India since 1952 have given considerable socio-economic awakening apart from political information to the people of India through their political programmes and manifestos, and the election shows and exercises have made the common man and masses much more enlightened as compared to their position in 1947. This oral education is done by the use of audio amplifiers, stage dramas, dance, popular folk music, posters and a variety of indigenous methods. To this the video-cassettes, and the television have added tremendous boost since 1980s. Somehow the Indian masses are attracted by this election time extravaganza and by this the older and younger generations, rural and urban populations and the future voters also become better informed citizens. Prior to twelfth and thirteenth general elections the television had done good and purposeful service to the nation by the education of people through programmes which projected that 'they must vote' and 'vote only for honest and sincere candidates who did not have criminal records'.

1.31B-1. As a result, present situation is that irrespective of the quality of literacy, the common or ordinary Indian citizen when he goes to cast his vote he understands his interests, remembers the hollow promises that the politicians had made previously and the general trends of the time. When he votes under corrupt practice pressure of political groups he remembers the situation and when the pressure is removed he is positively a different person, at least in urban constituencies.

1.31B-2. As such the elections are increasingly becoming difficult game for politicians. The uncertainty was discernible on the faces of politicians before and during eleventh general elections held in April-May 1996 when Model Code of Conduct had come down heavily and successfully against the use of ministerial privileges, money and muscle power for obtaining votes. In the eleventh general election (May 1996) and twelfth general election (March 1998) most of those people who earlier voted for money or favours and sometimes vitally influenced the verdict of election, preferred to abstain from voting altogether rather than to vote on the basis of past favours.[9] This is read generally as a socio-political balancing act on the whole. Increase in the political awareness of the masses is also a by-product of the confusion created by multiple party system which subsists with around forty political parties represented in Twelfth Parliament. When the 13th general elections were held in September-October 1999, there was little public display of convassing and motivation of voters by the political parties but the total number of votes cast in the election had increased.

1.31C. Fourthly, the competitive character of elections has rejuvenating effect within political parties also.

(i) It has been said that the political party is a fighting organisation and as such it has to take care of its own unity, party organisation and the quality of the representatives who are to contest election from various constituencies under its banner. There has to be a constant brushing up of political parties with every general election sometimes vigorously also by shedding spent-force, shady or undisciplined members who were occupying coveted posts, by inducting new cadres and by promoting the lower cadre leaders, that is, municipal corporators, panchayat office-holders, institutional union or trade union leaders to State Legislatures or Parliament. In fact there is abundance of career oriented new aspirants in politics and that is a cause for coming into existence of too many political parties

---

9 The study on this aspect has been made in some detail in Chapter VII, *infra*.

in India in place of two or three and also frequent migration or defection of individual politicians from one party to another.[10]

(ii) Further, the public contact system of political parties also gets competitively overhauled with every general election by the dropping of old issues and bringing up of new issues in the party programmes and election manifestos for public discussion or attention. Normally and ideally the capability of a political worker in making public contacts in the party interest is the measure of his political qualification. Somehow in India the nuisance value of a politician to the administration, education institutions or other establishments and also his capacity of unscrupulously organising disruptive activities like, strikes, closures, road blockades, *bandh* or *gherao,* is taken into account as a qualification for inducting him as party leader. Graduating from this background the politicians now become members of Parliament, State Legislatures, municipal corporations or *panchayat* institutions. The sad pictures of undisciplined behaviours in the Houses of Parliament or State Legislatures are the baneful result of the quality of basic training which goes to make a person a party worker and then a leader or politician. It is also a matter of regret that every political party maintains a long list of unemployed persons as casual party workers who have to be paid their daily subsistence allowance by the party or by a leader till full time job is managed for them. After that, just as aspiring young professionals change their corporate employer for better career prospects, junior and even senior politicians change their political parties for better prospects. Active politics provides good brokerage from public or from corrupt officials to the politicians or leaders at all levels which they either transfer to the party or use as their own election fund. With this working background every successful politician also becomes an educator for his standby juniors and *chelas* (devoted apprentices). These juniors and *chelas* in turn find unhappy, dissatisfied, incompetent but rich or cunning people

---

[10] See earlier comments under foot note 5.

who seek political help for consideration which is generally illegal or out of way. With the help of political leverage of their patron and with the aid of corrupt officers in the administration, the juniors and *chelas* complete the parasitic cycle. The unfortunate thing is that this vicious cycle has led to the vice of toleration of corruption in civil life by all political parties, this corruption is being increasingly let loose in the society by the lower and middle cadres of all the political parties.

(iii) However, the fact remains that during the last 50 years of Independence the education of public done by the political parties of India for their success during elections through their programmes and election manifestos has given tremendous uplift to the intelligence both of the urban and rural population. Whether to vote, not to vote and whom to vote are exercises which are now carefully and consciously done by simple looking or rustic voter also. Most of the political parties dread the prospect of facing the electorate in the elections and are now uncertain of the choice and preference of parties which will be finally made by the voting masses at the elections.

1.36. Fifthly, those political parties which have formed governments at the Union or in the States several times or for a number of years generally loose grass root level contact with masses since their lower cadre gets promoted slowly as Ministers, etc. Those who are not elected utilise the time and patronage of Ministers to get jobs, generally better than their qualifications or else drift to other political parties. The result is that successful or old political parties gradually develop top-heavy and middle-heavy frame but very weak lower cadre, that is the field workers. Also, there is less of rapport between party and people and often the promises made by upper crust leaders are not properly backed up with effective party cadre support and the party suffers at the elections. For example, this happened with the Congress Party which since 1980s is a party of ex-ministers, ex-MPs, ex-MLAs and the currently elected members of Parliament or State Legislatures or Local Bodies. These always think in terms of becoming Ministers generally at the cost of party loyalty, abhor field work and are ready to defect to other parties for positive prospects.

1.36A. On the other hand, the non-ruling political parties have had better manpower at lower cadre level and have more time for public relationship and have progressively done better in every successive election. The absence of the lower cadre was the reason for debacle of Congress in 1989 ninth general elections to the House of People and again in April 1996, March 1998 and October 1999 elections to the House of people. The Congress, the Magnus party, has since 1980s a very slender middle order and almost non-existent lower cadre. People found that during the election days no Congress party worker ever visited their area even once and their agents were also missing from the polling booths. The Congress Party, however, manages its public image through a comparative much better control of mass media and the past popularity of its leaders.

1.36B. In contrast, the Samajvadi Party, Samata Party or Bhartiya Janata Party and even the CPI(M) are bottom heavy and in 1998 they lacked leadership of top and middle range in sufficient number considering the size of Indian country. Yet, because of abundance in the lower order of field workers they are progressively performing better in elections, though it has had a steady record of improvement the BJP, even after the twelfth general election of March 1998 to the Lok Sabha, the party still lacks clear majority. It is, however, observed that the bottom heavy political parties, like Samajvadi Party, have gradually improved their strength in Parliament and in the State Legislatures.

1.37. Sixthly, with the exit of British rule in India, politics is now a whole time profession in nature. It provides full and part-time occupation to millions of people all over India. The multiparty system ensures regular induction of fresh entrants into this profession; qualitatively the active political cadres are generally from education and business profession both for rural and urban areas. It is observed that there is a change over from politics of patriotism and sacrifice to a professional politics of opportunism and cleverness. This may be a new situation for India but this kind of evolutionary process has always been part of materialistic and competitive 'survival of the fittest' character of the societies of the West. It is another thing that with the inevitable trend for globalisation in 1990s, this onslaught on nature of Indian political parties has to be faced and mastered with equanimity if the present democratic constitutional system is to subsist or survive.

4. THE PEOPLE AND ELECTIONS

1.38. The Preamble to the Constitution of India contemplates popular sovereignty as the base of the political system for the government of the country. The elections to the Lok Sabha (House of People) and the State Legislative Assemblies are held every five years on party lines.[11] The President or the Governor invites the majority party to form the Council of Ministers who are responsible to the people through the vote of confidence in the Lok Sabha or State Legislative Assembly. However, after election the elected members take oath of loyalty and allegiance to the Constitution under its Third Schedule[12], not to the political party or the people who had sent the, to the House. On the contact point between people and the elected representatives it id noteworthy that there is no right to recall the elected persons available to the constituencies. The Tenth Schedule to the Constitution has since 1985 created and introduced a limited concept of loyalty or allegiance of elected members towards their political party by restricting the right of elected members to change their affiliation to other political parties at their will. The integrity of the elected persons remains, however, subject to law.

1.39. The point creating conflict in the minds of common people is the fact of professional or career politicians taking

---

[11] *The Constitution of India,* Articles 83 and 172.

[12] *Ibid.,* Articles 99 and 188.

over the control of all the political parties. The traditional image of the Indian politician is that they lead a life of extreme sacrifice and devotion to the country, emotionally called the motherland, in *Vande Matram* spirit. This image of Indian politician was vainly tried to be resurrected when celebrations of '50 Years of Freedom' at the end of 1997 were held on a mass scale. The twelfth election to the Lok Sabha (March 1998) will be remembered for the openly pronounced ballot war fought for as to who should wield political power of the Country—the United Front, Congress (I) or B.J.P. The voting masses had deprecated the attitudes of the political parties and their leaders. The thirteenth general election of October 1999 had put the question marks for the people to decide (i) on the non-Indian or foreign origin of the leader of Congress Party, Sonia Gandhi, whom the Congress Party had earmarked to be the next Prime Minister of India and (ii) whether Congress Party was wrong in voting out the existing Government when it did not have capacity to provide or form alternative Government These two arguments had persisted as the main election issues before the electorate. It was observed by the people with some alarm that the political parties had forgotten the socio-economic aspects of community life, the importance of their election manifestos, the fast growing economic disparity within the society, the immense corruption or the choking shortages of drinking water, food and electricity resources. The parties had given best attention to the seat adjustments between the regional and national parties as the only important politics in ways as were never seen before.

1.40. Whatever be the form of government and the method of organising the Parliament, the democracy rests on the basic concept that people are the real sovereign and their representatives run the administration. According to the Press Information Bureau of the Government of India the Parliament in 1952 had a total electorate of 17,32,13,635 out of which 10,58,44,499 had actually voted. These figures became 35,55,90,700 for electorate and 20,24,05,413 for actual voters in 1980 and by 1998 these figures swelled to 60,58,64,103 for electorate and 37,54,54,034 for actual voters, giving the singular distinction to India of being the largest democracy in the world.

1.41. *The democratic temper:* It has its own peculiarities and it manifests itself in various forms, expectations and requirements from the political parties and also the representatives of people in the government. The elected representatives are representatives of people, members of political parties and members of the Parliament or legislatures, three characters rolled in one. As discussed, the power to administer in democracy is a delegated power with ultimate responsibility owed to the people. Democracy has always a national outlook, a social purpose towards egalitarian development in diversity and the participation of the individual in the formulation of the social purpose by his right to vote and to be elected in the election to the democratic institutions.

1.42. *Constitutional Status of the Individuals and the People*: While the country has adopted the democratic system of polity and the Constitution of India has provided for the Parliament and State Legislatures as the foundation of this democratic polity and the Election Commission of India conducts the elections to elected bodies and institutions under the Constitution contested by political parties and also by independent individuals, the inquiry here is as to what is the position of people in this process. Do the people have constitutional status in this political process? A government must have majority of members in the elected legislature, that is Union Parliament or State Legislature in case of States. It may be mentioned that the elected members of the Parliament, the State Legislatures and the Members of Council of Ministers have a constitutional status while the people cease to have a status in the political process once the elections are over.

1.42A. The political rights including the right to vote are available only to Indian citizens. Article 19 (1) of the Constitution which guarantees personal freedoms to Indian citizens as fundamental rights is conspicuous for being silent on the right of citizens to indulge in politics, though it is well recognised that every citizen has under the right to freedom of speech and expression the fundamental right to be informed, to learn, to mentally react alone, or to express and propagate his political views by speaking in any assembly of people or by forming an association for that purpose. This personal right to freedom is subject only to those restrictions which are expressly laid down in Article 19 by its Clauses (2) to (6). The Supreme Court has been categorical in saying that as such there is no fundamental right to vote or to take part in the political process under the Constitution of India. It is a constitutional right dependent on the name of a person being in the general election roll of a territorial constituency and on this aspect his right extends to the basic condition that his name should not be excluded from the election roll on grounds only of religion, race, caste, sex or any of them.[13] Beyond this, the right to vote of the people is only a statutory right subsisting under the Representation of People Act, 1951 though the right of people to elect is fundamental to democracy.[14] The convicts undergoing imprisonment term or suffering from disqualification as prescribed by Constitution, law or a verdict of Election Commission are in the interest of good people debarred from the right to vote.

1.42B. The right to vote is coupled with the duty to be discreet and to exercise the right to franchise with caution, responsibility and social purpose. The thirteenth general election held in October 1999, posed several problems at national level for the voters. Whether a recently naturalised Indian citizen could be Prime Minister of India, whether to vote for national parties or coalition or alliances of parties and whether success in Kargil war of May–August 1999 with Pakistan, a national and non-political issue supported by all political parties, should be deciding factor in favour of re-electing the political alliance

---

[13] *Constitution of India*, Article 325.

[14] Right to elect and right to be elected are only statutory rights and not common law right: G.K. Bapat *versus* D.R. Meghe (1995), 5 SCC 347.

forming the interim Government. The voters did, however, took note of the performance of the political party forming government in their respective States in deciding their vote for the election to the House of People. This element expressed as anti-incumbency factor or syndrome did vitally influence voters' behaviour in the elections to Lok Sabha held in October 1999 in several States, like Bihar, Delhi, Uttar Pradesh, Madhya Pradesh or Maharashtra, showing that voters are now turning critical, discreet and hard to be pleased by promises made by the political parties. The general awareness of Indian voters has increased with every general election beyond doubt but the voters also preferred to loyally vote for their favourite political parties or candidates. Actually this discreteness is the quality of mobile public opinion segment of Indian voters and by the end of this millennium this small section of Indian voters is confined to the educated news-media influenced urban middle class only.

1.43. It has been already emphasised that political parties are essential means for successful and efficient functioning of democracy in contemporary constitutional systems. These occupy a distinct and unique position. It is visualised that a political party is a creation of free men, acting according to its own wisdom and it is in no way a creation or department of the government,[15] the political party is to advise or run the government but it is not agency of or subservient in any way to the government. Also, that the political party is a group of human beings of similar views possessing a discernible stability which is organised for the achievement of the common political agenda or election manifesto, for securing or maintaining for its leaders the control of government and at the same time for providing to the members and leaders of the party through such control some material benefits and advantages.[16] By law these can be given benefits and privileges and modalities can be laid down for their proper functioning in public interest.[17] A political party

---

[15] Fellman, *The Constitutional Right of Association*, p. 39.
[16] Fredric, *Constitutional Government and Democracy*, p. 419.
[17] P.N.T. Terah *versus* Union of India, AIR 1985 SC 1133

need not be a platform for selfless sacrifice as was the case before independence in India when national politics was patriotism pure and simple for achievement of independence from foreign rule and political parties provided the directions for this movement.

1.43A. In all countries the political parties are professional "fighting organisations" which have to maintain internal unity, develop strategies for winning the elections and conducting the administration of the country when forming the government.[18] In England the existence of political parties had been second stage in development of parliamentary system beginning from the Prime Ministership of Walpole under King George I.[19]

1.43B. In India political party system had been taken for granted when the Constitution was being framed and so there is no recognition of the right to political association in the Constitution. It is rather an incidence of 'right to form associations and unions' which includes the right to work for achievement of the legitimate objectives of the association, but the Constitution does not guarantee that the State shall help or guarantee the successful achievement of the purposes of the association.

1.43C. The political parties under the Constitution of India and also under the political theory for democracy developed in the West are voluntary association of people formed by the free will. There is to be no compulsion to join or to continue to remain in the party. A member may quit the party for whatever reasons that prompt him. It is judicially recognised in India that the persons forming an association as a political party had a right under Article 19 (1) [c] to expect that its composition continued to remain voluntary or at least as much voluntary as

---

[18] Herman Finer, *The Theory and Practice of Modern Government,* iv ed. p. 241.

[19] The study has been pursued in Chapter III, *infra.*

they had agreed it to be at the time of formation.[20] The only restrictions on the association could be those reasonable restrictions which could be justified under clauses (2) to (6) of Article 19. It is not possible for the Government or any other authority to lay down that certain persons shall be admitted as members of a political party against the will of the existing members.

1.43D. Also, it is not possible for a political party to prevent defection of its successful members in any election who join other party or form a new party, since the right to association is voluntary and it includes the right to defect at all stages. The right of defection when the political party fails to inspire a member is part of freedom of association. However, the Indian political scene of 1970s and onwards became too much muddled because of too frequent defection of successful party members, and in order to bring some stability in politics the right of members of a party, after being successfully elected to a House on a party ticket, was restricted in 1985 by amending the Constitution.[21]

1.43E. By the anti–defection laws, as it will examined in detail in next Chapters, the defections have been sought to be made difficult by creating disqualifications for defecting elected members of Parliament or State Legislatures but the activity has not been completely prohibited. Within exceptions both defections from a party and splits in parties remain legal. It has not been possible to contain the spirit of freedom of association

---

[20] State of Madras *versus* V.G. Rao, 1952 SCR 597: AIR 1952 SC 196; Damayanti *versus* Union of India, AIR 1971 SC 966: the right of existing members of an association extends to the right to admit or not to admit particular individuals as members of the association; also, any law by which members can be introduced in voluntary association without option to the existing members (to keep them out) or any law which takes away the membership of those who have voluntarily joined it, will be unconstitutional for violating freedom of right to form an association.

[21] Tenth Schedule introduced by the Constitution (Fifty-second) Amendment Act, 1985.

and alongwith it the voluntary defections with reference to political parties by the amendment of the Constitution since the political morality has undergone change in India during the last fifty years of freedom and the Indian political parties continue to remain voluntary association of politics-minded people.

1.44. Viewing the democratic polity through the constitutional framework in India the right to take part in political process which includes right to elect or vote, right to be a candidate for election under the Constitution, right to canvass for others alone or in association, to dispute the result of an election and the right to wield the power of State for public administration on being elected are constitutional rights but subject to the limitations set by Articles 325, 326, 84, 191 and the laws enacted under Articles 327 and 328 for the purpose of elections.

2

Cabinet System for Democracy in India

2.01. The Constitution of India framed during 1947-1949, after the Second World War, was a unique political venture outside what is popularly known as West. It established parliamentary democracy in the East for the first instance for maintaining the people as political sovereign, the subjects of constitutional and legal systems and for providing a continuous system for the governance of the country by the mandate of the people. The envisaged democratic system provides a popularly elected political executive composed of the President and his Council of Ministers with the Prime Minister as the constitutional and legal chief executive. The President of India is part of Parliament[1] and he and both of the Houses of Parliament are directly or indirectly elected by the people periodically. While 'Cabinet' is a general term for the 'Council of Ministers' in England, the Constitution of India uses the latter term only. This body coexists along with the elected House of People except when the latter is dissolved for holding of fresh election.

2.02. In constitutional theory in the matter of laying down the relationship among the three constituents of Parliament for making the democracy work, the Constitution of India follows the British parliamentary system in spirit but with some notable reservations and adaptations. The British Constitution is unwritten and a large part of it in the context of parliamentary system and institutions is based on 'Conventions of the

[1] *Constitution of India,* Article 79.

Constitution'. The Constitution of India, on the other hand, has codified, though not exhaustively, most of the British 'conventions' on the inter-relationship between the Crown, the House of Commons and the House of Lords and the Cabinet. In the British system common law or customary law after codification evolves in a manner different from unwritten law. This pattern is followed in Indian legal system along with the status of pre-eminence given to the judiciary by which it is endowed with the constitutional status of being the final interpreter of the constitutional and legal norms. Indian Parliament is not master of its status, it has the powers available to it under the Constitution and it has to accept the interpretations of the constitutional provisions and its powers as made by the judiciary from time to time.

2.03. As such, there are some marked or obvious institutional differences in the British and the Indian systems which can be emphasised here since these indicate of the resulting deviations in the two parliamentary democracies.

First, the President of India is elected by an elected electoral college, has a fixed term and is regarded as part of Parliament and is representative of people, as much as the Prime Minister. The British Crown, on the other hand, is hereditary though when necessary by demise or abdication, British Parliament by law fixes the line of succession for the Crown. There is no term or retiring age for the King or Queen. The Crown has conventional and prerogative powers in the matter of British foreign relations and functions within parliamentary system which are sometimes different from the constitutional discretionary powers of the President of India. For example, when the Conservative Party[2] is returned in majority in House of Commons after an election, the King or Queen can exercise discretion and decide on the leader of the Party who is to be the Prime Minister. In India, the President is recognised to be an umpire in Union and State relations in the matter of propriety of decisions.

---

[2] It is not so in case of Labour Party which chooses its own leader.

Secondly, the House of Lords is not an elected body but it is partly hereditary and partly nominated generally from elderly statesmen, and has unlimited membership. It is supposed to represent elderly, mature and successful in life persons and not the units of the United Kingdom of England, Scotland, Northern Ireland or Wales, as in India or as in the U.S.A.[3] In status Indian Council of States is equal to House of People except in the matter of passage of financial bills but is less powerful than the Senate of U.S. Congress. The House of Lords is and has been rather ornamental in nature, a place of honour for its members.

Thirdly, in England all Ministers must be members of either House and the Prime Minister, since Lord Salisbury resigned in 1902, can only be from the House of Commons. This condition in case of Ministers is easily met since the membership of House of Lords is by nomination, not by election, and it is always possible for the Prime Minister to nominate a person to the House of Lords.[4] In India, the membership of Council of States is by election except for specified number of nominations laid down by the Constitution. The Prime Minister can be from the Council of States in India in the normal course.

---

[3] As at present the House of Lords has a predominant conservative character and can only delay passage of a bill. This power is generally not exercised when Conservative Party forms the Government, but when Labour Party forms the Government the House of Lords can and becomes obstructive of legislative programmes of the Government. This has led to the move for abolition of hereditary peers (Lords) so that by packing the House with its nominees the Labour Party may change or balance the political character of the House of Lords, see, f. n., below.
In December 1998, House of Lords had 759 hereditary peers, 512 life peers and 26 Lord Spirituals (archbishops and bishops); Queen's speech to joint session of Parliament in November1998, which is written by the Government, disclosed that the hereditary peers would be deprived of their rights to sit and vote in the House of Lords: "Democracy at Work", Warren Hoge, *Frontline*, December 18, 1998; The bill was introduced accordingly in House of Commons by the Labour Party Government of Prime Minister Tony Blair in January 1999.

Fourthly, Lord Chancellor[5] is a member of the Cabinet and a member of House of Lords. He presides over House of Lords when it functions as a House of Parliament, and also when it functions as the final Court of Appeal or as the Judicial Committee of Privy Council both of which are constituted out of the House of Lords. When the latter sits as a House of Parliament the Lord Chancellor functions as its Speaker. Unlike the Speaker of House of Commons he freely takes part in its deliberations and proceedings and he is an active and the principal spokesman of the ruling party in the House of Lords. There is no special position like that of Lord Chancellor in India and Vice-President of India is *ex-officio* Chairman of Council of States and the Chief Justice of Supreme Court is not a member either of Council of Minister or of Council of States.

Fifthly, the British Parliament has unrestricted legislative powers. In the course of the history of British monarchy since the thirteenth century Parliament has been the guardian and protector of the rights and liberties of the people as against the arbitrariness of the Kings. These rights and liberties are politically protected and the people express their voice for protection of their interests through the medium of House of Commons. It is believed that Parliament will never work against the welfare of the people and the laws made by it for this purpose. The laws made by it bind the government as well as the people. The Great Charters which guarantee the liberties of the people, namely, the Magna Carta of 1216, the Petition of Rights of 1628, the Bill of Rights of 1688 and the Act of Succession of 1701, are in the form of enactment of Parliament which can be amended by Parliament. In India, the legislative power of Parliament is subject to the Fundamental Rights of the people and Parliament cannot amend the basic structure of the Constitution.

Sixthly, the legislative supremacy of British Parliament is

---

[5] The Party forming the Government generally nominates a like-minded person having the capacity and qualifications of a Judge to the House of Lords and appoints him as Lord Chancellor.

also maintained by the absence of judicial power of review of the laws enacted by Parliament. The judicial writ extends to defining the statutes and enforcing them only. In India the position is markedly different on this aspect.

1. THE COUNCIL OF MINISTERS

2.04 In the Indian constitutional scheme for people's democracy, the Council of Ministers as a body occupies a unique position, which is at once distinct from and rather superior to the President, Vice-President and Prime Minister of India. To all those who are conversant with Cabinet system of England, the position of the Indian Council of Ministers with regard to Prime Minister will appear to be an exaggeration in the above statement since the British notion is that Cabinet provides helping hands to the Prime Minister and its composition is his handiwork.

2.05. The description of Cabinet in British constitutional setting given by Bagehot in 1867 that Cabinet is the hyphen of the buckle which on fastening provides a bridge between the Executive and Parliament is an apt simile.[6] It is also true for the position of the Council of Ministers in the Indian Constitution and the analogical description has been with approval adopted by the Supreme Court of India.[7] The 'Cabinet' and the 'Council of Ministers' represent the same kind of constitutional authority and there is no difference between them. The term Cabinet was a popular expression for Queen Anne's (1702-1714) Privy Counsellors who met in one of the interior chambers of the Queen which was known as cabinet room. The Privy Council was at that time the "sole supreme consultative council and executive authority in the state" and the monarch was the chairman of the council. The Act of Succession 1701 and its

---

[6] Bagehot, *The English Constitution*, p. 11.

[7] Ram Jawaya Kapur *versus* State of Punjab, A.I.R. 1955 SC 549; Shamsher Singh *versus* State of Punjab A.I.R. 1974 S.C. 2193; R.S. Nayak *versus* A.R. Antulay (1984) 2 SCC 184.

amendment by the Place Act of 1707 had together in effect already provided:

(a) that no Council office-holder shall be in a position to hold government contracts and so the cabinet minister cannot have any interest in any company which is concerned with government contracts and must resign or give up such an interest before joining the cabinet, and

(b) that pensioners or placeman or members of permanent Civil Service cannot sit in Parliament, therefore they cannot be in Cabinet also.

This was intended to separate the Cabinet from any kind of subordination to the executive. However, the successors of Anne, George I and II could not speak or understand English and therefore they did not attend the meetings of the Cabinet Council and the tradition of the Prime Minister presiding over the meetings of Cabinet was developed by the Whig Prime Minister Walpole. Significantly, Walpole was not only the first Prime Minister (from 1721 to 1742) to start the practice of presiding over the meetings of Privy Council which came to be known as Cabinet Council during his time, but he also insisted that Cabinet Council be composed of his nominees only that is Whig Party or one party, and he dismissed from the Cabinet those who did not agree with him. This was possible because George I was thankful to the Whig Party for giving him succession to the throne in 1714 as Queen Anne earlier had been.

2.06 The pattern of Indian political executive, combined in the President or Governor and the Council of Ministers, embodies in general form the British parliamentary and Cabinet system of government both for the Union and the States. This was consciously done in the Constituent Assembly of India where it was recognised that the contemporary Indian public life was largely drawn upon the working of the British Westminster system. It was observed:

> "Most of us have looked up to the British model as the best for the last thirty or forty years, some kind of

responsibility has been introduced in the governance of the Country. Our constitutional traditions have become Parliamentary and we have now all our Provinces functioning more or less on the British model."[8]

2.06A. The Supreme Court in Shamsher Singh *versus* State of Punjab, confirmed the above position when it stated that Indian "Constitution embodies generally the Parliamentary or Cabinet system of Government of British model both for the Union and the States."[9]

2.07. The Cabinet in England considered in historical perspective signifies as W.B. Munro has explained:

> "a body of the Privy Councillors, who have been chosen by the Prime Minister in the name of Crown, with the approval of the majority in the House of Commons."[10]

In 1867 Bagehot described it as a board of control created to rule the nation, chosen by the Legislature and composed of persons whom the Legislature trusts and knows.[11] But, when assessed functionally the Cabinet operates, in the words of Ivor Jennings, as "the supreme directing authority...(providing) unity to British system of Government."[12]

2.07A. In England all the members of the Cabinet at all times have to be Members of Parliament and by practice since 1902 the Prime Minister is invariably from the House of Commons. In 1963, Lord Home resigned from House of Lords and got elected to House of Commons before becoming Prime Minister. In 1966, the Indian Prime Minister Indira Gandhi also did the same thing.

2.08. *Functions of Cabinet or Council of Ministers*: The Cabinet in England has been the architect of the representative

---

[8] Shri K.M. Munshi, Member of the Drafting Committee: *Constituent Assembly Debates*, Vol. VII, p. 984.

[9] A.I.R. 1974 S.C. 2193.

[10] Munro, *The Government of Europe*, p. 74.

[11] Bagehot, *The English Constitution*, p. 12.

[12] Jennings, *Cabinet Government*, (1959), p. 1.

and responsible Government. It had always carried on the struggle against the King or the autocracy of the Chief Executive but more so since the beginning of seventeenth century. In this process it also created a system for expression of public opinion in Parliament which since the end of eighteenth century asserted itself to the extent of choosing between alternative counsellors in the form of Cabinet. When the political rivalry between Conservative Party and Liberal Party developed in middle of nineteenth century the swing from one party to another depending not on the will of the King but on the majority in the House of Commons, leading to formation of a different Cabinet, became established practice for parliamentary form of Government in England. The famous political chess games between Gladstone and Disraeli during later half of nineteenth century, constitute the firm foundation for Cabinet system of Government. In 1878, Lord Salisbury had on the functioning of a Cabinet significantly reiterated[13] and stated the principle, which is true even now, that

> "For all that passes in Cabinet every member of it who does not resign is absolutely and irretrievably responsible and has no right afterwards to say that he agreed in one case to a compromise, while in another he was persuaded by his colleagues...."[14]

2.09. The Report of the British Parliamentary Committee on Machinery of the Government (1918) during the tenure of Prime Minister Lloyd George, appears to be most pertinent document in order to explain the contemporary Indian constitutional scene. The Report assessed that the functions of the British Cabinet are threefold:

"(a) The final determination of the policy which is to be submitted to Parliament;

---

[13] Danby's Case (1679), 11 St, Tr. 599, established the principle that a minister cannot shelter himself from legal responsibility by a plea of obedience to the command of the Sovereign.

[14] *Life of Robert, Marquis of Salisbury*, Vol. II, pp. 219-220; Wade and Phillips, *Constitutional Law*, iv ed. p. 64.

(b) the supreme control of the national executive in accordance with the policy prescribed by Parliament; and

(c) the continuous co-operation and determination of the authorities of the several departments of the State."[15]

2.10. At the very outset, after the election when the Cabinet or the Council of Ministers has been formed the Cabinet formulates the general policies which it wants to pursue and the aims which it wants to achieve in order to redeem the promises which the party forming the cabinet had made to the people. The King or Queen in England at the opening of the session at a joint meeting of the two Houses of Parliament held in the House of Lords, addresses the Parliament setting out the policies of the new government. The same practice is followed in India when the President addresses both Houses of Parliament at a joint sitting at the commencement of the first session after each general election to the House of People and at the commencement of the first session each year.[16]

2.10A. Apart from this, each Ministry of the Government comes with a formulation of its policies on matters requiring legislation or grant of money or policies which are necessary to be considered in order that the departments concerned with the matter may function with definiteness during the term of the ministry and in future. For example, in India in 2002, the Defence Ministry might want to know whether it should go on with the nuclear programme, development or production of particular system of missiles or should update the main battle tanks manufactured indigenously or purchase them from abroad; the Ministry of Civil Aviation might be interested in purchase of a new fleet of commercial aeroplanes for which the Airlines may be pressing; the Ministry of Commerce might be anxious that some regulations for investment by foreign corporations should be made less stringent; the Ministry of Justice might be under

---

15 See Jennings, *Cabinet Government*, reference given, at p. 232.

16 *Constitution of India*, Article 87.

pressure to increase the number of judges in various High Courts; or the opposition parties might be pressing for permission to be given to foreign companies to do insurance business in India or start publication of newspapers in India.

2.11. In parliamentary government system, all such policy matters are first discussed by the experts and senior officials of the concerned Ministry, if the Minister agrees for further action the matter is referred to the Cabinet which in its own way through its Committees examines the policy matter and takes the clearance and advice from commonly or indirectly related Ministries including those of railways, Foreign affairs, Environment Protection, Finance or others as may be necessary. The consideration of a matter for evaluation or clarification of government's policy might also be forced upon the Council of Ministers by the Opposition through adjournment motion,[17] cut motions, censure or no-confidence motions.

2.11A. After this formulation before the House, through President's address, or through appropriation Bills or Bill for new enactment or amendment of an existing Act, the policy matter is referred to Parliament for its approval. Such approval of policies operates as vote of confidence and if the policy is disapproved by the House of Commons in England or House of People in India, this disapproval is a successful hostile vote and is taken to mean vote of no-confidence leading to the rejection of the Cabinet or Council of Minister *in toto* and a change of Government or general election to Parliament takes place. It is for the Cabinet or Council of Ministers to lay down and give final shape to all of the policies of the government and it is for the Parliament which represents the people to endorse or reject these policies as essential part of the democratic process. The

[17] For examples, the opposition forced the government to discuss the imposition of President's Rule in Bihar and the matter of the dismissal of Naval Chief Admiral Vishnu Bhagwat in the Budget Session of Parliament, February-March 1999, by adjournment motions. In 2002, the opposition forced discussion on 'Gujarat communal disturbance' situation in House of People by a motion which was defeated after voting.

ruling party has at all times to ensure majority in the House of People at the time of voting and this in India is ensured by the party whip.

2.11B. Thus, the relativity between people and the Cabinet and the subordination of Cabinet to the Legislature is maintained. However, whether the Council of Minister controls Parliament or latter controls the Council of Ministers in actual practice is always a matter of independent discussion but the theory is that people control the House of People and the House of People (Lok Sabha) controls the Council of Ministers which is the real executive since the negative vote or absence of majority in the House of People finishes the existence of the Council of Minister unceremoniously. As practical application of this principle (a) Prime Minister Charan Singh could not remain in office in 1979 since he could not show majority in the House of People, and (b) the same happened with Prime Minister Atal Bihari Vajpayee in June 1996, though both of them very much wanted to continue as Prime Minister.

2.11C. The other side of this constitutional relationship between Parliament and Council of Ministers is also significant, that is, by rejecting a Governmental measure the House of People also invites its own dissolution unless an alternative Council of Ministers is possible.

2.12. The second element in the formulation of the function of Council of Ministers under the *Report* (2.09) is not less basic and pertinent. It links the democratic process running through elected Parliament, its dependent Cabinet or Council of Ministers to the control of the executive for the good government for the people. It is a principle of democracy in parliamentary form of government that the executive through the Cabinet is responsible to the legislature.

2.12A. The first task of the Prime Minister after being designated by the President is to divide the executive or administration of the Union into different departments known as ministry headed by a Minister. By now this division is not a new thing since by experience the main ministries are well defined in England as well as in India, such as, Foreign Affairs, Home Affairs, Finance, Energy Development, Commerce, Railways or Defence Affairs. All that the Prime Minister does is to combine or sort out the various ministries into groups to be allocated to particular Ministers. As the number of Ministers is increased the departments are reallocated between the existing and new ministers.

2.12B. There is an important question as to the ready availability of qualified political manpower for controlling the Executive of the country and the administrative machinery for keeping the wheels of democracy moving. It is observed that in the presidential form of government as evolved in the U.S.A. there are political posts in the Executive to be occupied by politicians, available after the election of President in large numbers, apart from the ministers known as Secretaries. These political posts are spread from the Federal government machinery to State level since the federal executive and judiciary are separate from State executive and judiciary. It is, therefore, easy for the President's political party to accommodate its party workers in government paid positions but which end with the term of the President. Such Party workers are assets for the two political parties of U.S.A., they put in sincere work for retaining the party in power since that secures their positions also. At the same time the President of USA can develop his Cabinet out of experts who agree with him and whom the President regards worthy of the assignment. As the term of these Secretaries depends on the sweet will of the President, the Members of the Congress belonging to the President's Party are not eager for shifting to become members of Cabinet of the President which involves resignation of their membership of the Congress.

2.12C. Under the parliamentary system of government envisaged in India on British pattern, however, there are no such avenues for accommodating in government posts the party workers of the political party forming the Council of Ministers.

The control of administrative infra-structure is done only through the Ministers and the constitutional posts of Attorney General or State Advocate Generals. The result is that with the growth of multifarious welfare activities and public duties, the number of government departments and ministries has been steadily increasing. Now, in addition to the category of Cabinet ministers, their subordinates under the designations of Deputy Minister and Minister of State have been added. While the Cabinet Ministers are subject to the principle of ministerial responsibility and take part in basic formulations of policies, the ministers of subordinate category are in the charge of various departments coming under a Cabinet Minister and assist him in managing the affairs suitably and efficiently. At the Union level taken together the normal strength of all kinds of ministers inducted by the President after administering of oath of secrecy, should remain at a number around fifty. However, the realities of coalition front or alliance politics lead to the accommodation of a much large number of politicians as ministers.

2.12D. It is a negative aspect of parliamentary system that the party in power is over burdened since it has to (a) maintain its contact with the people or the constituencies, (b) keep the party prepared for the next election by showing positive results as achievements of the party, maintain party discipline particularly when there are more aspirants for the posts of minister, and (c) at the same time lay down and execute the policies of the government. The task of the party in power becomes much more stringent and difficult when there are party workers who could not get nominated as election candidates or failed to get elected as M.P. or M.L.A. It is a fact of political life in parliamentary form of politics that every aspiring politician has to maintain a large number of party supporters, elected or non-elected, behind him. This requires finances as well as making of various kinds of promises with the capacity of redeeming the promises. This in a natural way breeds parasitic phenomena or corruption atmosphere through political elements in the society, particularly since the Ministers can deny political patronage only at the cost of being left without supporters. The opposition parties take advantage of these maladies in order to bring down the image of the ruling party in the estimation of public. The freedom of press also plays important role in this process since the ruling party must have a helpful or sympathetic press, while the opposition led press always projects a dismal picture of the deeds of ruling party.

2.13. Are the defections of elected members of a House into or out of a party in national interest or beneficial to the health of parliamentary system of government? The answer to this inquiry cannot be definitive of the resulting situation. The defections into the ruling party for becoming ministers break the other political parties no doubt but simultaneously these create dissatisfaction in the rank and file of the ruling party. There is a question mark on the loyalty of the members of both the gaining and losing political parties. The voters and the public become the ultimate judge of the merits of the parties which come to them at the time of election. Also, breaking of the opposition party is not a mark or substitute of good and efficient administration expected from a Council of Ministers, the latter has to stand on its own merit.

2.14. The next inquiry in the process of control of executive by the Council of Ministers is about the requisite qualities of Ministers and this inquiry should be done by taking into the problems of their profession, that is, representing the people in the control of and giving of directions to the administration. The Constitution of India prescribes that a Minister must be a member of either House of legislature or become a member thereof within six months of his appointment as Minister or Prime Minister of India or Chief Minister of a State. This ensures a link between the people and the Minister.

2.14A. Under Articles 84 and 173 of the Constitution the pre-conditions for a person who seeks election to fill a seat in the Houses of Parliament or State Legislature, are that he:

(a) is a citizen of India and makes and subscribes an oath or affirmation according to prescribed form before a prescribed authority,

(b) is in case of lower House not less than 25 years of age and in case of upper House not less than 30 years of age, and

(c) possesses such other qualifications as may be prescribed under any law made by Parliament, that is Representation of peoples Act 1951.

Further, Article 102 and Article 191 define the disqualification of a person, either before or after being elected, from becoming a member of Parliament or the State Legislatures. These are:

(a) that he holds any office of profit other than one exempted by Parliament by law,

(b) that he is of unsound mind and stands so declared by a competent court,

(c) that he is an undischarged insolvent,

(d) that he ceases to be a citizen of India, or

(e) that he is so disqualified by or any law made by Parliament.

However, being a Minister of Union or of State is not holding an office of profit for disqualification under sub clause (a) above.

2.14B. The Tenth Schedule to the Constitution of India inserted in 1985 by the Fifty Second Amendment, 1985, further provides that an existing elected member of the House of People or a State Legislature would become disqualified and will lose his membership if he defects from his party under the conditions laid down therein. But, a member will defect from his party, understandably either to retire from politics or to become Minister, Prime Minister or Chief Minister, instead of resigning from the Party, Council of Ministers for difference of opinion with the Prime Minister or Chief Minister. In such case such member or Minister must have been assured of a large chunk of the legislative party members in the lower House forming another Party and of support from other parties either as a coalition government or with outside support of the other party.

2.15. What the people of India are resenting in the 1990s and onwards is the lack of any educational qualifications for Prime Minister, Chief Minister, Minister or Member of a Legislature.

(a) The Constituent Assembly had in 1947-49 felt that formal education was not a normal phenomenon with Indian masses particularly when during the struggle for freedom the patriots had left their jobs, professions and education to take up the fight against the alien rulers. A requirement of formal education would have deprived a vast section of political freedom fighters from continuing with their zeal for serving the motherland.

(b) By political theory also, the representatives of the people as ministers and legislators need not be experts or better informed than the persons whom they have to control or direct. The framers of the Constitution had left it for Parliament to introduce literacy as a qualification and had rejected an amendment to provide it constitutionally. It was felt that the fears that an illiterate regime might take over the legislatures was remote, and the Chairman of Drafting Committee Dr. Ambedkar had observed that:

> "With regard to the amendment of Professor K.T. Shah about literacy, I think that it is a matter which might as well be left to the Legislatures. If the Legislatures at the time of prescribing qualifications feel that literacy qualification is a necessary one, I no doubt think that they will do it."

However, after fifty years of Independence at the beginning of the Twenty First Century, lack of educational qualifications in the representatives of people in Parliament or State legislature, is regarded to be the main reason for criminals taking over control of politics, existence of puppet governments at the State level or 'government by proxy' situations.

2.16. With the controversial experiences of State of Bihar during 1997-98 in background,[18] which have defied normal understanding and functioning of the Constitution, now at the advent of twenty-first century, a minimum of educational qualification, graduation or its equivalent, for the elected representatives of the people in the Parliament or the State Legislatures, appears to be proper. According to statistics in the first House of People, 110 Members did not have any formal education but in the ninth House of People that number was 21 and in eleventh the number was 16 only. The highest number of graduates (245) were in tenth House of People. However, the picture is different in case of State Legislatures where the constituencies for election are small. One expects that the representatives of the people should be educated and experienced enough to understand the intricacies of the government when they become Ministers or Chief Ministers so that they do not become puppets in the hands of bureaucracy or mafia dons and thereby fail to direct and control the administration to fulfil the expectations of the people who elected them. In fact national integrity and well being are at all times more important and valuable than the rights of the

[18] The Rashtriya Janata Dal Government with outside support of Congress Party, in the State of Bihar since middle of 1997 has become an enigma in Indian politics for becoming a family affair and a government by proxy due to majority available to the Chief Minister who had little or no education but was maintained functional and stable by her husband the former Chief Minister quite for sometime even from Jail and with party support. In September 1998 this Government withstood the recommendations of Governor for imposition of President's Rule under Article356 for breakdown of constitutional machinery in the State mainly on the ground of majority rejecting a no-confidence motion. The Chief Minister Rabri Devi had no parliamentary experience and was not a member of the legislature but she was elected to the Legislative Assembly subsequently. She continued as Chief Minister till February 1999 when President's Rule was invoked in the State by the Central Government. But, she was reinstated on revocation of President's Rule on March 10, 1999.

individuals. It is necessary to recognise that the art and science of governing is intricate and is too difficult to be entrusted to ignorant and uninformed persons even though these might have been chosen by the majority of people of a constituency. The fear is legitimate when an era of criminal threats, muscle power, polling booth capturing or vote manipulation by other corrupt practices may appear to have set in.

2.17. It is also noticed since 1990s that politics is a profession now and the politicians are not self-less patriots as theses used to be in the earlier pre-independence days. Politics attracts young persons of dubious character and of poor worth more, who are generally a financial liability to everybody. Talented persons are not interested in this profession since the time and experience required for becoming a minister is much too disproportionate to his lawful earnings. The bureaucrats, technocrats, lawyers or businessmen have better social respect and income than the politicians. The direct nomination of retired or capable persons with wide experience of business or technical professions for election by political parties is almost negligible and party tickets are given to the party workers or else to those who can partly or fully bear the expenses of the election. Incidentally, the top political leaders of the political party forming the Council of Ministers are more at ease with party backbenchers and feel that too much talent causes indiscipline in the party since all elected party men cannot be made ministers.

2.18. In national interest, however, it is necessary for a minister to be more intelligent, far-sighted and altruistic than the highly talented bureaucracy and the technocrats and professionals in the contemporary society with whom he has to come into contact. The Ministers have the power of choosing their immediate subordinates from the civil services, deciding on their promotions, suspending or transferring them when dissatisfied with their performance. They also regulate the officers on the key posts so that the policies of the government are properly and efficiently carried out. If any minister suffers from inferiority complex, he will quarrel with his tools and indulge in exercising his powers of mass transfer of the civil servants and will, thereby make a mess of the administrative machinery. The task of Ministers is further made difficult when the bureaucracy is corrupt or where the officers are used as 'middlemen' in receiving pay-off or kickbacks by political figures in high places.

2.19. As controller of administration the Prime Minister, a national and international figure, has not only to lay down the policy but also to see that the policies are properly executed and the results are seen and felt by the voters. He must have vision to know what the people desire within the constitutional framework, the existing pattern of law and situation dealing with the desired matter, a power of convincing speech making on the floor of the House and a persuasive and receptive disposition when meeting the people who voted for him. A Prime Minister helped by his party and the other members of the Council of Ministers has to meet all sections of people and members of administrative machinery to know the state of affairs and problems or the hurdles in smooth working of the schemes. Every Minister has to be vigilant with his public image since the opposition parties are always ready to expose his weakness in order to harm him and his party. Now with multimedia active in political circles purity in life and behaviour is to be assiduously maintained by the Minister. A Minister with poor public image may continue to remain in his chair for various reasons but he cannot win the confidence of and control the administrative machinery since in democracy things are achieved by persuasion and co-operation and cannot be achieved by creating awe in the public and in the bureaucracy. In England sex scandals and in India criminal graft charges are taking heavy toll of the Ministers. In the U.S.A. the same is the position with the President and the members of his cabinet where both public and the media take interest in the purity of public men.

2.19A. However, the collective wisdom and integrity of the Council of Ministers has of necessity to be efficiently mobilised and harnessed to the satisfaction of Parliament and the people. Within the functional framework of supervising the work of administrative machinery comes the ability of the Council of Ministers to select proper officers on the key posts, to define their work and to co-ordinate heir functions so as to achieve prompt and efficient implementations of the policies. Every Council of Ministers which wants to make a headway, has to tackle the bureaucratic inertia and red tape before the effects reach the people.

2.20. Thirdly, the *Report* (2.09) emphasises that in the indoor management of the government the Council of Ministers has to ensure a continuous co-operation between different departments and ministries of which the Cabinet Secretary, Chief Secretary and the Secretaries of the different ministries are required to take care. At the ministerial level there are several Cabinet Committees in which two or more Cabinet members participate in order to fix up the share of burden or to remove the objections which the other ministries might have in adoption or implementation of any scheme or policy. However, these Cabinet Committees are of confidential nature since the principle of collective responsibility prevents public display of differences between different ministers while a matter is on the stage of formulation. This confidentiality is particularly maintained because the Opposition is always interested in playing up dissension in the ruling party to emphasise that the government is weak and incoherent. Further even if there is a collective decision of the cabinet on a matter coming in the sphere of a particular ministry, the principle of individual responsibility of the Minister continues to be applicable in the Parliament in case anything goes wrong.

2. THE PRINCIPLE OF MINISTERIAL RESPONSIBILITY

2.21. The principle of ministerial or individual responsibility is an integral part of parliamentary democratic government system which entrenches the status of the Cabinet or the Council of Ministers in between the Chief Executive and the Chief Legislature, that is, the President of India and Parliament. As such the principle of ministerial responsibility has dual implications. First, as part of executive and *second,* as part of Parliament and as representative of the people.

2.22. When the principle of individual responsibility of a minister is considered in the first context, that is as part of executive, it means that for whatever is done by a minister the legal liability shifts from the President or the State to the minister concerned. Since the principle of ministerial responsibility has emerged out of the practices of British Parliament, this background is part Indian parliamentary practice.

2.22A. In England, there has been an established principle that 'The King can do no wrong' since he is sovereign and is vested with regal characteristics which separates him from his subjects. This principle has now been changed by the Crown Proceedings Act of 1947, under which the Crown is also responsible like individuals for legal actions subject to certain preconditions. Since, the King was deprived politically of his regal powers by British Parliament and all such powers were exercised by the Càbinet on his behalf, Parliament regarded his ministers to be politically responsible for all the policies and decisions of the government, and when censured by Parliament a minister had to resign from the Cabinet and could not continue even if the King wanted him.

2.22B. As early as in 1679, in the Case of Danby[19] it had been in England held that for all advice given to the King the Minister is responsible and he cannot take shelter behind the plea that he was working under the command of the King even when the King expressly takes upon himself the responsibility for the act. Earl of Danby was Lord Treasurer and leader of Country Party (1674-79) and the Danby Ministry was supporter

---

[19] F.N. 13, above.

of the royal authority. He is said to be the first English minister who maintained his ministry by organised bribery and the Parliament had earned the name as 'Pensionary Parliament'. Charles II did not want war with France and he was interested in enhancement of his pension from France. He compelled Danby to negotiate a treaty with France secretly which he failed to do but Louis XIV published the correspondence with Danby. The House of Commons impeached Danby for high treason. The King acknowledged that he was responsible for the negotiation of treaty with France and for the demand for increase in his pension and that Danby signed the letters for the treaty at his command. Charles II issued a pardon under the Great Seal, but the House of Commons held that no such pardon can be pleaded in bar of the impeachment by the House of Commons. Charles II dissolved the House of Commons in 1679 in order to save Danby and the question arose if impeachment ceased with the dissolution or prorogation of Parliament.

2.22C. The Act of Settlement of 1701 of Britain laid down emphatically that 'No pardon under the Great Seal should stop impeachment by the Commons', and that 'all public business should be done by the Privy Council, the decisions of which should be signed by all its members' among other things. The other question whether impeachment ceased with the dissolution or prorogation of Parliament it was finally settled in the case of Impeachment of Warren Hastings in 1791, in the negative, that is it shall remain alive. By the end of eighteenth century, the convention and practice of a minister including Prime Minister resigning on the censure by the House of Commons developed which is now known as individual or ministerial responsibility and the complex procedure of impeachment of a Minister came into disuse. Maitland has in brief stated the nature of individual liability in British system in the words that the Ministers are responsible:

> "before the Courts of law and they are responsible even for the highest acts of State; for those acts of State they can

be sued or prosecuted, and the High Court of Justice will have to decide whether they (acts) are legal or not. Law, specially modern statute law, has endowed them with many great powers, but, the question whether they have overstepped those powers can be brought before a court of law, and the plea 'this is an official act, an act of state' will not serve them".[20]

2.23. In India, the Constitution of India provides that 'the Ministers appointed by the President on the advice of Prime Minister shall hold office during the pleasure of the President'.[21] All executive actions of the Government of India are taken in the name of the President, by means of orders and other instruments which are authenticated by the Ministers in accordance with the rules made by the President of India.[22] The President makes the rules for convenient transaction of the business of the Government of India, and for the allocation of the said business among the Ministers.[23] If the President so requires any matter on which a decision has been taken by a minister but which has not been considered by the Council of Ministers, such a matter is submitted to the Council for its decision before President executes any document or issues any order on it.[24] Accordingly, for all that takes place in the name of Government of India is signed by the President on the advice of some Minister or Council of Ministers and each of such documents has to be authenticated by a Minister. The liability if any, on the actions taken under the document rests on the Minister concerned. Where the Minister makes any unlawful gain or when there is unjust enrichment of the Minister out of any matter arising out

---

20 Maitland, *Constitutional History*, p. 484.

21 Article 75 (1), (2).

22 Article 77 (1), (2). Rules, *vide* Notification No. S.O. 2297, 3-11-1958, *Gazette of India, Extraordinary* 1958, Part II, Sec. 3(ii), p. 1315, as amended from time to time.

23 Article 77 (3).

24 Article 78 (c).

of the authenticated document the liability of the Minister ceases to be political and becomes legal.

2.24. The ruling party or the ruling coalition can decide on a Deputy Prime Minister, who shall be additional Prime Minister in effect but will be subordinate to Prime minister. He can in absence of Prime Minister preside over the meetings of the Council of Ministers. When there is no Deputy Prime Minister and the Prime Minister is away from the country or for some reason unable to attend to the work, one or more senior members of the Council can be identified by the Prime Minister to look after the work in his absence so that decisions by the Council of Ministers are taken in emergency.

2.24A. Prime Ministers Jawahar Lal Nehru, Indira Gandhi, Rajiv Gandhi and P.V. Narasimha Rao had designated their deputies to work in their absence as and when it became necessary. When Prime Minister Atal Bihari Vajpayee was hospitalised for knee surgery in a hospital with medical advice to refrain from any work and not to meet any visitor in October 2000, he had refrained from identifying any Minister for chairing the cabinet meetings during his hospitalisation. The President also did not ask him to make such arrangement. The inter se politics of coalition National Democratic Alliance government ostensibly made it difficult for him to make such a nomination since this act would have been equivalent to naming his successor in the coalition National Democratic Alliance which only the Alliance could do.

2.25. The political liability of a Minister under the Cabinet System arises for:

(i) any policy decisions taken by his Ministry without consultation or approval of the Council of Ministers and where the subsequent approval is denied and

(ii) wrong or disastrous implementation of any matter which is likely to be censured by the House of People and which will confirm a lapse on the part of his Ministry.

2.25A. In either of such eventuality either the Prime Minister should make the lapse a responsibility of the entire Council of Minister and face a no confidence or censure motion squarely or, else, the Minister should resign. Since a censure of a Minister by the House of People when the Minister is being protected by the Prime Minister or the Council of Ministers means censure of the Council of Ministers.

2.25B. Under these circumstances constitutional provisions that "the Council of Ministers shall be collectively responsible to the House of People"[25] shall apply and the whole Council of Ministers will have to be replaced. Accordingly, because of the extended consequences this situation has become an internal matter for the party forming the Council of Ministers and the resignation of an erring Minister either as a matter of grace or as a scapegoat before there is formal accusation in the House of People in India or in the House of Commons in England has become unwritten part of constitutional system.

2.25C. In India this was taken seriously by the Ministers and some Ministers had assumed responsibility for the mishaps and as a moral choice have resigned from the Council of Ministers.

(a) When the Budget was suspected to have leaked before being presented in House of People the Finance Minister John Mathai had resigned but ostensibly on the issue of his disagreement on the setting up of Planning Commission around 1953.

(b) The Railway Minister L.B. Shastri had resigned in 1957 on the issue of successive train accidents.

(c) The Defence Minister V.K. Krishna Menon resigned from the Cabinet for the Indian humiliation in 1962 successful aggression on Indian territory by China.

(d) The Railway Minister Nitish Kumar resigned from care-taker Union Government of Prime Minister Vajpayee

---

[25] *Constitution of India,* Article 75 (3).

in early August 1999 following a disastrous train accident in West Bengal costing more than 400 lives.

2.25C. However, now in the era around the end of twentieth century, the Ministers have ceased to be guided by considerations of grace and prefer to continue as long as possible since politics has become a matter of profession and career. The result is that as in eleventh Parliament poor performances by Ministers were allowed to become no-confidence motions against the Council of Ministers eventually to be defeated under the threat of House of People being dissolved for another election which even the Opposition did not want. A saving grace to this moral responsibility of a minister for malfunctioning in his ministry was somewhat salvaged by Minister Nitish Kumar.

2.26. The considerations of grace for ministerial responsibility resulting in resignation also apply to the charges of moral turpitude against and charge sheeting for a crime of any Prime Minister or Chief Minister or Minister. The argument of the Opposition parties in Parliament proceeds on he ground that such individuals cannot provide a clean administration and so also the Council of Ministers. The Opposition normally puts pressure for the matter to be placed before a parliamentary committee and the discussions in media or in Parliament on the character of a minister. Such proposition becomes highly embarrassing for the ruling political party or coalition alliance in their relationship with the public for votes.

2.26A. Impact of corruption on political parties was felt when in the 1990s the public image of Congress(I) and Janata Dal suffered very much because of public discussions of the charges of accepting of kick-backs by and transfer of public money to personal accounts of the ministers. After 1996 both of these parties faced the deserting of the party by members or setting in of the breaking process with their followers joining other parties or making independent political parties in States. Even the names of two former Prime Ministers and three prominent Chief Ministers and two Governors had figured during Tenth and Eleventh Parliaments (1991-97) in about twenty scams and scandals of the decade including pay-off to MPs of a regional party for voting against no confidence motion in House of People. Most of the Ministers and Chief Ministers resigned after charge sheets were filed against them in law courts. Former Prime Minister P.V. Narasimha Rao and a Minister of his Cabinet were convicted five years later in the year 2000 for the conspiracy for making pay-off to some Members of House of People for voting against no confidence motion against the Ministry in 1993, and were sentenced to three year imprisonment and fine by the Trial Court. On appeal, P.V. Narasimha Rao was later acquitted in 2002 of the changes by the High Court

2.26B. In England Ministers have often resigned on sex scandals. On mismanagement or disapproval of actions taken by the Cabinet, resignation have also followed. In 1917, Austen Chamberlain had resigned from the Cabinet for disastrous Mesopotamian campaign for which a judicial inquiry held him responsible technically. Samuel Hoare in 1935 resigned from Cabinet when his compromise on Abyssinia was not recognised *ex post facto* by the Cabinet.

2.27. A Minister is usually a very busy party man, heavily burdened with the obligation to oblige and repay his constituency supporters and he cannot attend personally to all of his duties every day. Most of his duties of a Ministry in the first instance are carried out by the civil service Secretaries and other staff who are technically highly qualified and experienced persons and are experts where specialised knowledge is required for understanding the matter. This ministerial staff from the Executive represents the particular Ministry of the government but all their *decisions and conclusions* have to be endorsed by the Minister as part of the concept of popular government under Article 75 of the Constitution. Only where by Constitution or by law a decision is to be taken by the Minister himself but the Minister delegates the exercise of the functions to the officers after laying down the basic policy, there is a delegation of power and the decisions of the officer become the decisions of the Minister and can be directly challenged.[26]

2.28. Under the parliamentary process as it stands in contemporary times, now-a-days it is difficult to separate decisions of a Minister from those of the Cabinet since most of the Ministers are professional politicians and prefer to side track individual responsibility. This they do by making all important matters of the Ministry involving any policy element to be a matter to be considered by the Cabinet Committees, since in one way or other many ministries, Finance, Commerce, Human Resource, etc., may be connected or involved side by side in the project at hand. In this way the final decision becomes the decision of the Prime Minister or of the whole Cabinet.

2.28A. Further, if there is any mishap in the working process under the Ministry, the Minister immediately, blames the government officers, makes their transfer or suspension and announces compensation or other remedial measures if the people are involved,[27] but does not offer to resign, in the

26 Sanjivee Naidu *versus* State of Madras, A.I.R. 1970 S.C. 1102 at 1106; Shamsher Singh *versus* State of Punjab, A.I.R. 1974 S.C. 2192 at 2199.

27 For example, in a suspected Naxalite fomented protest agitation by farmers for government aid on heavy crop losses due to severe hailstorm and unusual heavy winter rains in the region in Madhya Pradesh in January 1998, the tehsil office of Multai with Superintendent of Police and other officials inside, was alleged to be surrounded by about 5,000 strong irate mob of armed farmers. In the shoot out 75 policemen and 45 farmers were seriously injured and more than 17 farmers were killed by police firing. Political demands were made for resignation of three ministers for not taking timely preventive action against the fomenting unrest among local population after the natural calamities. The Congress (I) Chief Minister of Madhya Pradesh Digvijay Singh took responsibility, if any, on himself and the State Government, refused to sack the concerned three Ministers, blamed the local administration for the incident, ordered their charge-sheeting, announced payment of compensation to the dead, and demanded Union Government to defer recovery of loans from the State along with immediate payment of its due share of funds in order to meet the ongoing problems on different fronts: *Hindustan Times*, January 15, 16, and 17, 1998.

manner Railway Minister L.B. Shastri had done in 1957 when there were frequent train accidents.

2.29. The question, therefore, arises as to what is the utility of the principle of individual or ministerial responsibility of the ministers in the present era. The answer to this inquiry may be found to a great extent in the realist exposition by a British jurist:

> "The most common political meaning (of the principle) is that a certain minister will answer parliamentary questions on a given subject. A second sense arises when those in political circles appreciate that a particular policy is largely the idea of the minister, rather than the traditional policy of the party in power, and they may single out the minister as responsible even if the policy is the work of the Cabinet as a whole but his colleagues choose to place the burden on him."[28]

2.30. It is for the House of People ultimately to assess a Minister for his efficiency and sincerity in the discharge of his functions, and to put pressure on the Prime Minister to tone up the things by shuffling the work among the Ministers or by replacing one or the other. The situation is always intricate in a coalition ministry where the Ministers may happen to be the leaders of the constituent parties and on whose support the entire ministry depends. For example, In the eleventh Parliament (1996-98) in the United Front coalition governments under Prime Ministers H.D. Deve Gowda and I.K. Gujral, in reality there were more than three[29] additional or virtual prime ministers at all times. The peculiarity of this coalition was that the constitutional Prime Minister was simply a spokesman for the Council of Ministers, he could not have in reality removed any

---

[28] Mackintosh, *The British Cabinet*, p. 529.

[29] The Home Minister, Defence Minister and Finance Minister could not have been dismissed by the United Front Prime Ministers since these three Ministers were leaders of important constituents of the coalition.

of these three from the Council of Ministers or changed their portfolio at his will without endangering the coalition itself. The same was the position of Prime Minister Vajpayee in the twelfth Parliament when his government fell in April 1999 because he did not make compromise with the demands of one of the constituent of the coalition. The Prime Minister or Chief Minister is quite often a symbol of unity for the Council of Ministers, when a majority party is ridden with inside turmoil or when the coalition of several parties forming the government is wild or wayward.

3. THE COLLECTIVE RESPONSIBILITY OF COUNCIL OF MINISTERS

2.31. The constitutional requirement that "the Council of Ministers shall be collectively responsible to the House of People"[30] presupposes a deep rooted firm unity within the Council of Ministers, right from the composition and functioning of the Council of Ministers. This unity has two bases, first, the way the Council of Ministers is composed, and secondly, the way the unity of views, objectives to be achieved and the relationship with President and the people is maintained. In short, this unity within the Council of Ministers is ensured through the constitutional institution of Prime Minister who has been accorded a special position of par excellence in the Council of Minister as the leader of the team.

2.32. Constitutionally, if the Government suffers a defeat on any policy matter in the House of People, this includes official resolutions, passage of bills, cut motions, motion of thanks to the President's Address to Parliament, but not the approval by the Government of any action taken by the President under Article 356 of the Constitution, the government has to resign under the principle of collective responsibility for expression of no-confidence in Prime Minister and the Council of Ministers.

---

[30] *The Constitution of India,* Article 75.

2.33. *The Prime Minister*: The Constitution provides that 'There shall be a Council of Ministers with the Prime Minister at its head to aid and advise the President who shall, in the exercise of his functions, act in accordance with such advice'.[31] This in short sets the status of the Prime Minister *vis-à-vis* the President and the Council of Ministers. All the three are constitutional institutions and have to co-exist together. President cannot exercise his powers himself, he must have at all times a Council of Ministers,[32] and when there is a Council of Ministers it must have a leader or captain at its head, so there has at all times to be a Prime Minister. The Supreme Court in the U.N. Rao Case[33] noted that the Constituent Assembly had rejected presidential form of government and so there could not be any situation in which President could directly administer the country.

2.33A. The Prime Minister is one of the Council of Ministers and the principle of collective responsibility makes them to exist or to fall together.[34] His position in the Council has a speciality since on his advice the President appoints other ministers and the President cannot ignore the advice of Prime Minister recommending dismissal of a Minister from the Council. In civil service jurisprudence, power of appointment carries with it the power of dismissal but ultimately Article 75 (1) and (2)[35] rest both powers with the President in the matter of ministers but he cannot act independently and so the advice of Prime Minister precedes the dismissal of a Minister. However, the constitutional provisions do not make the Prime Minister a dictator since there

---

[31] *Ibid.*, Article 74 (1).

[32] U.N. Rao *versus* Indira Gandhi (1971) 2 SCC 63, at 67.

[33] *Ibid.*

[34] S.P. Anand *versus* H.D. Deve Gowda (1996) 6 SCC 734 at 743 f-g.

[35] "(1) The Prime Minister shall be appointed by the President and the other Ministers shall be appointed by the President on the advice of the prime Minister.

(2) The Ministers shall hold office during the pleasure of the President."

are several checks and balances, such as, the inter-party struggles, need for coalition for majority, personal standing of a Minister who has a large number of supporters, fear of break up of the party and so on. It has been observed in the modern context, that the Council of Minister or the:

> "Cabinet is a democracy, not an autocracy; each member of it, including the Prime Minister, seeks to convince his colleagues as to the course to follow. The Cabinet bears his stamp, it is true, on each and every policy issue, but it is the Cabinet not the Prime Minister who decides."

> "The growth of the Cabinet committee system is one factor which would restrain the overweening desires of a would be dictator. More and more decisions have to be taken there, or prepared there for the Cabinet. Where there is a general agreement on the Committee, he would have to be a brave or rash Prime Minister who sought to over-ride such a decision. He would not last long."[36]

2.33B. Normally, the party in majority in the House of People chooses its leader who is a senior and respected leader and considered to be capable of commanding better numerical strength *vis-à-vis* the opposition party. In this process of selection of Prime Minister, the elected Members, the bureaucracy and the public or the people whose approval or votes matter in the next election have to be reckoned and taken care of.

2.33C. L.M. Singhvi, an eminent Indian jurist, makes a strong case for evolution of general practice among Indian political parties of naming their prime ministerial choice before the election. He emphasises:[37]

> "Political realism and the operational premises of our parliamentary system require a party or a coalition of

---

[36] Wilson, *Governance of Britain*, at pp. 8, 9.

[37] L.M. Singhvi, former MP and former Indian High Commissioner to U.K., 'For PM Name the Man' *The Hindustan Times*, New Delhi, February 8, 1998, p. 13.

parties aspiring to form or participate in the national government to disclose their prime ministerial candidate (before the election). A party manifesto would be seen as an insufficient manifestation of the intentions of the party if it fails to present its prime ministerial choice." He further adds:

"The logic of asking every major political party, national or regional, to make a pre-poll declaration of its prime ministerial candidate is unanswerable. It would reduce the intrigue, the contradictions and the wheeling dealing after the polls. It would make party policies more clear and coherent both within the parties and in terms of inter-party equations. There would be greater political transparency and accountability. Most importantly, the people have a right to know and to judge the merit of each party and each claimant on the basis of quality of leadership it offers for the prime ministerial office. *Political parties have to learn to reckon with the host, that is, the electorate*" (Italics added).

2.33D. Since the Prime Minister chooses the other members for his team and in the beginning he has almost free hand in the formation of his Cabinet. However, he has to be and is discreet in many ways, and the plus point with him is that the selected Ministers also feel their future to be dependent on the continued favours from the Prime Minister. The party plays silent role and has persuasive but not a dictating approach in the formation of the Council of Ministers since after the general election the future of the party shifts into the hands of the Prime Minister. In India, in order to stabilise his position, the Prime Minister has to take various steps, such as, providing important positions for influential members of the party who have lost in the election to the House of People, out of these some are made Governor of a State or Indian Ambassador to a country or are given chance to be elected for the Council of States or they are given party organisation posts.

2.34. Accordingly, in single party ministry having safe majority or in a coalition ministry, the Ministers think first of building their own reputation as a Minister. Often, a Minister who resigns showing disagreement with or disapproval of any of the policy of the Prime Minister does so when he hopes to become Prime Minister himself, fears that he will be dropped from the Ministry or does not expect the Prime Minister to win in the next election. There have been various precedents of this nature:

(a) Jagjiwan Ram resigned from Indira Gandhi Ministry in 1977 to form a new party and became Minister in next Janata Party Ministry while Congress(I) of Indira Gandhi lost the 1977 election,

(b) Charan Singh resigned from Morarji Desai Ministry in 1979 to form his own party and to become Prime Minister,

(c) Chandrashekhar resigned from National Front Ministry of V.P. Singh in 1990 to form a new party and to become Prime Minister.

(d) After tenth Parliament in 1996, a number of Ministers from Congress(I) Ministry under Prime Minister P.V. Narasimha Rao deserted and formed regional parties and succeeded in being elected to the House of People or in becoming Minister again in the United Front Government in 1996-98.

2.35. Understandably, therefore, the position and status of Prime Minister is significant, and it is good to have become Prime Minister of India even for thirteen days,[38] but at the beginning of present century there is little or no element of dictatorship attached to this singular post. Now, under the convention that has developed, a Prime Minister designate in

---

[38] In June 1996, on the convening of eleventh Parliament, A.B. Vajpayee became Prime Minister for 13 days. He again became Prime Minister in March 1998 for next thirteen months after the twelfth and in October 1999 after thirteenth general election to Lok Sabha. In all circumstances he headed a coalition of political parties.

'Hung Parliament' is given 14 days to prove his majority on the floor of Lok Sabha till then he is Prime Minister of caretaker government.

2.36. Considering the uncertainties attached to the office of Prime Minister, in the first half of twentieth century the British experts assessed him to be *primus inter pares,* 'first among equals', like captain of a cricket or football team. In the written Constitution of India, the Prime Minister has a singular status of *par excellence* as

(i) he is first to be appointed,

(ii) he recommends the names of Minister for the Council of Ministers to the President,

(iii) he recommends the dismissal of Ministers from the Council of Ministers,

(iv) he allocates ministries among the Ministers and can at any time reshuffle the work among them,

(v) he presides over the meetings of the Council of Ministers and decides as to the collective view of the Cabinet on all policy matters,

(vi) he is the symbol of the policies of the government and any Minister who disagrees with the policies of the Council of Ministers or with him, has to resign,

(vii) he decides on the business to be taken up in a session of the Parliament,

(viii) in Parliament he is the leader of the House of People to which he is elected,

(ix) he can speak at any time, even out of order, in Parliament on matter pertaining to any ministry and when Prime Minister is speaking others give precedence to him,

(x) he has the right to reply in the end of debates particularly when no confidence motion is discussed in the House of People,

(xi) he has always a right to meet the President, has the duties to communicate the decisions of the Council of

Ministers to him and to furnish such information to him as he (President) may call for and

(xii) only he is to advise President on dissolution of the House of People before the five year term is over.

2.37. In England during the Second World War a national or 'war cabinet' was constituted which was a national government under Prime minister Winston Churchill. This war cabinet had an inner cabinet which used to take decisions on vital questions connected with the war but its decisions were regarded to be the decisions of the cabinet and practice had grown that Prime Minister would do a lot of field work involving taking of national policy decisions for victory in Second World War on the assurance of endorsement by the war cabinet subsequently. This enhanced the status of Prime Minister of England temporarily during the War, but the spirit has continued further though in a subdued form during normal conditions. The subsequent Prime Ministers, *viz.*, Clement Atlee, Winston Churchill, Anthony Eden, Harold Wilson or Margaret Thatcher, had forceful dominating personalities both within their party and in their cabinets. About the resulting change in character of cabinet members, Lord Home, subsequently Prime Minister of Britain had observed:

"Every Cabinet Minister is in a sense the Prime Minister's agent—his assistant. There is no question about that. It is the Prime Ministers Cabinet, if the Cabinet discusses anything it is the Prime Minister who decides what the collective view of the Cabinet is. A Minister's job is to save the Prime Minister of all the work he can. But no Minister could make a really important move without consulting the Prime Minister, and if the Prime Minister wanted to take a certain step, that Cabinet Minister concerned would either have to agree, argue it out in Cabinet or resign."[39]

2.38. The status of Prime Minister has been assessed and commented upon by L.M. Singhvi in the words:

---

[39] See, Mackintosh, *British Cabinet*, p. 628.

"...Obviously, an effective Prime Minister is *sine qua non* for effective governance."

"As inevitable consequence of the rise of political parties as the key to electoral systems, the locus of real power shifted first from Parliament to the Cabinet and then from the Cabinet to the Prime Minister. It is true that bureaucracy has wielded real power behind what a commentator called the cloak of cabinet dictatorship. *A major shift in the institutional equation has made the office of Prime Minister unquestionably the pivot of power."*[40]

2.39. The Prime Minister can be removed from his position by his party or the coalition before and by the people after a general election. No Prime Minister has ever assumed an autocratic or dictatorial posture within the party or in the country except for Indian Prime Minister Indira Gandhi during 1975-77 when she imposed 'internal emergency' in the country. She placed most of opposition leaders under preventive detention and asked for full submission from her party men. However, she also eventually submitted her fate to be decided by the people at the general elections to the House of People which had become due in 1977. In the elections she lost her majority and gracefully resigned leading to formation of a new government of a pre-election coalition, Janata Party, led by Prime Minister Morarji Desai after the election.

2.40. It is obvious that parliamentary form of government operates under several checks and balances and no single authority has a permanent superiority over others. President is handicapped by the advice of Council of Ministers, latter is handicapped by the need for finances for implementation of its policies which only Parliament can sanction The Prime Minister is the navigator of Parliament and at the same time survives on its support. President has to be advised by the whole of Council

---

[40] See, Foot Note 37, above.

of Ministers and fir this he can ask the Prime Minister to refer any matter for decision of the Council.[41]

2.40A. *The Check and Balance Web*: The Prime Minister cannot dismiss a Minister but can only advise the President to dismiss the Minister. The Prime minister depends on the support of his party for the passage of any Bill and defeat in House of People on this issue means dismissal of the Ministry and therefore he has to maintain the confidence and support of his Minister and each Cabinet Minister has some Members of Parliament in his pocket as his staunch followers. Since the Prime Minister recommends dissolution of the House of People when this to be done prematurely, the House also does not easily adopt a no confidence motion. The tenth Parliament completed its term (1991-96) under this danger when Prime Minister P. V. Narasimha Rao was heading a minority government with outside support of several parties. The United Front coalition governments (1996-1998) of Prime Ministers H. D. Deve Gowda and I.K. Gujral could function under eleventh Parliament for the time they did, since no party wanted fresh elections and rejection of Ministry meant dissolution of House of People for mid-term election. The British Prime Minister Harold Wilson has pertinently observed in his Book that in Parliamentary system:

> "the checks and balances operate not only as long-term safeguards, but also, in one way or another (often unpredictably), almost every day".[42]

2.41. *Appointment of Prime Minister:* In India the selection of a person for appointment as Prime Minister is intra-party matter normally. When there is single party majority the Party nominates or votes the most acceptable or charismatic leader of the party for the post and the elected members of the party in the House of People also formally project him as their leader and the name is referred to the President for appointment as

[41] *Constitution of India*, Article 78 (C).

[42] Wilson, *The Governance of Britain*, p. 8.

Prime Minister. In such circumstance the President has little or no scrutinising power since the Prime Minister can be a Member of any of the two Houses or even may not be a Member of either House but who has to become a Member within six months of his appointment as Prime Minister.

(a) After the elections to the tenth Parliament in May 1991, Congress (I) the single largest party elected P.V. Narasimha Rao as the leader of the Congress legislative party for Prime Ministership when he was not a member of either House. He became Prime Minister and was later elected to the House of People within the prescribed period.

(b) Again, after election to the eleventh Parliament in June 1966, the United Front was formed by the National Front and Left Front which decided on accepting H.D. Deve Gowda, Chief Minister of Karnataka State, as Prime Minister who was not a Member of Parliament. Later Prime Minister H.D. Deve Gowda preferred to become a Member of Council of States, obviously because he was not certain as to how long he will remain a Prime Minister.

2.42. The Supreme Court[43] in a public interest litigation petition challenging the appointment of H.D. Gowda as Prime Minister on the ground that the Prime Minister must be a Member of Parliament at the time of appointment, held that in view of Article 75(5) and Article 164(4) of the Constitution, the frequent appointment of Chief Ministers in States who are not members of either House of State Legislature, the earlier decisions of the Supreme Court[44] on the issues under Article 164(4), the proceedings of the Constituent Assembly and the normal democratic safeguards envisaged in the Constitution, such an appointment does not militate against the democratic principles

---

43 S.P. Anand *versus* H.D. Deve Gowda (1996) 6 SCC 734.

44 H.S. Verma *versus* T.N. Singh (1971) 1 SCC 616; H.S. Verma *versus* State of U.P. (1985) 2SCC 48; H.S. Verma *versus* Union of India, (1987) Supp SCC 310.

embodied in our Constitution. In the Judgement it was observed that:

> "(The) President has to act in accordance with the advice of the Council of Ministers as a body and not go by the advice of any single individual. Only a person who, the President thinks, commands the confidence of the Lok Sabha would be appointed the Prime Minister who in turn would choose the other Ministers. The Council of Ministers is collectively responsible to the House of People. The form of oath prescribed in the third schedule under Article 74(4) is the same for the Prime Minister as well as a Minister. In other words, *the Constitution does not draw any distinction between the Prime Minister and any other Minister in this behalf.* This is not to say that the Prime Minister does not enjoy a special status; he does as the head of the Council of Ministers but the responsibility of the Council of Ministers to the House of People is collective."[45]

2.43. *Stop Gap Prime Minister*: Since President cannot be without a Council of Ministers with Prime minister at its head, there are circumstances when in order to maintain the Constitution, President himself appoints a Prime Minister as a stop gap arrangement without waiting for the party in majority to forward the name to him.

(a) When Jawahar Lal Nehru died on 27-05-1964, President appointed senior most member of the Cabinet, Gulzari Lal Nanda as Prime Minister who remained in office for fourteen days till Congress Party nominated Lal Bahadur Shastri as Prime Minister.

(b) Again on the death of Prime Minister Lal Bahadur Shastri in Tashkant on 11-01-1966, Gulzari Lal Nanda was appointed Prime Minister and after fourteen days Indira Gandhi took over the post as nominee of the Congress Party.

---

[45] S.P. Anand *versus* H.D. Deve Gowda (1996) 6 SCC 734 at p. 743 e-f.

(c) On the losing of majority in House of People due to defections Prime Minister Morarji Desai resigned on 28.07.1979 and President appointed Charan Singh as Prime Minister subject to proving his majority in the House of People within the stipulated time, which he could not do and the House of People was dissolved for fresh mandate.

(d) On the assassination of Prime Minister Indira Gandhi on 31.10.1984, President appointed Rajiv Gandhi as Prime Minister without consulting anybody, but, the Congress (I) Party and its legislative party members approved the appointment and he continued on the post.

(e) At the outset of eleventh Parliament when no party had earned a majority in the House of People after the election, President invited Atal Bihari Vajpayee leader of single largest party B.J.P. to form the government on 16.05.1996 subject to proving majority within 14 days (and when this did not happen, he appointed nominee of United Front H.D. Deve Gowda to take over as Prime Minister).

2.45. Sometimes it happens that the political party in majority party wants to change the Prime Minister or Chief Minister and withdraws its support. In such a case, from the point of view of President or Governor the members of that Party in the legislature, *viz.*, House of People or State Legislative Assembly, have to withdraw support. If they remain behind the Prime Minister or the Chief Minister, giving him necessary majority in the House, latter survives.

For example, it happened in 1969 with Prime Minister Indira Gandhi when the Indian National Congress had become hostile to her because she was disregarding and was disrespectful the old stalwarts of the party who were in her Council of Ministers. The party censored her and expelled her from the party itself. However, the majority of Congress Legislative Party members in House of People supported her and expressed their confidence in her. She formed her new political party

Congress (I) and continued as Prime Minister without any break.

2.46. *Coalition or Minority Governments*: The choice of Prime Minister becomes a heady or tricky matter when after an election or on defection from a majority party, there is no clear cut situation in the House of People. There may be:

(1) several parties with varying numbers of elected members but none of them having majority of the total strength of the House of People; or

(2) a coalition of some parties which took place *before* the election but the coalition is without a majority; or

(3) a coalition of some parties which took place *after* the election but the coalition is without a majority.

In all such conditions the question before the President or the Governor is whether to dissolve the House, of course this he cannot do except on the advice of Prime Minister or Chief Minister or else he has to go on exploring the possibility of formation of some kind of make-shift government. This was done presumably by the President (i) in 1979 when Charan Singh was asked to form the Government or (ii) in 1990 when Chandra Shekhar was given opportunity to form the Government, but in both cases this was done subject to proving of their respective majority in the House of People of Parliament. In England, the defeated Prime Ministers seek dissolution of House of Commons in natural course, for example, Lord Melbourne in 1841, Lord Palmerston in 1857, Lord Derby in 1859, Disraeli in 1868, Gladstone in 1886 or Macdonald in 1924.

2.47. The defeated British Prime Minister does not lose the right to advise the King or Queen to dissolve the House of Commons.[46] This position is repeated in India also subject to certain constitutional contingencies providing a burden on President of India.

---

[46] Keith, *Constitutional Law*, (1939), pp. 51-52; Dicey, *The Law of Constitution*, (9th ed.), 432

(a) When any of the three conditions mentioned in paragraph 2.46 above arises or when the ruling majority party gets disintegrated at a late stage, say after two or three years, there is little hesitation in accepting the advice for dissolution of the House of People or a Legislative Assembly coming from the Prime Minister or Chief Minister who has lost confidence of majority in the House after a vote or due to patent defections from the majority party or the coalition of parties since the democratic process has had sufficient time to show results. A dissolution of the House of People means that the people should assess the situation and give clear verdict on the conditions of uncertainty and stalemate.

(b) However, when either of the above conditions surface at the very outset, that is, on verdict of election, the situation is differently viewed. The reason is that a process of re-election immediately means incurring of heavy expenditure on elections which at the end of twentieth century is estimated to be more than eight hundred crores of rupees. Along with this there is a feeling of national fatigue and frustration since the politicians are not favourite or likeable part of Indian society any longer. Accordingly the political parties are given chance to form alliances or get 'out side support' for acquiring a working majority to run the Government.

2.48. Normally the single largest party is given the first chance failing which the second largest party or a coalition gets the chance, and so on.

(1) In 1989 after the ninth election Congress(I) was invited to form the government and on it refusal, the National Front under V.P. Singh as Prime Minister with the outside support of B.J.P. formed the Government.

(2) When the National Front lost no confidence motion in 1990 due to defections from Janata Dal, Chandrashekhar with outside support of Congress(I) became the Prime Minister being the leader of next largest political party Janata Dal (S). When Congress (I) withdrew its support to Prime Minister

Chandrashekhar the tenth general election to House of People became unavoidable in 1991. The House of People was dissolved by the President on the advice of Prime Minister as no alternative government was possible.

(3) After tenth general election again there was no party with clear majority and the same process as above was repeated. This time in 1991, Congress(I), the largest single party, decided to form the government with outside support of National Front and Left Front and completed the five year term.

(4) After elections to eleventh House of People B.J.P. emerged as first single largest party, the United Front forged after elections came out as second largest party and Congress(I) as the third largest party. The President invited the formation of government in the same order, and only after B.J.P. Prime Minister failed to show majority in the House of People, was the United Front given the chance to form the Government which it did with the outside support of Congress (I). It had to change the Prime Minister when Congress(I) threatened to withdraw its support in 1997 and finally the Ministry collapsed after the support was finally withdrawn. On the advice of Prime Minister I.K Gujral, the House of People was dissolved by the President in December 1997 and fresh elections for twelfth Parliament were announced.

(5) Same process was followed after the twelfth general election and when invited by the President Prime Minister Vajpayee formed a coalition government in 1998 supported by some parties from outside. When the outside support was materially withdrawn after thirteen months, Prime Minister Vajpayee advised the President to dissolve the House which the latter did in April 1999.

2.49. *Minority Government:* When a party without majority in the House of People forms Government with outside support, such government is popularly known as minority government in the media. Its existence is always precarious and uncertain and it becomes a politicians paradise particularly for the party on whose outside support it survives. The extent of its independence depends on the personality of the Prime Minister and the extent to which the supporting parties are fearful of next parliamentary election.

(i) Prime Minister P.V. Narasimha Rao (1991-96) could manage for the full term with the outside support of anti-BJP parties and without visible compromises on policy matters.

(ii) The two (13 party coalition) United Front Governments under Prime Ministers H.D. Gowda and I.K. Gujral precariously existed on the outside support of the Congress Party which always kept the Ministry on toes for survival and successfully dictated formulation of national or foreign policies or appointments such as of Governors.

(iii) The subsequent BJP Government of PM Vajpayee in 1998 had better stand on this aspect though the Government was much harassed for survival not so much by opposition parties but by its inside supporters Shiva Sena Party and Akali Dal and outside supporters AIADMK and Trinamul Congress. However, Prime Minister apparently weathered the storms by rejecting their demands on the silent threat of inevitability of general elections if the coalition was ruptured. This neither the opposition nor the coalition partners desired. However, when AIADMK finally withdrew support to the coalition, the Vajpayee Government lost vote of confidence by a margin of one vote and resigned in March 1999.

2.49A. The minority and coalition governments are based on consensus of its members having parallel or even conflicting programmes and so by nature these are unstable governments and so these generally do not take strong governmental steps. Besides constant efforts directed towards the mending of internal disagreements their tenure is marked with reduced legislative activities and dependence on the goodwill of the President or in case of States on the goodwill of Governors. Both, Prime Minister Gujral in 1997 and Prime Minister Vajpayee in 1998 had their Cabinet recommendations for imposition of President's Rule in Uttar Pradesh and Bihar respectively under Article 356 of the

Constitution referred back by the President, as procedurally immature, for reconsideration by the Council of Ministers and the propositions were dropped.

2.49B. Whether the defeat of a coalition partner in general election in States held within the term of the coalition government at the Union amount to show of non-confidence in the ruling coalition. The answer to this query is in negative, obviously since Parliament and State Legislatures are distinct constitutional bodies and the constituencies are differently defined. Interestingly, after the debacle of BJP in two States, Rajasthan and Delhi, in the general elections held therein November 1998 in favour of Congress, the opposition claimed that it was general disapproval of BJP Government by the electorate and PM Vajpayee should resign on ethical and moral grounds. Prime Minister assessed the position of Coalition Government in Lok Sabha and he squarely asked CPI-M and Rashtriya Loktantrik Morcha (RLM) to bring a non-confidence motion in the House which the opposition did not do as no political party wanted general elections.[47]

2.50. The significance of a coalition lies (a) in the non-application of anti-defection provisions of the Constitution when a partner of coalition leaves it and (b) in the manoeuvrability of minor parties in joining one or the other major party which is likely to form the government for gaining places in the Council of Ministers.

2.50A. The latter element is obviously unethical from the point of view of people who vote for a party or candidate but for career politicians of India in 1990s it is now valid opportunism which does not carry any feeling of shame. During the period for twelfth election to the House of People the leaders of United Front including the Prime Minister I.K. Gujral defended coalition Government as a normal political system with all that goes with coalition formation emphasising that the people should accept

[47] "Government dares Opposition to no-confidence vote": *The Hindustan Times*, New Delhi, December 3, 1998.

as valid alternative to stability slogan by parties claiming capacity to provide single party rule but without having absolute majority.

2.51. When coalition of political parties takes place before election, the coalition is treated as a single political party for the purpose of invitation to form government whether its strength crosses the majority mark or not. After the thirteenth general election result in October 1999, the President had no hesitation in calling Atal Bihari Vajpayee to form the government as leader of National Democratic Alliance, a pre-election alliance of 16 national and regional political parties which had secured 296 seats out of 538 seats in House of People, for which polls had been held. However, when the coalition of parties takes place *after* the election or after a change of government is indicated, it does not get precedence over the original single largest party according to the conventions which have grown both at the Union and in the States under the Constitution of India.

4. THE INCIDENCES OF COLLECTIVE RESPONSIBILITY

2.52. As discussed above the system of collective responsibility operates through the medium of the Prime Minister who is symbol and leader of the Council of Ministers. In a single party or coalition having absolute majority in the House the Prime Minister also commands loyalty from the Ministers apart from the loyalty for the party since a disagreement with the policies of the leader means resignation from the cabinet. The party or coalition also stakes its prestige on the prestige of the Prime Minister and now this situation is well understood by the Ministers. However, this loyalty towards the Prime Minister is much diluted in coalition governments since the coalition partners bargain positions for their leaders in the coalition and the dismissal or shuffling of the portfolio by the Prime Minister of such coalition ministers is subject to difficult riders.[48]

---

[48] See, at f.n. 28, above also.

2.53. The first incidence of collective responsibility is that no Minister can project or call any policy decision as his own and if he does so he can be pulled up by the Prime Minister since the primary function of a Minister is to implement the decisions of the Council of Ministers and to oversee the work of the departments under his Ministry. Normally a minister has no direct link with the President or the Governor except for the documents requiring his signature coming from a ministry on which executive action has to be taken which must be authenticated by the Minister and the Secretary of the Ministry. Where the President or the Governor feels that a matter presented to him under the signature of a minister should also have been discussed by the Council of Ministers, he can refer it back accordingly. The Council of Ministers belongs to the President or the Governor whereas the Ministers belong to the Prime Minister or the Chief Minister.[49]

2.54. The second incidence of the principle of collective responsibility is that there should be complete harmony in the Council of Ministers. Normally the majority party or the coalition provides the general guidelines to its legislative party group and the loyalty to the party or coalition in the first instance and to the Prime Minister in the second instance provide the foundation for the harmony in the cabinet. In coalition government, there is of necessity a common minimum programme which becomes the working basis for harmony.

(i) In early 1950s on the issues relating to States reorganisation, the Congress suffered resignation from the Union Cabinet of C.D. Deshmukh,

---

49 The Constitution of India, Article 78: It shall be the duty of the Prime Minister:

(a) ......

(b) ......

(c) if the President so requires, to submit for the consideration of the Council of Ministers any matter on which a decision has been taken by a Minister but which has not been considered by the Council.

(ii) On the question of setting up of Planning Commission the Finance Minister John Mathai left the Cabinet.

(iii) When the Congress decided on nationalisation process and development of public sector by its 1958 Nagpur Resolution, T.T. Krishnamchari and K.M. Munshi along with a sizeable group of Congressmen left the Cabinet and formed independent Swatantra Party with rightist ideology.

(iv) An interesting case arose when the President accepted the resignation of Law Minister Ram Jethmalani on the recommendation of Prime Minister Vajpayee in July 2000. The Supreme Court was examining the Sri Krishna Report which had probed the Mumbai communal riots of 1992-93 and had indicted Shiva Sena chief Bal Thackeray for his role in the riots. The Chief Justice had castigated the Minister for making statements which were contradictory to the affidavit filed by the Central Government. Shri Jethmalani had reacted to the comments and had stated that 'he knew the law as well as anyone else'.

2.54A. Prime Minister made the following statement in Parliament in Jethmalani Case which is significant from the point of view of the Principle of Ministerial Responsibility:

> "Certain Statements have been made by Shri Ram Jethmalani, former Union Minister for Law, Justice and Company with regard to the Chief Justice of India and the Attorney General of India.
>
> I have gone through those statements. My government does not share the views of Sri Jethmalani with regard to the subject matter on which he has spoken, We completely disagree with his perception of facts.
>
> The government believes in promoting a harmonious relationship between different wings of the State. Without going into the question of correctness of any possible view involved on the issue on which Shri Jethmalani corresponded with honourable Chief Justice of India, I was of the opinion that even the differences of opinion between the Chief Justice and the Law Minister should not

create any imbalance in the harmonious relationship (between different wings of the State).

Thus in order to ensure that his harmony is not only maintained but strengthened, I exercised my prerogative and asked Shri Jethmalani to resign.

I have gone into the text of his statements issued yesterday, *i.e.*, 27th July, against the Chief Justice of India and the Attorney General of India. I reiterate that my government completely disagrees with his perception"[50]

2.55. The loyalty to the Prime Minister or acceptance of his pre-eminence by the members of the Council of Ministers is an important consequence of the Principle of collective responsibility. It is pertinently accepted principle that once a decision has been taken by the Cabinet on an issue whatever different views may have been expressed or asserted in the cabinet come to an end and all the members must collectively accept the responsibility for the decision. All the members of the cabinet must thereafter refrain from criticising the decision even when individually they may remain unconvinced. The alternative to this is clear, that is, resignation.[51] An anomalous situation on this principle occurred in October 2000. After the prices of petrol and its products were raised in India after a Cabinet decision, on sudden increase in their prices in world market, the Trinamul Congress Party members of Cabinet resigned in protest. This was done inspite of the consensus among the member parties of the National Democratic Alliance Government of Prime Minister Vajpayee when the matter had been earlier discussed in that forum. It was contended by the Trinamul Congress Party that consensus among members of NDA was one thing but Cabinet decision was another aspect. The Prime Minister did not accept the resignations. However, on the assurance of Prime Minister to review the enhancement of price of some of the

---

[50] *The Hindustan Times,* New Delhi, Saturday, dated July 20, 2000.

[51] Keaton, *British Commonwealth.* See, f. n. 14, above.

petro-products used by poor, not petrol, the resignations were withdrawn.

2.56. Usually when members of the cabinet in large numbers lose faith in the leadership of the Prime Minister, it is seen that the party itself suffers a break down.

(i) In 1969, in Congress Ministry at the Union under Indira Gandhi there was an inside conflict between 'old guards' of the party and the 'young Turks' in the party. The Congress Party was dominated by the former while in the House of People the Congress legislative party had young Turks in majority. In the turmoil which followed Prime Minister Indira Gandhi and young Turks quit the Indian National Congress and formed Congress(I) but continued to have their Council of Ministers against the Congress (O) odds.

(ii) In 1979, in the Janata Ministry under Prime Minister Morarji Desai came to an end when dissension developed and Charan Singh group of MPs separated and formed a new party. With promised Congress(I) outside support Charan Singh formed his Council of Ministers but his government fell because Congress(I) withdrew support before the House of People met for the confidence vote.

(iii) Similarly, in 1990 National Front Prime Minister V.P. Singh suffered a defeat in House of People when Chandrashekhar led big group of Ministers and MPs left Janata Dal. Subsequently, Chandrashekhar with outside support of Congress(I) for some time functioned as Prime Minister himself.

These illustrative examples establish that the party obtaining majority in the House has to be very much practical and judicious in the choice of person who has to form the government as Prime Minister or Chief Minister. If and when the Prime Minister or Chief Minister fails to command respect and loyalty and the party does not or fails to change the leader for the Council of Ministers in time the party itself suffers a break or serious upheaval.

2.57. The coalition Governments in India seem to have evolved a new pattern, slightly more democratic, in the matter of allegiance to the Prime Minister while not contradicting his policy stand. Here the continued existence of the coalition appears to be more acceptable both to Prime Minister and the Cabinet Ministers.

(i) During the United Front Ministry (1996-98), the Finance Minister or the Home Minister laid down and announced the policy while the two Prime Ministers, H. Deve Gowda and I.K. Gujral meekly followed the policies without showing any embarrassment. The United Front Government also often compromised principles by submitting to the dictates of Congress Party which was giving it support from outside.

(ii) In the BJP led coalition (March 1998) the Samata Party supremo Defence Minister George Fernandes aired freely his views on friends and foes of India while the Prime Minister and Government had their own stands. But, there was no acrimony of any kind to show disharmony in the Cabinet since the views of Samata Party leader were taken to be his personal or that of his party. His party also led the movement for imposition of President's Rule in Bihar which the Government just ignored.

2.57A. On the other hand AIADMK and Trinamool Congress which were supporting the BJP coalition (March 1998) from outside felt rather humiliated or embarrassed when the coalition preferred to suffer ouster rather than to compromise with the status of Prime Minister and principles of Government's policies and rejected the dictates of these supporting parties on the issue of imposition of President's Rule in Tamil Nadu and West Bengal respectively.

2.58. After a decade of the working of coalition or minority governments, now it is recognised that such governments work on consensus of coalition partners or those parties which extend support to the government from outside and so mutual criticism outside the House does not *ipso facto* violate principle of harmony in the Council of Ministers. The media and the people have to reconcile with this change and should not read much in contradictory or inconsistent statements of the coalition partners.

2.59. The third incidence of collective responsibility concept is that the Ministers have to take up an overall view of the performance of the government and the individual thrusts of particular Ministers have to be contained. The objective approach of the Cabinet is to harmonise the election manifesto on which the party had contested the election with the policies being pursued by the government, to make best use of the parliamentary platforms for highlighting the achievements of the party and to justify the peoples choice of the party through public speeches and the media with an eye on the next election. Therefore, the Ministers have to lend support to each other. In this process the cabinet committees and the Prime Minister become a sort of forum for compromises between the demands made by different ministries both for allocation of finances and setting up priorities.

2.60. It is the function of the administrative machinery under the ministries to project the policies based on community needs and public demands. Such needs, innovations or modifications are accepted, modified, postponed or shelved by the Minister or the Council of Ministers taking into account the wishes expressed in the Parliament and the priorities based on availability of finances. The administration provides the feasibility report, the reactions of the different departments or ministries involved and the position of finances whereas the Council of Ministers filter or process the schemes in accordance with the wishes of the Members of the Parliament. The net outcome of these interaction and process determines the achievement or failure of the Cabinet based on collective responsibility.

2.61. Fourthly, in the field of policy making or policy enforcement and pursuance, such as in foreign affairs, making of treaties, import or export strategies or economic planning for the country, the collective responsibility is presumed to be cent per cent unless the Cabinet disowns the decision as the decision of a particular Minister. For example,

(i) in the matter of faulty Indian foreign policy based on full trust of Communist China in the late 1950s and leaving Indian northern borders undefended while China quietly went on occupying Indian territory, Indian Defence Minister V.K. Krishna Menon was regarded to be responsible since no other Minister had associated himself with the involved policy decisions.

(ii) Similarly, in January 1998 on the eve of twelfth mid-term poll for the House of People, the Congress(I) party in a Constitution-like manner *ex post facto* held the then Prime Minister P.V. Narasimha Rao personally responsible for governmental laxity which led to the demolition of Babri Masjid complex in Ayodhya in December 1992 and debarred him from contesting in the ensuing elections. This Babri Masjid incident had caused a long lasting animosity between Hindu and Muslim communities which created a visible wedge between Congress (I) Party and Muslim voters in the sequence.

2.62. It is certain and well established constitutional principle now that a recommendation by Council of Ministers for imposition of President's Rule in a State is not fully its policy decision since the President has to examine its validity and viability on objective grounds before he approves it under Article 356. When he approves the recommendation it ceases to be an exclusive decision of the Council of Ministers. Subsequently, if either House of Parliament does not approve the proclamation, the responsibility is shared by the President alongwith the Council of Ministers. The supervisory role of President under Article 356 of the Constitution was established in 1997, 1998, and 1999 in the matters relating to the States of Uttar Pradesh and Bihar.

2.63. The collective responsibility of the Council of Ministers is towards the House of People only and exclusively under the Constitution. If any matter, whatever be its nature, is rejected by the majority in the Council of States, that is, Rajya Sabha, the government does not fall.

2.64. Lastly, all the Ministers are presumed to have agreed to all that has been done by the Council of Ministers whether they actually participated in the decision or action or not. If at any stage a Minister has any reservations this should be accompanied with offer of resignation from the Council of Ministers.[52]

2.65. To *conclude* it may be reiterated that the principle of collective responsibility is an *entrenched* provision of the Constitution of India, much of the pre-conditions, incidents and consequences of it are written in the Constitution and the conventions regulate it only marginally. The composition of the Council of States depends on Prime Minister,[53] it is collectively responsible to the House of People,[54] all the decisions of the Council of Ministers have to be communicated to the President by the Prime Minister[55] and the Prime Minister *has to submit* for the Consideration of the Council of Ministers any matter on which a decision has been taken by a Minister including the Prime Minister but which has not been considered by the Council when so directed by the President.[56]

2.65A. However, the Constitution does not provide that the Prime Minister alone or all or some Ministers shall exit when the Council of Ministers has lost the confidence of the House of People. It is a presumed hypothesis that the vote on no-confidence motion is directed against the whole team based on party lines and that there shall be consistency in the House in

52 Foot notes 14 and 49, above.
53 *The Constitution of India,* Article 75 (1).
54 *Ibid.,* Article 75 (3).
55 *Ibid.,* Article 78 (a).
56 *Ibid.,* Article 78 [c].

voting against the ruling party forming the Government which as a consequence is defeated. This hypothesis is fortified from the consequences of consistent opposition majority in voting and the consequent non-workability of the constitutional government since the grants have to be periodically voted by Parliament without which the government cannot last long, among other factors. Similarly, the Constitution does not provide that the President can *suo moto* dissolve the House of People at his discretion sooner than its five year term.[57] The mid-term dissolution of the House of People when the Cabinet has lost the confidence of the House of People proceeds on the advice of Prime Minister and the Council of Ministers. The normal procedure has been that the President explores the possibility of forming alternate Council of Ministers but when this is not possible he accepts the advice of such Prime Minister on dissolution of Lok Sabha and fresh elections are announced along with installation of a care-taker government.

2.65B. By convention this care-taker Council of Ministers is the same Council of Ministers headed by the same Prime Minister which continues till next Council of Ministers is formed after general election. This practice was followed in 1979, 1990 and 1997 while dissolving the sixth, ninth and eleventh House of People.

2.65C. Under the Constitution the care-taker Council of Ministers and the Prime Minister have all the normal constitutional powers since the Constitution does not specifically provide for any institution like 'care-taker government'.

---

[57] *Ibid.*, Article 83 (2).

3

LAW AND INDIAN POLITICAL PARTIES IN PARLIAMENT

3.01. The Constitution of India has constituted a democratic polity for the country wherein the government represents the common will, aspirations, concerns and intelligence of the people. Parliament and State Legislatures are platforms where different views are expressed, projected and debated by the representatives of the people for the good of the country. The decisions of State Legislatures are binding both on the people and the government. In practice, the Council of Ministers guides the Parliament but at the same time the censor of the government by the House of People of the Parliament sets the process for change of government into motion. The Union Government is carried on by the Prime Minister and State Government by the Chief Ministers. The Council of Ministers in turn are responsible for their performances and decisions to the House of People or the State Legislatures.

3.02. Parliament and State Legislatures represent the people through the Members elected by the people normally after every five years. Every government has to face the people for approval, so as to say, through the election process. Though the democracy can be run by independent members also but by general trends the political party system is functional in all democracies of the world. The Constitution of India has not expressly prescribed party system for achievement of democratic polity but its Tenth Schedule of the Constitution and the

Representation of Peoples Act 1951 in various ways regulate the political parties that there may be for participation in election and governance processes. For the democratic process to be successful and enduring there have to be a lot of common aspirations among the political parties and unbending loyalty towards the Indian nation and the Constitution.

1. A PRE-VIEW OF INDIAN POLITICAL PARTIES

3.03. In the middle of twentieth century when the struggle for Independence was taking place and when the Constituent Assembly in 1947-49 was framing the Constitution of India, the party system for forming the base for parliamentary democracy was presumed. The harmful effects of single party democratic system operating in Communist counties were known. So also the problems faced by Fourth French Republic due to many small political parties were known. At the same time the British and American constitutional law and political science experts had praised the multiparty system in theory but were limited to two parties only in practice. India had intimate links with British Parliament and Indian leaders most of whom had been educated in England were familiar with the way in which the party system was operating in England. In British India also prior to Independence the Indian National Congress, the Muslim League, Hindu Mahasabha, Communist Part of India the Socialist Party among others, were actively projecting their view points.

3.04. Under the Constitution of India side by side with political parties independent politicians have also been taking part in democratic process in good number. In Parliament there have always been independents in the House of People, while the procedure for election to the Council of States makes it practically impossible for independents to find a seat there, and therefore, it is almost entirely represented by political parties. In the eleventh House of People elected in 1996 there were nine independent or unattached elected members. The success of independents in elections is generally based on their personal popularity, connection with erstwhile princely families or zamindars. Sometimes the political parties decide to support independents by not fielding their own candidates against them for tactical reasons. The political worth of independent members is enhanced or is felt when there is a 'Hung Parliament' or the majority party has marginal or slender majority. Since Ninth Parliament of 1989 the independents have acquired significance because they can vote for any party in case if a division. They can join any coalition government but not a political party because in the latter case they become subject to the anti-defection provisions. Otherwise, the independents are unable to show or bring about achievements to their credit to the view of the electorate so as to justify themselves in the next election.

3.05. The party system for parliamentary democracy in India is significantly recognised now by various statutory provisions and the Tenth Schedule to the Constitution of India inducted in 1985 by the Fifty Second Amendment. The Tenth Schedule regulates in detail the situation arising from defection from one political party to another of members elected as candidates of a particular political party. It provides for the conditions in which a member elected as a nominee of one political party will lose his membership of Parliament or State Legislature or when can a group of members can split from their political party to join another political party or form a new political party. It also deals with the case of joining of a political party after six months by an independent member under the scheme for preventing defections.

3.06. The Representation of People (Amendment) Act of 1988 recognises political parties for the purpose of compulsory registration with the Election Commission. The Elections Symbols (Reservation and Allotment) Order 1969 provides for categorisation of political parties into "National Party", 'State Party' and Unrecognised Party. In absence of proper legislation, the Election Commission has with consensus evolved the Model Code of Conduct which among other matters significantly regulates election expenses by political parties and also the candidates for parliamentary and state legislature elections. The finances and funds of the political parties including the donations received by them are subject to Income Tax Act. At the time of elections, the Election Commission gets significant jurisdiction on the income and expenditures of the political parties much against their desire. The Election Commission also obligates the political parties to maintain intra-party democratic processes before these participate in any election. Lastly, under the Representation of People's Act 1951 and the Order of 1969, a party can be de-recognised for boycotting elections or for corrupt practices during the election period. The existence of political parties is implicit in the Indian democracy.[1] Interestingly, for boycotting the democratic process, the election to Lok Sabha or State Assembly, the Election Commission de-recognised Shiromani Akali Dal (Badal) and Shiromani Akali Dal (Mann) in 1992 and Nagaland Peoples' Council in 1998. The Election Commission held the candid view that the political parties, particularly the recognised political parties, should always carry forward the democratic process rather than negate the same.

3.07. *Political Parties in British India:* The party system of democracy was taken for granted both by the British and the Indian freedom movement as natural to democracy. Of course, as mentioned earlier the All India Congress represented the platform on which all shades of Indian politicians had assembled for the same quest, that is, for freedom from alien rule of British. The British rulers had backed sectional and religion based political parties by making propaganda that Hindu Caste system was very rigid and the Congress represented Hindu initiative. Once Congress would be in power the Hindu caste system would prevail with the result that the Scheduled Castes, Muslims, Sikh and Christians all will be second class citizens. That the non-Hindu people were safe under British rule and that they should oppose the moves of Congress in their own interest. This made the spying process also streamlined since Englishmen could not mix freely with Indian population. The British

[1] Kanhiya Lal Omar *versus* R.K. Trivedi: (1985) 4 SCC 628.

Government as Imperial power found the pattern of Indian freedom movement as one against which bullets were of no consequence and it recognised that political counter offensive was required. In order to counter freedom movement the British had actively helped emergence of sectarian parties like, Muslim League, Scheduled Caste Federation or Akali Party and very much succeeded in balancing and thwarting the demand for self-rule and later for full freedom put forth by Mahatma Gandhi through Indian National Congress as common platform for the freedom of country from alien rule. Thus, the freedom movement was also a two party affair, Congress for freedom and most of the rest parties playing the game for the British preservation. The British democratic tradition through debates in Parliament had significantly asserted itself even against their own administration after the Jalianawala Bag massacre of 1919, that lawful opposition was to be tolerated unlike the communist tradition where opposition was to be exterminated. While British tolerated Indian thinking for freedom below the crime of sedition which was of course very favourably defined for the rulers and very strictly defined for the Indian people. Under the law of sedition laid own by section 124-A of Indian Penal Code, 'disaffection' was interpreted to hold that spoken words without any incitement to commit offence were sufficient to commit sedition if they created disaffection for the British rule.[2] The Indians also tolerated the opposition by fellow Indians to the freedom movement as part of rule of law.

3.07A. Politics and political thought though very hazardous for Indians under the British alien rule were the monopoly of educated class of major cities of India of late nineteenth and first half of twentieth centuries. Most of the political leaders of

---

[2] B.G. Tilak *versus* Emperor (1897) 22 Bom.L.R. 528 Privy Council; Besant *versus* Advocate General (1919) I.L.R. 43 Mad. 146 Privy Council. The law as above has been finally over-ruled by Indian Supreme Court in Kedar Nath *versus* State of Bihar, A.I.R. 1962 S.C. 955: Now incitement to commit offence is part of 'disaffection' under section 124-A of I.P.C.

this era were educated in England where they were imparted the same liberal education as Englishmen. These Indian experienced the great difference in their civil rights and treatment at the hands of the British administration when they were on the soil of England and when in the Colonies. If the British had provided same treatment in Colonies and India also, involving dignity of the individual there would not have been any freedom movement which Mahatma Gandhi had spearheaded only after suffering from insults in South Africa. For this ends, to the England educated Indian elite in the first quarter of twentieth century, the comprehension of democracy included British parliamentary system where the Conservative, Liberal and Labour Parties debated administrative problems and policy matters concerning and extending to all areas of British Empire. These British political parties hotly contested elections to the House of Commons with open speeches and freely advocated their points of view and celebrated their victory at the elections without any acrimony and violent retribution unlike as was meted out to the political opponents in the contemporary autocracies functioning on the European Continent. The Indian educated class had with interest noticed how the Liberal Party and the Labour Party in England had rather peacefully merged in stages between 1916 and 1931.

3.07B. The educated Indian elite of pre-independence era had also developed emotional interest in the democratic views of Rousseau, Thomas Paine and Jefferson leading to American War of Independence (1776-83) and the principles of equality pursued by Lincoln for which the Civil war had taken place in the U.S.A., during 1860-64 leading to the glory for natural rights for man and democratic principles. The French Revolution of 1789 and the narration of it by Carlyle were favourite study material for this elite group. All scholars of law and politics in India during British Period were fully familiar with the American federal constitutional form, the doctrine of separation of powers, the powers of review, due process of law doctrine, and a constitutional guarantee of freedoms of individual which even

American legislatures could not violate particularly under the First, Fifth and Fourteenth Amendments of the U.S. Constitution. They highly appreciated the Fabian socialist thought of England, had immense respect for Laski and George Bernard Shaw which at the outset of twentieth century had asserted that the welfare of people was a matter of positive concern for the government of the day. The revolutionary spark in India against the British had been very much present during the last two decades of nineteenth century along with peaceful *satyagrah*[3] process of Mahatma Gandhi and Indian National Congress and the revolutionary spirit found followers among the elite as well particularly after the Soviet Revolution of 1917.

3.07C. However, the Soviet revolutionary experiment was looked at with admiration only by a good proportion of Indian freedom fighters while the U.S. presidential form of government and dual party system for democratic set up were keenly desired for India. In the debates which took place in the Constituent Assembly (1946-49) and also in the critical thinking of post-independence era whenever parliamentary system has appeared to be difficult or failing, the U.S. presidential form of government has appeared to be a plausible alternative. The Constituent Assembly had as it members not only freedom fighters and lawyers but also had, as advisors, Indian administrators and a host of eminent persons from Indian Civil Service to think about the ultimately adopted parliamentary form based on party system.

2. ORIGINS AND EVOLUTION OF INDIAN POLITICAL PARTIES

3.08. *Indian National Congress—First Phase*: The British rulers of India had under the wisdom of Lord Macaulay around 1840 adopted the policy of giving English education to Indians with the hope that this education will develop Indians into useful and loyal subjects. To a good extent the policy was

[3] Non-violent insistence on truth and righteousness.

successful but by the end of Nineteenth Century the British found that it was a mixed blessing. It was realised that liberal education of Indians in England and in India under Macaulay's Plan was producing considerable number of revolutionaries set against the Imperial policies. The wise among the British rulers under the patronage of Lord Rippon who was the Governor General of India during 1883-85 founded the Indian National Congress in 1885 in order to 'ascertaining the real wishes of the people' and to get 'the best public opinion' for and against governmental policies so that revolutionary extremism should not develop among the Indian elite, while at the same time the progressive civilisation of the West should continue to flow into India unhindered.

3.08A. The British Government sponsored Indian National Congress was intended to be a kind of informal one chamber parliament providing a platform for discussions and it used to meet annually as a Conference. After about 20 years in 1905, Bengal which had parts of adjacent Bihar and Assam in it was partitioned. This had placed the Bengali language speaking people in a revolutionary mood. In the 1905 Session of the Congress this partition was opposed and the Congress turned into a political platform henceforth against British Government's policy of repression. This partition was ultimately withdrawn in 1910-11.

3.09. *Extremist and Para-Extremist Political Parties*: The revolutionary and extremist group of Lala Lajpat Rai, Gopal Krishna Gokhale and Bal Gangadhar Tilak had come into existence as a leftist wing of Congress in its 1905 session. In the first two decades of Twentieth Century, Lala Har Dayal and his Ghadar Party which was banned evolved revolutionary thinking that the end justified the means and *swaraj* or home-rule must be won from British for Indians. What these groups believed in common was that the *swaraj* for Indians could never be achieved by methods of begging, prayers or in Councils. Self-reliant action involving forceful methods would only be effective against the British rulers for which bombs and fire arms had to be used by the Indians. However, Mahatma Gandhi's non-violence had more appeal and the extremists were isolated from Indian political process.

3.09A. By 1930, this revolutionary movement was violently suppressed by the British Government leaving the name of martyrs for Indian freedom, like, Chandra Shekhar Azad, for memory. Subsequently, in moderated form the revolutionary spirit was revived in 1934 by the formation of Congress Socialist Party by Jai Prakash Narayan which was promptly banned by the British Government. This ban was lifted in 1946 by the Indian Interim Government and the Congress Socialist Party was renamed Socialist Party of India. It fought the election in 1951 for the First House of People of Parliament constituted under the Constitution of India.

3.10. *The Indian National Congress with politics of Satyagrah—Second Phase:* Mahatma Gandhi entered into Indian politics in second decade of Twentieth Century advocating and seeking support of all Indian political intelligentsia for his movement in South Africa against racial discrimination. In 1918 he became leader of moderate extremist group in Congress and advocated positive methods against the British, not of violence but of active non co-operation, boycott of foreign goods, fostering of spirit for *swadeshi*[4], reliance on Indian culture by rejecting western way of life, and maintenance of village cottage industries and economics. He effectively advocated the ideals of non-violence and passive suffering in the form of *satyagrah.* In retrospect it can be said that if Mahatma Gandhi had not appeared as leader of extremist group in Congress, the course of Indian politics would have drifted to freedom though revolution based on use of arms and bombs very much on the Irish pattern. Mahatma Gandhi continued to have active and effective leadership and hold over Indian National Congress in

[4] (Indian) Country made things or Indian ideas.

one way or the other till Interim Government was formed under Jawahar Lal Nehru in 1945.

3.11. *Political Parties at the time of Independence*: In 1947 at the time of Independence the Indian National Congress had been the main all India political party. Other political parties did not have all India organisation set up. They were more of ideological affinity among individuals type loosely organised as association rather. The Communist Party had territorial bases but in particular areas of the country only. Socialist Party had been organised separately from Congress after ban was lifted from it in 1946. Only Hindu Mahasabha which represented Hindu political interests had an enduring past. However, when the Constitution of India came into existence, many constituents of Congress started thinking of developing separate identity. Apart from this, there had been in existence since 1925 a socio-religious but politically conscious organisation *Rashtriya Swayamsewak Sangh* (popularly known as R.S.S.) which had the feeling that the Hindus had a national identity which needed to be asserted properly. The division of country between India and Pakistan in 1947 was ostensibly disapproved by R.S.S. on emotional and historical ground. When Mahatma Gandhi was assassinated in 1947, the R.S.S. was dubbed as a communal organisation and was banned but was soon exonerated from the charge. The R.S.S. organised a political wing under the name Jan Sangh with national and non-communal outlook which has been on political scene since first election to the House of People of 1951. Later in 1980, it changed itself into Bhartiya Janata Party after a brief stint as one of the constituents of Janata Party between 1977 and 1980.

3.12. *Need for Organised Opposition in Parliament*: Since 1950 for effective parliamentary system under the Constitution of India the need for a well organised opposition on the pattern of two party systems operating in England and in the U.S.A. has been felt and desired. As all the Indian politicians were trained only for seeking and working for independence against an alien rule, the practical problem faced for a two party system was how to evolve a political party in independent India having a political programme parallel to the Indian National Congress within the framework of the Indian Constitution. The situation was made difficult since the All India Congress had developed the psychology of identifying itself with the Constitution of India, had developed leftist programmes and had declared itself saviour of all the Indian virtues past or present. In order to remain in power it projected other political parties anti-national or as opposed to constitutional ideals on one point or other. The Congress had high flexibility to change its ideals from natural rights and individualism in 1946-47 to welfare state conception in 1952, from state ownership and development of public economy in 1958 to a system of free trade, de-nationalisation and liberal economy in 1991, or from the ideal of liberties for individual to a police state in 1975-77. Since the Congress was always in power except for brief interludes between 1977-80 and 1989-91 till 1995, it did not from its side leave any innovative scope for other political parties. Only Bhartiya Janata Party, Communist Parties and some regional parties could establish themselves with separate and parallel programmes in the course of first 50 years of Independence.

3.12A. *Indian National Congress—Third Phase*: Congress has had notable ups and downs during the last fifty years. It was continuously in power except for a three year interlude, 1977-1980. It has not been returned to Lok Sabha (House of People) as majority party since 1989. In 1991, it formed a minority government. Its State units have revolted in large numbers and have organised themselves as regional Congress parties. But, Indian National Congress has immense goodwill of Indian people, the bureaucracy and mass media. The Congress leaders have often by their corrupt deeds alienated public support for the party but generally Indian people forget the failures of Congress Party when there is a change in top leadership. The past history of its leaders for sacrifices made for the nation prevails ultimately over its dubious immediate past. This helps new leadership of Congress Party to stage comeback from time to time; the interlude depends on the failures of other parties to provide clean and efficient administration. In 1998, in the general elections held in some States, notably, Rajasthan and Delhi, it staged a come back as reaction against or as alternative to the BJP State Governments. In 2002, it came back into power in Punjab.

3.13. *Politics for Indian Muslims*: In Indian politics of 1940s, in 1947 all politics minded Muslims had to be either of secular thinking if they wanted to stay in India or they were expected to migrate to Pakistan which was and is the embodiment of Muslim brotherhood on Indian sub-continent. Pakistan is a religion oriented Islamic state and had its existence under the two nation theory of British rulers which was given credibility by partition of the country in 1947. Muslim community is highly spiritualistic and religious in approach. It has not been able to digest culture of West and Muslim fundamentalism in militant form has become a problem in all Muslim states of the world. In India the situation after 50 years of Independence remains to a good extent of the pattern in which Muslims in India have not been able to separate politics from religion which is necessary in secular Indian state. It has been significantly observed by EMS Namboodiripad, former two times communist Chief Minister of the State of Kerala, that after Independence:[5]

> "Unfortunately, however, Muslim leaders in several parts of the country continued to pursue the line of the pre-independence Muslim League, setting Muslims off from non-Muslims. They continued to keep alive not only the political traditions of the pre-Independence Muslim League but the organisation as well. Renaming their party as the Indian Union Muslim League, they started operating in that name in several States, notably in Kerala and Tamil Nadu".

---

[5] EMS Namboodiripad, "Muslim Politics—Before and after Independence", *Frontline*, July 15, 1994, 107; Namboodiripad, a communist leader, was twice Chief Minister of Kerala in 1958 and 1967.

3.13A. As a result the majority of Muslims for long continued to look to Pakistan, Saudi Arabia and Emirates of Middle East as the lands of their ultimate destiny. But, the rejection of Pakistan as embodiment of the nationhood for Bengali Muslims, by the people of present Bangladesh which was East Pakistan as well as the socio-political non-acceptance by Pakistan of Muslims who had migrated there on partition of India, known as *mujahirs,* has forced Hindustani Muslims to think again about their identity.

3.13B. Now, since late 1980s the Indian Muslims are taking advantage of minority rights provisions of the Constitution of India and are trying to develop themselves as a distinct vote bank for influencing the political parties to their political advantage. In this process they suffer from a feeling of isolation and they feel shy even of those Muslim community reforms which have taken place in Pakistan or in Middle East Muslim States. In choosing their candidates and political parties for voting in General Elections to Parliament or State Legislatures the Muslims voters often appear to wait for the *fatwa(s)*[6] issued by their religious leaders. For example, the Imam of Jama Masjid had on the eve of 1996 elections issued a *fatwa* in favour of United Front—B.S.P.—Congress combine.

3.13C. It can be politically said that such a *fatwa* to Muslim voters by a religious head signifies only an appeal for voting according to some political compromise with some hopes with secular parties which may or may not be fielding Muslim candidates. But from the point of view of law, a *fatwa* which has evidently a religious content issued to Muslims for voting a Muslim candidate only or not to vote for non-Muslims in name of religion will have different implication under section 123(3A) of Representation of Peoples' Act 1951, which penalises corrupt practices. The Supreme Court in Suryakant Venkat Mahadik *versus* S.S. Naik[7], has held that where the returned candidate

---

[6] Edicts, directions or appeals issued by a *mufti* who knows Sharia and Hadith.

[7] (1996) 1 SCC 384.

being a Hindu had invoked the support for the Hindus and Hindu religion in a religious gathering of Hindus during an election campaign, the charge of "corrupt practice" was established.

3.13D. The separation of Bangladesh from Pakistan and the establishment of Islamic States in Central Asia after the demise of Soviet Union has further confused the Muslim community of India and in presence of Pakistan they feel neither here nor there. There was a period upto 1971 when Pakistan used to project itself as patron of Muslims in India but now it has shifted itself to Afghanistan and Middle East Muslims. However, it is gradually found that Indian educated Muslims are joining established mainstream political parties in significant numbers and have begun to occupy important party posts. In other occupational fields, like, judiciary, armed forces, business or central services the Muslim community is significantly represented in the highest of the posts.

3.14. *Hindustani and Hindutva Politics*: For the rest of Indian communities, other than Muslims there has not been any doubt as to the place to which they belong. Hindu, Sikh, Christian, Parsi or people belonging to other religious faiths have regarded India to be their homeland. The question before them has been how much interest to take in politics or the democratic process. Of Course the Anglo-Indian community which is on the side of one of the parents of British heritage was confused after the British decided to leave India after the 15th of August 1947. However this numerically small community had no problem of adjustment.

3.15. While 'India' is a term which originated in English language, Bharat is basically an ancient or Sanskrit nomenclature for our country but has not been used by people in general before Independence. Muslim rulers during last five centuries or so, called India as Hindustan, the people living on this land as Hindustani, and, later the language of masses of northern India as Hindi which is an admixture of Sanskrit, Persian and Arabic and the dialect spoken by the people. In Urdu language spoken by Muslim rulers all over the country, the land was known as Hindustan. Since Hindustan leads to Hindi for language of the people, and since the Constitution of India in the Preamble mentions, 'India, that is, Bharat' and also because Pakistani leaders found that Pakistan was part of Hindustan and Pakistan and Bharat refer properly to the effects of partition of the country, the nomenclature Hindustan has gone out of use progressively. For a secular country composed of different religious denominations, cultures or languages but having a common past, the term Hindustani refers to a composite heritage of the people. In the evolutionary pressures of democratic process in India, the term Hindustani is generalising itself as the quality of being 'Indian', like, 'French', 'American' or 'British'. In the evolutionary process hastened by international mixing of people and the cultures the English language has not been banned in or expelled from India but continues as link language for the country where more than twenty regional languages are recognised to be spoken. Now in addition to Hindi and Urdu a third dialect is fast developing to which many refer as 'Hindi-English' which half English and half Hindi and Urdu. This new dialect is readily understood and is accepted in non-Hindi speaking areas of India also. In the same strain 'Hindutva' has come to mean the essence of being 'Indian' or 'Hindustani', that is, a toleration and peaceful coexistence of different Hindustani cultures irrespective of religious cults, somewhat akin to Sufi or of pan-theistic character.

3.16. During the Maharashtra State Legislative Assembly elections held in December 1987, in public speeches made in favour of regional Shiva Sena Party, fervent appeals for casting of votes for protection of 'Hindutva' and 'Hinduism' were made. The Supreme Court in the case, Dr. Ramesh Yashwant Prabhoo *versus* Prabhakar K. Kunte[8], (Hon'ble Justice J.S. Verma for the Court) examined in detail the implications of these two terms from the point of view of adoption of corrupt practices by way

[8] (1996) 1 SCC 130 at pp.153-162.

of exploiting religious feelings of the voters under section 123 (3) & (3-A) of the Representation of People Act and held that unless a speech "can be construed as an appeal to vote for a candidate on the ground that he is a Hindu or to refrain from voting for a candidate on the ground of his religion, *i.e.*, he not being a Hindu" there is no electoral corrupt practice involved in the case[9].

3.16A. The Supreme Court further examined if appeal to 'Hindutva' and 'Hinduism' are religious matters. It noted with approval the observations in earlier case, Sastri Yagnapurushdasji *versus* Muldas[10], that Hindus are "that part of great Aryan race" as narrated by Monier Williams, which "immigrated from Central Asia, through the mountain passes into India, settled first in the districts near the River Sindhu (now called Indus). The Persians pronounced this word Hindu and named their Aryan brethren Hindus, The Greeks, who probably gained their first ideas of India from the Persians, dropped the hard aspirate, and called the Hindus 'Indoi'."[11] Hon'ble Justice Verma who delivered the judgment for the Supreme Court quoted with approval the observations of Dr. Radhakrishnan that "(T)he people on the Indian side of the Sindhu were called Hindu by the Persian and the later western invaders",[12] and that "(T)he term 'Hindu', according to Dr. Radhakrishnan, had originally a territorial and not a credal significance. It implied residence in a well defined geographical area".[13]

3.16B Examining how much the term 'Hindu' had religious content, Justice Verma[14] held that the scriptures as well as the

---

[9] *Ibid.*, p. 153g.

[10] (1966) 3 SCR 242 at pp. 259-66.

[11] Monier Williams, *Hinduism*, p. 1.

[12] Dr. Radhakrishnan, *The Hindu View of Life*, p. 12.

[13] *Ibid.* p. 12.

[14] Later, Justice Verma became Chief Justice of Supreme Court of India, and currently, in April 2002, he is Chairman of National Human Rights Commission.

view of modern learned has been that Hinduism refers to a way of life, the...

> "history of Indian thought emphatically brings out the fact that the development of Hindu religion has always been inspired by an endless quest of mind for truth based on the consciousness that truth has many facets. Truth is one, but wise men describe it differently." ..."When we consider this broad sweep of Hindu philosophic concepts, it would be realised that under Hindu philosophy, there is no scope for excommunicating any notion or principle as heretical or rejecting it as such."[15]

3.16C. Justice Verma quoted with approval the Webster's Third *New International Dictionary of the English Language* for concentrating on the meaning of 'Hinduism' according to which, it is:

> "a complex body of social, cultural and religious beliefs and practices evolved in and largely confined to the Indian subcontinent and marked by a caste system, an outlook tending to view all forms and theories as aspects of one eternal being and truth, a belief in *ahimsa, karma, dharma, sanskara,* and *moksha,* and the practice of the way of works, the way of knowledge, or the way of devotion as the means of release from the bonds of rebirth; the way of life and form of thought of a Hindu."

The Judgement further elucidated the point by quoting from *Encyclopaedia Britannica* (15th ed.), to observe that the term Hinduism....

> "is an utterly diverse conglomerate of doctrines, cults, and way of life.... In principle, Hinduism incorporates all forms of beliefs and worship without necessitating the selection or elimination of any. The Hindu is inclined to revere the divine in every manifestation, whatever it may be, and is doctrinally tolerant, leaving others—including

[15] *Op. cit.,* f.n. 5, at p. 156 (b,c).

> both Hindus and non-Hindus—whatever creed and worship practices suit them best. A Hindu may embrace a non-Hindu religion without ceasing to be a Hindu...."

Finally, the Judgement declared the legal position on 'Hindutva' in the words:

> "Hindutva is understood as a way of life or a state of mind and it is not to be equated with or understood as religious Hindu fundamentalism...the word 'Hindutva' is used and understood as a synonym of 'Indianization', *i.e.*, the development of uniform culture by obliterating the differences between all the cultures coexisting in the country".[16]

3.17. The political balance between secularism, religious fervour in general and during elections and the disqualification for political parties and the candidates seeking election for adoption of 'corrupt practices' under section 123 of the R.P. Act has thus been resolved by the Supreme Court.[17] On academic or journalistic plane also some commentators have tried to harmonise the problem of interaction of religion and politics. With reference to the above judgement of the Supreme Court, it has been observed,[18]...

> 'to judge the real nature of any religion, one has to go into its theological aspects, not its political and sociological aspects. What (is meant) by political and sociological aspect is that a section of the followers of any religion has its political ambitions and it misuses religion to fulfil its ambition and, if need be, makes it appear intolerant of

---

16 *Ibid.*, at p. 159, para. 39.

17 The *ratio decidendi* of the case was applied with approval by the Supreme Court in Manohar Joshi *versus* Nitin B. Patil (1996) 1 SCC 69, and latter case was confirmed in Mohd. Aslam *versus* Union of India (1996) 2 SCC 749.

18 Asghar Ali Engineer, 'Islam, Hindutva and Pluralism', *The Hindu*. September 5, 1996. The writer is/was Director of the Institute of Islamic Studies and is/was Chairperson of the Committee for Communal Harmony.

other faiths if they come in the way of achieving the ambitions. ...Looking from a theological angle, Hinduism, Islam or Christianity have respect of other religions provided they are studied in a holistic perspective, not through purposely chosen quotations from the scriptures....Islam is as pluralistic as Hinduism, and if one goes by Quaranic spirit, as tolerant as Hinduism, one should also remember that in every religion there are people with different tendencies and mindsets and they interpret religion accordingly. Tolerance is not a religions but a psychological category. We have tolerant and intolerant Hindus and Muslims.... Sufi Islam was in general much more liberal and the Islam projected by the Ulema.... Ibn Arabi, for example, maintained that his heart was a mosque, a synagogue, a church and a temple, *i.e.*, he was equally inspired by spiritual traditions of all these religions.... In fact, the Quaran goes one step further and declares that Allah created pluralism to test our ability to live in peace...." For every one of you We have appointed a law and a way. And if Allah had pleased He would have made you a single community but He might try you in what he gave you (many religious groups and communities). So vie one with another in good deeds (5:48), ..."And everyone has direction in which he turns, so vie with one another in good deeds" (2:148).

3.17A. Thus, 'Hindutva' is a new socio-political term which is a state of secularised peaceful coexistence of different Hindustani cultures irrespective of religious cults and represents a spirit for toleration but with a progressive Hindustani attitude of Sufi or pantheistic nature. It cannot be limited to a conceptual generalisation of Vedic or Puranic *devi-devta(s)* and the wisdom of Upanishad(s).

3.18. The Indian legal system regards God, *Khuda* and *Bhagwan* as non-religious and secular concepts. Constitutionally, the State is required to treat all religions equally, it is not an atheistic State. There is no wall of separation between the State and the religion. To this extent the Indian secularism is different from U.S. Constitution secularism under First Amendment.

3.18A. As mentioned, the 'Hindutva' as a political slogan is patronised by the regional Shiva Sena Party which thrives on fears of Muslim fundamentalism and partly on this regional party being a constituent of the coalition government at the Union led by BJP Prime Minister Atal Bihari Vajpayee.

3.19. *Anti-Religiosity in Indian Politics.* As a matter of fact, Indian National Congress being a platform for freedom movement was inert on religious aspects. Its members were Hindu, Muslim, Christian, Sikh or Parsi.

3.19A. The Marxism and the Communist Party have an anti-religion attitude as in erstwhile Soviet Union or Mao's China. The Marxism is an aggressive materialistic politics which does not mix with Indian culture. Its first principle that ends justify the means is a-moral philosophy according to Hindu mind wherein *ahimsa* and coexistence are essential way of life. Muslims believe in good deeds and vigorous religious life in preference over Godless materialism. The Communism could not become part of Indian thinking apart from its hard core leaders and except for Kerala, Andhra Pradesh and West Bengal where poverty ridden and much exploited agricultural farmers have found solace in communism.

3.19B. Anti-Brahmin attitude in South India had produced parties like, Dravida Munnetra Kazhagam (D.M.K.) which were obviously hostile to the orthodox religious practices of majority community. Further, Prime Minister Jawahar Lal Nehru was known to be a karma-yogi but without exhibition of dependence on God's grace and he dominated both Congress and Indian political scene till his death in 1964. He had faith in hard work, and worked for heavy industrialisation and scientific temper for the country. His successors, both Prime Minister Lal Bahadur Shastri and Prime Minister Indira Gandhi were religious in personal life but had successfully separated politics from their religion and the latter had more faith in the loyalty of non-Hindu colleagues. Prime Minister Rajiv Gandhi was a aeroplane pilot turned into politician and had visions of scientific transformations for the country for entering into twenty-first century and had no time for prayers. The political parties which had evolved by fragmentation of Congress were also conglomerates of Indian religions. In fact this group of political parties had since 1980s found Bhartiya Janata Party (B.J.P.) as its main opponent and had rather thought of prospering by B.J.P. baiting in place of having their own programmes. In this process they had dubbed B.J.P. as a religion based communal organisation, as banking for the support of people on fundamentalist Hindu organisations for its votes and for a rigid anti-Pakistan stance, by not accepting the partition of India in 1947 as *fait accompli*, and which charges the latter was all the time trying to shake off. Paradoxically, because of this baiting the B.J.P. has become more and more known to the masses and less and less communal in outlook by the end of 1997.

3.19C. As for the masses and the intelligentsia who vote, being part of Indian society, the economic prosperity and economic everyday problems have been more important to them. The present generation after 50 years of freedom has no or little idea of communal frenzy which British had unleashed in India and had left it as a legacy. Neither Hindu nor Muslim young generation is emotionally attached to religion, though the Muslim fundamentalist have in the context of Kashmir now and then tried to make an impact on Muslims. The job market and economic considerations ultimately decide the flow of votes. The role of electronic or satellite multimedia on creation of non-religious but sex oriented culture through cheap entertainment has in 1990s with the use of mixed or spicy scenes and language eclipsed both the Indian traditions and the political issues. Under the new technological and social pressures, therefore, those political parties which will bank on religious issues are most likely to get shelved by the new voters in the electorate in the early twenty-first century.

3.19D. It may be mentioned that after Independence in 1947, the Hindu Mahasabha or Ram Rajya Parishad, which took part in elections by depending on Hindu votes, were soon driven out of democratic process. Almost similar was the position of Jan Sangh which had a very slow growth rate till 1977 but had kept surviving in North and Central India more as a front organisation of R.S.S. but not so much on its own worth. On the other hand, Prime Minister Nehru kept the Congress in the forefront by achieving the ideals of international status for India as a non-aligned nation and as leader of this movement along with the industrial development of the country based on Five-Year Plans which reached the people at the grass root level election base, something prestigious for the country. This kept the All India Congress in power in Parliament till he remained alive and beyond that till the Congress Party got ridden by chronic corruption.

3.20. Again, taking help of *religion* by the political parties for getting votes or for denying votes to other political parties, is now a settled corrupt practice. However, there are charges that some parties indirectly create images in public mind that they are for a particular religion and therefore, the members of that religious community should vote for them only. There are many leaders who as individuals invoke blessings of their God in temples, shrines or *mazaars* in presence of Press and T.V. cameras for success for themselves or for their Party so that they become Prime Minister or Chief Minister, etc. Do these aspirants commit 'corrupt Practice'? There were charges against minority government Prime Minister P. V. Narasimha Rao for "exhibitionist religiosity" before elections to eleventh House of People in June 1996. Such situations are marginally situated and whether corrupt practice can be fixed for the actions becomes a matter to be established in each case but ordinarily it is the *paparazzi* press which is more interested in the behaviour or actions rather than the individual projecting himself to the society for seeking votes on the consideration of his devotional disposition.

3.20A. As for the masses and the intelligentsia who vote, being part of Indian society, the economic prosperity and economic everyday problems have been more important to them. The present generation after 50 years of freedom has no or little idea of communal frenzy which the British had unleashed in India through their divide and rule policy, and had left it as an ulcerous legacy. Neither Hindu nor Muslim young generation is emotionally attached to religion, though Muslim fundamentalists have in the context of Kashmir now and then tried unsuccessfully to make an impact on Muslim community. The job market and economic and economic considerations ultimately decide the flow of votes. The role of electronic or satellite multimedia on the creation of non-religious but sex oriented culture of West through cheap entertainment with the use of spicy scenes, traditionally vulgar, has in 1990s eclipsed both the Indian culture and political issues of the time. Under the impact of the new technological and social pressures, therefore, those political parties which bank on religious issues and slogans are most likely to get shelved by the new set of voters in the early twenty-first century.

3. POLITICAL PARTIES BY FRAGMENTATION OF CONGRESS

3.21. The Indian National Congress was established in 1885 on the initiative of British citizens who were friends of India in order to understand Indian reactions to the British policy measure undertaken in the country. The idea was to provide a better administration which did not create feelings of animosity between government and the people and thereby the production of revolutionaries was prevented. However, as a sequence of the Partition of Bengal in 1905, the Indian National Congress became a political platform for voicing dissatisfaction against the government. In 1918 after joining of Indian politics by Mahatma Gandhi the Congress came under the influence and control of moderate extremists and also of constitutional experts like Sir Tej Bahadur Sapru with demands for *swaraj* or home-rule and to oppose the changes brought into the administration of the Country by the Government of India Act of 1919.

3.22. After the British succeeded in suppressing revolutionaries around 1930, the socialist revolutionary groups led by J.P. Narayan had joined Congress in 1934. When India became independent in 1947 they were the first to come out of Congress fold in order to establish their identity in democratic India and the Socialist Party of India was formed.

3.22A. The next fragmentation of Congress based on the functions and its policies for Government in independent India took place in 1951, when Acharya Kriplani, a staunch Gandhian aggrieved by the heavy industrialisation policy of Congress which was at the cost of Gandhian concept of cottage and village industries, formed Kasan Mazdoor Party (KMP). After the experience of 1952 First Elections to the House of People it amalgamated with the Socialist Party of India to form Praja Socialist Party (PSP). The new party had several top class former Congress leaders, particularly, Acharya Kriplani, Narendra Deva, J.P.Narayan, Ashok Mehta, and Ram Manohar Lohia. The P.S.P. promised to provide a viable opposition to Indian National Congress. However, it failed to achieve with the people the status alternative to or equal to the Congress and practically failed in its mission in 1957 and 1962 General Elections to the House of People. In 1963 and 1964 the P.S.P. was divided into three factions. The P.S.P. failed because the Congress which was at the helm of Government could not be outdone in leftist programmes for the masses. The Congress had a rural vote bank base with public welfare ideology under comprehensive heavy industrialisation and development of public sector through nationalisation programmes. These promised government jobs of every nature and money for rural development. In the face of these the socialist programmes of Congress which was forming government both at the Union and in States, the promises of the P.S.P. could not be placed before the people effectively and meaningfully. Moreover, after the 1962 war with China, the

Congress had strong support of Soviet Union in international politics and the people felt that this effectively provided security against Pakistani and Chinese aggressive postures. People of India did not find any political party as having the capability of tackling over all these situations. Of the three factions of P.S.P. only Samyukta Socialist Party (S.S.P.) under the leadership of Ram Manohar Lohia remained vocal and prominent but S.S.P. could not overshadow the socialism of Congress beyond making criticisms in public.

3.22B. The Indian National Congress always had a prominent group of thinkers, supporters and politicians who were advocates for maximum possible liberties and freedom of action for the people. This lobby had been successful in incorporating the right to property and other fundamental liberties in the Part III of the Constitution of India while members of the Constituent Assembly. Many of them were not supporters of the socialist approach but had been interested in the struggle for the freedom of the Country along with the Congress. These politicians were rather disappointed when at the Avadi Congress session of January 1955 it was resolved to link the planning with the establishment of a socialist pattern of society. The project for more equitable distribution of wealth by increased taxation burden, curtailment of the landlord system beyond abolition of zamindari and enlargement of public sector by excluding private enterprises from the same field, caused adverse reactions in the liberties minded politicians in the Congress. Then, at the Nagpur Session of Congress in 1959, the Resolutions in furtherance of co-operative movement, nationalisation of resources and financial institutions in the interest of socialistic pattern of society finally led to the formation of a new political party named as Swatantra Party in 1959. The Party was led by C. Rajagopalachari, N.G. Ranga, K.M. Munshi, Minoo Masani, S.K.D. Paliwal, V.P. Menon among others.

3.22C. The Swatantra Party stood for maximum freedom for individual, minimum interference by the State in society, maximum sanctity for Fundamental Rights, just compensation for property compulsorily acquired, competitive industrial private enterprise and least possible regulation by the State of industries etc. Thus, the Swatantra Party was to be a conservative political party and was intended to develop into an alternative to Congress. It made successful alliances with Krishak Lok Party in Andhra Pradesh, Akali Party in Punjab and Ganatantra Parishad in Orissa, and had adjustments with Jan Sangh for distribution of seats. However, the Swatantra Party had only moderate success in elections since it could not bank on rural votes and ultimately it merged with Janata Party in 1977 for election to the Sixth House of People.

3.23. *Congress Party Split of 1967-69:* The Congress Party had after five years of internecine problems split vertically into two parts, not on different ideological bases but on the matter of the ongoing power struggle in the party under the caption—'After Nehru—Who?', since Prime Minister Nehru died in 1964. This split in Congress is significant because it devastated the legendary Indian National Congress and gave rise to various situations of constitutional importance for the future, giving chance to the evolutionary process for two or more party parliamentary system in India to develop.

3.23A. After the demise of Prime Minister Nehru in 1964 which was rather unexpected several veteran Congress leaders wanted to be approached for the Prime Ministership. However, the desire for respectability helped the Working Committee and Kamraj, a senior Congress leader, succeeded in a consensus formula under which L.B. Shastri was accepted as Prime Minister. Later when L.B. Shastri unexpectedly died in early 1966, Morarji Desai insisted for Prime Ministership and ultimately there was voting which decided the issue in favour of Indira Gandhi. After the 1967 General Elections for Fourth House of People, again the same problem arose within Congress Party on the choice of Prime Minister. This time the old veteran leaders were better organised but the legislative members of the Congress who were younger set were in favour of Indira Gandhi. A consensus arrangement for Deputy Prime Ministership for Morarji Desai was made ultimately. However, a wedge between senior members who were known as *syndicate* and the supporters if Indira Gandhi known as *young turks* had come into existence. After the death of President Zakir Husain in May 1969 the syndicate wanted to make Sanjiva Reddy a member of the group, President of India. Jan Sangh and Swatantra Party wanted C.D. Deshmukh while Indira Gandhi wanted V.V. Giri or Jagjivan Ram as President of India. In the election which ensued Congress M.P.s were allowed to cast free 'conscience' vote. In August 1969 as candidate of Indira Gandhi, Giri was elected as President of India. However, this did not end the conflict and after a series of reprisals on both sides on 12th of November 1969 Indira Gandhi was expelled from the Indian National Congress. She had the support of about three fourth Members of Parliament from Congress and of the majority of Congress Chief Ministers. The Congress was divided vertically thereafter between Congress(O)[19] and Congress (I).[20]

3.23A. In 1971 general elections for the fifth House of People, the Congress(O) had major set back which retired most of the veteran Congress leaders. This Party later merged with Janata Party on the eve of elections to the sixth House of People in 1977 for providing a combined opposition to the Congress (I).

3.24. *Internal Emergency of 1975 and New Party Order*: In 1974, in anticipation of elections to the House of People due in 1976 all earlier splinter parties from Congress formed a new political party under the name Bhartiya Lok Dal (B.L.D). Its main constituents were Swatantra Party, Samyukya Socialist Party, Kisan Mazdoor Party and the Utkal Congress. Jan Sangh and Communist Parties were the notable exceptions from this B.L.D. which was supposed to be a formidable development at that

---

19 Congress(O) signified Congress Organisation.

20 Congress(I) signified Congress of Indira Gandhi

time and which somewhat unsettled Prime Minister Indira Gandhi. In 1975 Proclamation of Internal Emergency, a doubtful proposition, under Article 352 of the Constitution of India was made by the President and soon the life of the House of People was extended by one year and most of the leaders of all political parties were placed under preventive detention.

3.24A. When elections for the House of People were announced in 1977, Bhartiya Lok Dal along with Jan Sangh, Congress(O) and Congress for Democracy of Jagjivan Ram (1976) combined together to form a new coalition Janata Party in order to raise a combined platform against Congress (I). In the elections to the sixth House of People Janata Party secured 296 seats as against 153 of the Congress(I). Latter had majority in the Council of States and had most of the Chief Ministers in its fold and so it was not a washed out party. The new Janata Party had practically no country-wide organisational spread out except for what its earlier constituents could provide and so it was a top heavy political Party. The top layer itself suffered from personal ambitions of the leaders and all of them wanted to permanently get rid of Indira Gandhi.

3.24B. The Janata Party started breaking in 1979 when Charan Singh left Janata Party and formed Janata (Secular) Party. With outside support of Congress (I) Charan Singh replaced Morarji Desai as Prime Minister. However, Prime Minister Charan Singh could not face the House of People for confidence motion and resigned but continued as caretaker Prime Minister for the next seventh general election to the House of People. After the 1980 general election Congress (I) again came into power with majority of 352 out of 544 . This set into motion a disintegration process for Janata Party.

3.24C. In July 1981 Congress (O) separated itself from Janata Party and became Congress (U), then Congress (J) and then Congress (S). In 1982, Jan Sangh left Janata Party and regrouped itself as Bhartiya Janata Party, and H.N. Bahuguna formed Democratic Socialist Party. The basic Janata Party did not dissolve itself but continued to function as such with Chandrashekhar as its President. It had 31 seats in the House of People elected in 1980 and it joined Janata Dal in October 1988 on the eve of ninth general election. Janata Dal was formed in October 1988 as a combined new political party to counter Congress(I), It had the earlier constituents of broken Janata Party who were like minded and were prepared to bury their differences, *viz.*, Lok Dal (Charan Singh), Janata Morcha (V.P. Singh) and Janata Party (Chandrashekhar). V.P. Singh was elected as its President.

3.25. Later in 1988, seven opposition parties, notably, Janata Dal, Congress (S), Telgu Desam Party, D.M.K. and Assom Gana Parishad, came together to form a coalition named National Peoples Front with N.T. Rama Rao as Chairman and V.P. Singh as Convenor. It was a coalition formed before the election with adjustment of seats for avoiding internal conflict. In the next ninth general election this Front emerged as second largest Party, it had 141 seats while Congress (I) had 193 seats but not majority in the House of People and B.J.P. emerged as third largest party with 88 seats. The National Front formed the minority government with V.P. Singh as Prime Minister with outside support of B.J.P.

3.26. On November 1, 1990, Chandrashekhar defected from Janata Dal along with 58 members and formed Janata Dal (S). National Peoples Front lost vote of confidence in the House of People on November 7, 1990 after B.J.P. withdrew support on October 23, 1990 on the arrest of B.J.P. President in Samastipur. Janata Dal (S) formed the minority government with Chandrashekhar as Prime Minister with outside support of Congress (I) on November 10, 1990.

3.27. After May-June 1991 tenth general election to the House of People again a 'Hung Parliament' as after the 1989 general election, had come into existence. The minority government of Congress (I) Party with P.V. Narsimha Rao as its leader becoming Prime Minister completed the five year term.

It had outside support of National Front and was also helped by abstention from voting whenever no confidence motion was tabled by all those members who did not want fresh elections. However, when fresh elections were announced and the House of People was adjourned sine die the Congress(I) suffered significant splits both qualitatively and quantitatively.

3.28. In the State of Tamil Nadu, all the Congress (I) M.Ps defected and formed Tamil Mannila Congress (T.M.C.) as a result of which Congress (I) became non-existent in Tamil Nadu. Several important Congress(I) Union Cabinet Ministers had their names in graft scandals and prosecutions who had been charge-sheeted but were not convicted, they had resigned or were denied Congress(I) nominations and they formed new parties instead of joining opposition parties, in order to contest 1996 eleventh general election. Thus Congress(T) and Madhya Pradesh Vikas Congress came into existence. Subsequently, Congress(I) had splits due to State level politics also. In October 1997 Congress (I) split with 22 out of its 37 Congress (I) Legislative Party, forming a new U.P. Lok Tantrik Congress which supported Kalyan Singh as Chief Minister. On December 7, 1997 Manipur State the Congress (I) Legislative Party had a split with the Speaker forming a new party Manipur State Congress and formed own Government in the State. Before twelfth general elections in early 1998, West Bengal unit of Congress Party had split and had formed a separate Trinamul Congress on the issue of relationship between Congress (I) and C.P.I. (M) in the State under the leadership of Ms Mamata Banerji. In the twelfth general elections Trinamul Congress had 7 seats in House of People and became an important outside supporter of B.J.P. coalition government under Prime Minister Vajpayee.

3.29. Interestingly, after the Congress Party forced dissolution of the twelfth Lok Sabha for fresh elections, which took place under the Presidential Order of 25th April 1999, Congress President Ms Sonia Gandhi, a naturalised Indian, was projected as Congress Party candidate for next Prime Minister of India. This led to a public debate whether a person of foreign origin should hold such vital office involving security of India. Fearing that the other parties will get better over Congress Party in the general election because of this sensitive issue, three top leaders, Sharad Pawar, P.A. Sangma and Tariq Anwar proposed to the Congress Working Committee for consideration that the Party should propose a constitutional amendment that the President, Vice-President and Prime Minister of India should be natural-born citizens of India. The Congress Party expelled the three from its membership and the three formed a new political party, Nationalist Congress Party.

3.30. After May 1996 election to the Eleventh House of People, B.J.P. emerged as the single largest party, followed by the United Front, a combination of National Front and Left Front formed after the elections and with Congress(I) becoming the third largest Party. The United Front formed the coalition government after the President had invited B.J.P. as single largest party in Parliament to form the government subject to proving its majority on the floor of the House of People within fourteen days. The B.J.P. failed and so on June 1, 1996 United Front with outside support of Congress formed the Government which remained in office till the House of People was dissolved in December 1997 after the withdrawal of support by Congress (I)

4. THE LEFTIST POLITICAL PARTIES

3.31. The leftist political movement essentially based on Marxism has taken political aspirations from Soviet Revolution of 1917. It is based on hostility towards the existing society and political patterns which are founded on acceptance of religion, private property and enterprise and landed aristocracy, the latter values in one form or other are pursued by the rightist political parties.

3.32. At the time of Independence of India in 1947, distinct from Indian National Congress and the Socialist Party of

J.P. Narayan there was in existence the Communist Party of India (C.P.I.). This C.P.I. had been formed as a party in 1934, was pro Soviet Union and had been banned by the British Government of India. When Soviet Russia joined the Second World War the ban was lifted in 1943 under Soviet pressure. Subsequently it projected the Soviet-British friendship and was not concerned with freedom movement except on personal basis. The C.P.I. had inherent hostility to both capitalist system of England and the U.S.A. and the agricultural landlord or *zamindari* system prevailing under British Indian regime. Like as the Soviet international policy the C.P.I. was also against any trade relationship with capitalist countries or the Western Power Bloc. After Indian Independence, it stood for nationalisation of all industries and confiscation of foreign companies Regarding Indian industrialists it did not advocate their extermination but taking of their services and co-operation. Basically, C.P.I. advocated revolutionary methods for extermination of land aristocracy and also the Government machinery. However, under Soviet pressure it had forsaken disruptive tactics but the dissidence on this score within the Party was growing and which reflected the same level of hostility for each other as between Soviet Russia and Maoist China. The Communist Party of India took part in the first general elections held in 1952. In State of Madras *versus* Gopalan,[21] the Supreme Court found that the members of this party could take part in the elections provided they adhered to the constitutional requirements under Article 19, and that the power of State for preventive detention under an Act was not against political justice ideal enshrined in the Preamble to the Constitution of India.

3.32A. Later by 1967 the Communists were clearly divided into two completely hostile and separate political Organisations, C.P.I. and C.P.I. (Marxist). The C.P.I.(M) was pro-Peking and was waiting for Indian Mao to emerge who would take over the Indian Government on the lines of communist revolution in

---

[21] 1950 SCR 88.

China of 1949 but they had under advice from Communist China under Bandung formula of co-existence of 1956, undertaken to accept the parliamentary system as an internal compromise. While C.P.I. generally remained quiet and friendly to the Congress, the C.P.I.(M) had success in forming governments in the States of Kerala (1958) and West Bengal (1967) within the framework of the Constitution of India. However, the Nexalite communists known initially for their 'land grab' movement and terrorist attack on C.P.I. and police outposts, have come to be identified as C.P.I. (ML) Party.[22] All the three factions of communist movement in India have now been taking part in democratic process prevailing for membership of Parliament and State Assemblies with the C.P.I. (M) acting as the Big Brother. However, with the increasing closeness between capitalist USA and communist China since 1970s alongwith acceptance of economic liberalisation and global trade in 1990s as a means of progress by the communist China has badly shaken the ideological base of CPI(M). Recently in October 2000 it updated its 1964 party programme, which now recognises the impact of new world economy with a mobile finance capital as a serious setback for Marxist movement. In prospect, it wants to mobilise the Indian working people, including industrial workers, agricultural labour, rural and urban middle class and peasants, as a working class and through its victory at the polls, the CPI(M) has set itself to achieve the aim of people's democratic revolution.[23]

3.32B. The CPI(M) has been forming the Left Front Government in State of West Bengal continuously since 1967 and had also participated in the Union Government Ministries in 1977-98. The Left Front has had no specific legal or social programmes under the constitutional set up of India for the reasons mentioned above. Marxism as a political philosophy

---

[22] Now, it has two factions CPI(ML) (Party Unity) which is banned and CPI(ML) (Liberation) which is taking part in elections.

[23] *Frontline*, November 10, 2000, 127-131.

had ceased to influence leftist parties since universal acceptance of global trade and economic liberalisation. In West Bengal after stepping down as Chief Minister Jyoti Basu admitted that he and his Government had persistent fear that the Union Government will not permit it to continue for long and this fear prevented the Left Front Government from taking development and administrative work in the State seriously, thereby the impoverished State could not be transformed into a prosperous one like other States. This communist regime of State of West Bengal is regarded to represent a period of regression and of missed opportunities.[24] In reality, communism and multiparty democracy of the Constitution of India, the fundamental rights of people and the judicial sanctity of the basis structure of the Constitution are to be always at cross roads to the disadvantage of communism unless the CPI and CPI(M) remove the word 'Communist' from their titles.

5. THE RIGHTIST POLITICAL PARTIES

3.33. Under the Constitution of India the nature of Indian polity is also defined. The Chapter on Fundamental Rights for the people is followed by the Directive Principles of State Policy which lay down the direction in which the activities of any government will be expected to be channelled. The Constitution of India by itself lays down a middle course. The Congress governments found the Constitution to be hindrance in their leftist or welfare and land reform measures and evolved the technique of amending the Constitution very frequently, making it a highly flexible Constitution like the British Constitution. It also evolved the Ninth Schedule technique under which any enactment placed in it would become immune of Fundamental Right constraints. Thus the leftist movement for a revolution against the rigidity of conservatism was thwarted.

---

[24] Editorial: 'Autumn of the Patriarch': *The Hindustan Times*, New Delhi, dated 29 October 2000; "Another 'historic blunder' of the Left Front": *The Times of India*, Lucknow *ed.*, November 4, 2000, p. 7.

3.34. There have been only two main political approaches in India which can properly be labelled as rightist political parties or movement. These approaches have to be identified in contradistinction with the leftist movement which is anti-tradition, anti-religion, anti-past social institutions including kingship and land aristocracy in their pursuit for the rule of proletariat and extermination of bourgeois class. The authority of the State cannot also be limited by law. The Constitution of India is based on republican form, rule of law and supremacy of the Constitution over the citizens and the political institutions, and therefore a political party of 'right' is supposed to work for protection of democratic rights of the people, established religion and traditions along with Indian heritage of five thousand years now referred to as 'Hindutva' by some rightist parties.

3.34A. Examined in the above perspective, there were in existence in 1940s two political parties Hindu Mahasabha and Ram Rajya Parishad. The former party under Savarkar was partly of a militant nature in its promises for a Hindu Nation on the motherland operating mainly in Central India, while the latter functioning in Hindi language areas of North promised to usher the highly democratic golden era of rule of equality before law for the people for which the Kingdom of Ram (*Ram Rajya*) is a legendary example. These two political parties did not get much support since the British had dubbed ancient Indian culture and religion as one of bigotry, idol worship, rigid caste system which had given rise to depressed classes and one which had no place for Muslims and Christians whom the Hindus regarded as alien invaders. The Constitution of India promised a secular state and so Congress had the votes of non-Hindu population safe for its majority in Parliament and State Legislatures. Both parties had exhausted themselves by the time the Fifth House of People was formed in 1971.

3.24B. In addition to the above two political parties, Jan Sangh was formed in 1951 as a political front of Rashtriya Swayamsevak Sangh (R.S.S.) after ban imposed on it following the assassination of Mahatma Gandhi in 1948 was lifted. Jan Sangh stood for traditional values of India, unity of nation and a Hindu *Rashtra* by which they included extreme reverence and loyalty to Indian culture and nation as their ideal. In the 1967 Fourth House of People they had third place having won 35 seats, after the Congress Party and the Swatantra Party. In 1971 elections the Jan Sangh had only 16 seats. Before 1977 election, Jan Sangh had merged itself with Janata Party to form an alliance against Congress(I). Later after coming back into power in the Union of Congress (I) after 1980 election, the Janata Party started breaking and the Jan Sangh emerged as Bhartiya Janata Party in 1982. Since then it has had a steady progressive character both in ideology and popularity. In the eleventh House of People elected in 1996 it was the single largest party with 163 seats to its credit. It has formed State Governments in Uttar Pradesh, Gujarat, Rajasthan and Madhya Pradesh also. The B.J.P. has its allies in Akali Dal in Punjab, Shiva Sena Party and Samata Party.

3.25. The Supreme Court of India has vindicated the stand of B.J.P. and Shiva Sena Party that 'Hindutva' stands for the essence of being Indian and 'Hinduism' is not a religion but a tolerant secular way of life.[25] The B.J.P. has steadily improved its position in the elections and the United Front which appears to stand for negative politics for its unity, that is, tries to justify itself by denouncing a political party which used to be Congress (I) till 1991, has targeted B.J.P. instead since then. The B.J.P. professes to stand for the spirit of sacrifice by people for their country, the value of *dharma*, the unity of nation and for effective protection of boundaries of the country. All these factors make it a *rightist political party*. Except for Gujarat where 46 out of its 120 members in Legislative Assembly of 180 defected in September 1996 on leadership issue and formed Rashtriya Janata Party and later with Congress(I) support formed the Government, there have not been major defections from the Party.

---

[25] Foot notes 7, 12 & 13, *supra*.

3.26. The other rightist political party, the Swatantra Party, was consciously formed in 1959 after the Congress (I) at the Nagpur session adopted an actively leftist resolution for the future development of the Country. The Swatantra Party under the influence of K.M. Munshi laid heavy stress on *dharma*, private enterprise, non-interference by government in industries, least possible control and governmental regulation of companies, protection of private property, and no ceiling on land holdings, among other rightist programmes. The Swatantra Party did fairly well in elections till 1971, and along with its allies in Orissa, Andhra Pradesh and Rajasthan in the States also. In 1977 it became one of the constituents of Janata Party and after the splits in Janata Party the Swatantra Party did not revive itself but its leaders only remained in Janata Party to keep it alive. Now in 1990s, there is practically no political party which stands for private property as such. However, the new political philosophy adopted by all political parties now is for liberal economics, privatisation of industries and progressive minimisation of public sector except for core industrial sectors. Yet, the rightist politics continues to stand for religious fundamentalism, Hindu, Muslim or Sikh, for getting votes.

6. QUEST FOR PARLIAMENTARY OPPOSITION

3.27. The democracy of parliamentary kind is incomplete unless there are at least two political parties of almost equal strength and popularity which pose the threat of ousting each other at the elections. This depends on a mobile public opinion which shifts from one party to another on the basis of their future programmes and the past achievements or failures when forming and running the government. The recognised Opposition party has membership number next to the ruling party strength in the House and has a politically recognised role of keeping the ruling party on its toes. Its leader holds the privileges of a Cabinet Minister.

3.28. Existence of 'Opposition' to the ruling party in the working of democracy whether of parliamentary or presidential kind, is a normal feature. The U.S.A. has always had two political parties among which the swing of public opinion takes place to give a political stability which the Country possesses. In England the Conservative Party and the Labour Party since 1930 provide the alternative governments. It is generally believed that to get re-elected after completing one term is commendable and to get elected for a third term is a great achievement. It is historic success to continue to be in power for 15 years without a break for any particular party or Prime Minister. In India only Jawahar Lal Nehru remained Prime Minister for 15 plus years and the Indian National Congress had continuously won the first four general elections to the House of People. But this remarkable success was also due to the fact that there was no organised Opposition party which could have provided alternative government.

3.28A. Till 1947 the Indian National Congress was a common platform for the struggle for independence against the British. The British Government had lifted ban from the Communist Party of India but it was friendly to the British and became revolution minded during the period of 1947-51. It had some success in the House of People elections held in 1952 with 16 seats in 1952 and 27 seats in 1957 and 29 seats in 1962 elections. The Socialist revolutionary group led by J.P. Narayan was first to come out of the Congress fold in 1947 and the Socialist Party of India was formed with the object to provide Opposition to Congress by building socialist programmes for India. It earned 12 seats in 1952 and later joined with Kisan Mazdoor Party (K.M.P.) of Acharya Kriplani to form Praja Socialist Party (P.S.P.) for 1957 elections. The K.M.P. formed in 1951 had won 9 seats of the House of People in 1951. But the P.S.P. foundered with 19 seats in 1957 and 12 seats in 1962 elections. After C.P.I. (Marxist) came into existence as separate Party in 1964, the Communist group had 42 seats in 1967 election to the House of People. Also, when Samyukta Socialist Party was formed it had won 23 sets in 1967 election. Thus the *leftist opposition* remained week with a downward trend on the whole in the first three general elections to the House of People but had gained only after the demise of Prime Minister Nehru in 1964. As the results of 1967 election showed the leftist parties were not in a position to raise a voice of opposition to the Congress which had 284 out of 516 seats in the House of People.

3.28B. Jan Sangh, a rightist organisation, established in 1951 by Dr. Shyama Prasad Mookerji before the elections of 1952 functioned as a front organisation of R.S.S. It had a very slow rate of success with 3, 4, 14, 35 and 16 seats in first five elections to the House of People. The Swatantra Party another organisation of the right, formed in 1959 had done better with 18 and 44 seats in the elections of 1962 and 1967, but the position of rightist parties on the whole was dismal though both of them had made their place felt in the Indian polity.

3.28C. The development of Opposition in the House of People with a feeling of mission took place in 1974 with the formation of Bhartiya Lok Dal (B.L.D.). Its main constituents were Swatantra Party, Samyukta Socialist Party, Kasan Mazdoor Party and Utkal Congress. When elections for the House of People were announced in 1977 while the internal emergency Proclamation promulgated under Article 352 of the Constitution in 1975 was in operation, B.L.D. along with Jan Sangh, Congress(O) and Congress for Democracy of Jagjivan Ram combined together to form Janata Party to raise a common platform against Congress(I). In the ensuing sixth election to the House of People this Janata Party had surprising victory with 296 seats against 153 of the Congress (I) and formed the Government.

3.28D. Indira Gandhi became leader of the Opposition in House of People with Morarji Desai as Prime Minister. The opposition excelled the ruling Janata Party because of their experience in running the government. The ruling Janta Party did not understand how public opinion sways from one political party to another and mistakenly took the public sympathy and support for it to be permanent, that is, for all future times. The

Janata Party started breaking in 1979 when Charan Singh left it to form Janata (Secular) Party and with Congress(I) support replaced Morarji Desai as Prime Minister. In the 1980 seventh general election held after the failure of Janata (S) Party to show majority in the House of People Congress(I) again became ruling party with 352 out of 544 seats. The Janta Party led the Opposition but soon became demoralised and disorganised and got into a process of disintegration.

3.28E. In 1982 Jan Sangh faction of Janata Party regrouped itself as Bhartiya Janata Party. In October 1988 on the eve of ninth general election Janata Dal was formed by the splinter groups of Janata Party, namely, Lok Dal (Charan Singh), Janata Morcha (V.P. Singh) alongwith Janata Party (Chandrashekhar) itself, as Opposition. This grouping was enlarged and a coalition before election was formed by Janata Dal, Congress (S), Telgu Desam Party, D.M.K., and Assom Gana Parishad which came to be known as National Peoples Front with V.P. Singh as Convenor.

3.28F. The Ninth House of People (1989) resulted in 'Hung Parliament' with 193 seats for (Congress (I), 141 seats for National Peoples Front and 88 seats for B.J.P. Since this triangular division of membership, the role of Opposition in the House of People has emerged significantly since two of these three have combined to form the government and dreaded the third party all the time which formed the Opposition Party.

3.28G. After the ninth elections, in 1989, Congress(I) emerged as single largest legislative party but did not accept the invitation to form the government. The National Peoples Front led by V.P. Singh with outside support of B.J.P. formed the Government. Congress (I) became chief Opposition Party and its politics led to the division of Janata Dal faction of National Peoples Front and from which Janata Dal (S) emerged. When its leader Chandrashekhar became Prime Minister on November 8, 1990 with outside support of Congress(I), the B.J.P. became chief Opposition Party. The turmoil within the Janata Dal had led to its disintegration in U.P. and Bihar where (U.P.) Samajwadi Party and (Bihar) Rashtriya Janata Dal were eventually formed out of its State units.

3.29. The tenth general election held in May 1991 had again produced a 'Hung Parliament', but Congress(I) with outside support of National Front, formed the government with P.V. Narasimha Rao as the Prime Minister. The B.J.P. became the Opposition Party and for the first time in Indian parliamentary history the democratic system in the House of People appeared to have functioned as desirable. The government remained on the edge with the result that maximum number of corruption scams by ministers and misuse of governmental powers and privileges were exposed to the public scrutiny. This exposure badly hit the public image both of Congress(I) Party and Janata Dal faction of National Front.

3.30. After the eleventh House of People elections held in May 1996, the results did not produce any single party with clear majority but B.J.P. emerged as the single largest party with 193 members including its electoral allies. It was followed by the post election alliance of National Front and Left Democratic Front, named as the United Front as the second and Congress(I) as the third largest party in the House of People. When B.J.P. was invited to form government and confirm majority in the House, both United Front and Congress (I) combined to form a united Opposition to B.J.P. interim Ministry. Latter failed to acquire and prove its majority in the House of People and resigned before division in the House. On June 1, 1996 the United Front with the outside support of Congress(I) formed the government. The B.J.P. became chief Opposition party. Later when Congress (I) withdrew its support from the United Front coalition government on the issue of Jain Commission report the House of People was dissolved for fresh mandate in December 1997. The B.J.P. had performed well the role of opposition party again during the brief tenure of the eleventh Parliament. Now, since the thirteenth Parliament, 2000, the Congress (I) constitutes official opposition with Sonia Gandhi as its leader.

3.31. *Value of Opposition Party in Indian Parliamentary system*: One thing is clear that no party in Indian politics attaches value to the role of Opposition in Parliament. Political parties believe that forming of Ministry is a prestigious matter and it enhances the image of the political party or at least of a Minister with regard to the electorate. The sustainable political ethics is low and only law and legal restraints matter. Actually it is quite different with the people. The ruling party is always looked upon with too much expectations and with severe criticism by the people both at the performance and political morality levels and the recognised Opposition party makes use of this opportunity or public psychology to its advantage.

3.31A. Congress(I) has on its part always used this opportunity for breaking the ruling party by creating dissentious but without gaining a long term advantage for itself. The situation with Indira Gandhi as leader of Opposition in 1977 was interesting and different, due to the misplaced policies of Janata Party Government of Prime Minister Morarji Desai under which instead of utilising the opportunity of forming the government for public good, the Janata Party had indulged in undoing constitutional amendments, changing the legal structure and in witch hunting for the excesses during Internal Emergency of 1975-77 through the Shah Commission. This exercise had a look more of a personal attack on Indira Gandhi, leader of Opposition, by those individuals who had to suffer imprisonment during the internal emergency of 1975-77. People realised soon that the new Government was least interested in its approach towards public good or on any national issue. The people compared the sincerity towards the causes of nation by Indira Gandhi on one hand and the Janata Party on the other. They took into account the dedication, achievements or pursuits of Indira Gandhi on *Garibi Hatao* (removal of poverty) front, the shattering defeat given to Pakistan in 1971-72 war and what Emergency had achieved for the people on positive side, if the miseries caused to imprisoned opposition leaders were ignored. The result was that when Janata Party broke down on leadership issue the people made a negative marking of the administrative and organisational capacities of non-Congress parties and the result was landslide victory for Indira Gandhi in the 1980 elections. It was a personal victory for Indira Gandhi and not so much of a victory for Congress (I).

3.32. To be the leading Opposition party is in no way less important than to be a ruling party. The internal politics of United Front Ministries during 1996-97 and its dependence on Congress (I) for continuing the Ministries had deprived its fourteen constituents from developing into independent or mature political parties. Earlier in 1989, in a similar situation B.J.P. had fared better later when it did not join National Front and its Ministry.

3.32A. It is interesting to note that in 1952 there were fifteen political parties in the House of People, there were 26 political parties which represented the people in House of People in 1996 and 44 political parties in 1999. The natural question, therefore, is how far are we in our goal of having two or three mature political parties representing the people in the Parliament. At one time we lament rightly on not having an organised opposition party to criticise and correct the ruling party but at the same time we have to justify the presence of multiple political parties along with 'independents' in the House of People. It is said that the coalitions and Fronts reduce the number of active units in the House but this brings into existence the malady of defections from one group to another which is looked upon as political immorality, scar on the integrity of members and making a joke of Indian politics.

3.33. The rampant political immorality which undermines the nobility of the Constitution of India was brought about in Indian national politics since the middle of 1990s by two factors in particular. First, no political party had a stable standing before the masses. All politicians want to be successful politicians by being in a Ministry. A politician loyal to the party on whose nomination he got elected had become a rarity. In 1990s a professional politician could not be sure of his future along with any political party particularly when the continued existence of the party or a coalition or front was uncertain. All politicians had to be self-reliant in funds and supporters which is a very costly proposition.

3.33A. Further, a political party for elections to the House of People of Parliament has to organise its position in at least 475 out of 545 constituencies spread all over India and with voluntary service to them by people being almost nil, a huge investment and expenditure for contesting an election is required, which in conservative average estimates runs to be around 30 Crore rupees with 1997 base for an all India political party.

3.33B. It is thus seen for an idealistic working of parliamentary government in India that a political party or the coalition of parties would be all the time be trying to accumulate funds for the next election for each of its constituents. This is apart from the building of personal funds by the active politicians for their own standing with their supporters who will work for them unconcerned with the party which the active politicians may chose to represent. A similar additional burden is on a political party when it has to contest elections for the Legislatures of States as well. Political corruption, therefore, in an idealistic working of parliamentary government is rather to be anticipated.

3.33C. The political immorality set since middle of 1990s by the leaders of the ruling party consists in transferring people's money from national and State projects to the ruling party or to the personal possessions of ministers or giving illegal advantages to the donors including foreign companies for 'commissions' or 'kick-backs' received.[26] When criminals enter into politics they terrorise and force people and businessmen by violence to contribute generously to their election fund also, thereby vitiating the sanctity of the constitutional processes. Unless and until the parties have collected necessary funds these do not agree for

---

[26] The efforts of the Election Commission of India in this direction are discussed in detail in Chapter VII, *infra.*

fresh elections and force the President or the Governors to explore formation of coalitions making the situation move in a sort of vicious circle. So actually the public and the tax payers are financing both the government and the political ambitions of parties or the serious individual contestants for maintaining the democratic constitutional process. It is analysed that for a decade since 1988 no long term projects of national importance, like, power projects for meeting energy shortage in the country, have been undertaken and that all funds are generally being allocated to community development and other such schemes from which siphoning out of money is easily possible by the political parties when in partnership with bureaucracy. Prime Minister Rajiv Gandhi had publicly lamented that hardly 16 per cent of allocated fund were being used properly or were reaching the objective.

3.33D. A national debate on purifying politics sustained by the Constitution by giving a free play to the political parties for running parliamentary system and purifying the bureaucracy of corruption and criminal ends will always remain imperative for survival of democracy. As at present at the beginning of the century, unfortunately, the ruling political party has to be at peace with corruption if it is to succeed in remaining in office. The situation in the U.S.A.[27], England and other democracies on

[27] The cost of electing George W Bush or Gore on Tuesday (November 7, 2000) as the United states President comes to a record of almost a third of a billion dollars — and that is without taking into account millions more in 'soft money' contributions that are unregulated and hard to track.
Mr. Bush has raised $ 187 million for his republican campaign, all but $ 20 million of it spent by a fortnight ago. Mr. Gore raised $133 million for his democratic campaign, and Ralph Nader of Green Party raised 6 million, according to latest official figures.
The Republican national committee has raised another $214 million on top of that and the Democrats $179 million in unregulated soft money which was spent across a range of campaigns for presidential, congressional and local state elections : Michael Ellison and Martin Kettle—"US Election 2000 Spending Shatters All Records": *The Hindustan Times* New Delhi, November 6, 2000, p. 12.

the question of funding of political parties is enormous, equally appalling, sad and lamentable but this fact is no consolation for a developing poor country. The problem with Indian political leaders is that they do not see to the realities or make any introspection but blame the form of government and the Constitution.

7. THE REGIONAL POLITICAL PARTIES

3.34. *The Background*: Apart from the official classification of political parties between National and State parties which is made by the Election Commission on the basis of their performance at the previous election[28], the *popular* classification proceeds on the basis of the objectives of the political party, viz., it is taking up doctrinaire and all India wider outlook or else it

---

"The increasing role of money in the political system (of U.S.) is a growing problem, yes, This election will go down as the most expensive by far": Statement by Douglas Weber of the non-partisan Centre for Responsive Politics, which monitors contributions to candidates in U.S. elections: quoted: *Ibid.*

[28] The Election Commission of India had laid down under Election Symbols (Reservation and Allotment) Order, 1968 till December 2, 2000 a party to be a State Party if it managed to win four percent of the total votes polled in the State or had one out of every twenty five House of People seats from the State or had one M.L.A. for every 30 seats of M.L.As in the State Legislature. The Party became a National Party if the Party repeated this performance in at least four States.

Since amendment of the Order on December 2, 2000, a State Party should poll six per cent of the votes in a State during the general or Assembly polls and should also win at least two seats in the Assembly of the State, or, as an alternarive it should win at least three percent of the total number of assembly seats or a minimum of three seats, whichever is more. The Party became a National Party if it secured at least six percent of polled votes in four or more Ststes during general or Assembly polls, or, it should secure a minimum of two per cent (11/543) of the Lok Sabha seats from not less than three States.

The Election Commission has also laid down that a Party losing National or State Party status would not lose its symbol for six years during which it can retrieve its status.

wants to serve a local, State or linguistic interest only. In the latter case it is generally known as a regional party. A regional party may also have a title which reflects a general trend or political ideology but on account of its limited following or popularity confined to a particular region it might not be having a wider organisational capacity and might become known as a regional party only. Subsequently such a party may qualify as 'National Party' as per assessment chart of the Election Commission.

3.35. India has been the resting place of scores of civilisations and cultures during the last four thousand years or more. Sanskrit and dravidian languages have dominated the dialect development in India. The incoming communities who settled in Indian sub-continent adopted the cultures and languages of the local people but their impact breaded new dialects and cultural innovations in the areas of their settlement. On the mainland the Negroid were supplemented by austric, dravidians and nordic-aryans. In north and eastern hilly areas of India, the Sino-Tebatian and Mongoloid cultures and languages have also had their impact on local surroundings, along with internal indigenous evolutionary changes and development.

3.36. The Eighth Schedule of the Constitution of India recognises fifteen major languages of India out of 1652 listed mother tongues of people in the 1961 and 1971 Census Reports. The religious cults have the character moulding impact and these give rise to a regimented pattern morals laden community life. In the course of last five thousand years India has produced vedic, shivait, brahmanical, Buddhist, Jain or Sikh religions in their original form. The Indian way of thinking and pattern of life has also been enriched by the Zoroastrian, Parsee, Christian and Muslim religions of the Middle East Asia.

3.36A. The Indian political thought of pre-independence years was of cosmopolitan nature and the Constituent Assembly by the Preamble and Article 25 of the Constitution established a 'secular' and 'federal' polity. In such a polity the religion is to be the personal faith of the people in their relationship to God or wish for salvation and *nirvana* while politics for the control and direction of the governmental machinery is to be kept fully segregated from religious faith of the people. Democracy under Constitution of India is population-wise and constituency-wise and not religion based as it was during British regime.

3.37. Why and Where-from the Linguistic Regionalism? During the era of freedom struggle, the British rulers had countered the upsurge of Indian nationalism by what is known as a divide and rule politics. This British policy and politics did not function on individual level but through the efforts directed towards isolating the freedom struggle movement of Indian National Congress. To a great extent this divide and rule policy had been a success. The Christians and Anglo-Indian were taken care of by the Churches and by the political patronage and so these communities were loyal to the British. The Muslims remained divided but they were in general alienated from the main nationalist movement by British promise of fulfilment of parallel political ambition for them based on the two nation theory and on the hatred for Hindu way of life.

3.37A. The British took all necessary initiative to give equal footing to the Muslim League with regard to Congress and by insisting on a mutually agreed solution of every issue at a Conference table which was just not possible under the British policy of divide and rule. Sikhs were also prompted and motivated for similar separate religious identity and for a separate Khalistan. Sikhs were subsequently deserted by the British since Sikh masses could not understand this separatism. The reason was that Sikh community had similar culture and religious rituals as of Hindu population though they had a separate holy book like Muslims and Christians and unlike them they had not migrated into India from outside. The British also gave to the depressed classes among Hindu population a separate identity by magnifying caste and 'untouchable-bigotry' of Hindu Brahmins which the latter applied equally to Muslims and Christians.

3.37B. In the communal franchise system evolved in the first decade of twentieth century, however, the British gave due place to all the four and thereby made vertical splits in the Indian society. The leaders of these communal organisations which developed accordingly, were thus set against any united Indian approach against the British. The fight against this separatist politics which was being constitutionally implemented by the British, particularly by the Indian Councils Act 1909 and the Government of India Act of 1919, was taken up by Mahatma Gandhi in 1919, and the Congress thereafter tended to be an elitist secular movement for freedom of the country to which elite of all communities had responded.

3.38. The Indian National Congress had countered the vertical communal division of the Indian population by a nationalism which was based on the linguistic and cultural identity of people by taking advantage of the fact that all of the Indian languages were either of Sanskrit or of Dravidian origin and both were foundations of Indian identity. Culturally the South India was more orthodox Hindu under Krishna and Shivait cults while North India had mixed Vaishnav and Shivait cults. In Eastern India, the Bengali language had been the base of Indian militant nationalism against the British since the middle of Nineteenth Century which Congress appropriated for nationalist politics. In Central India the language of Marathas, was Maharashtrian. The Marathas had taken part in the first war of independence of 1857 and it was the language of Veer Savarkar, a popular patriot and the revolutionary leader of Hindu Mahasabha of early Twentieth Century.

3.39. The emphasis of Indian National Congress was that through the languages other than English, people should feel a national identity and that the alien British and their English language were set only to oppress the Indian people. The Indian National Congress in its 1920 Nagpur Session recognised and demanded the linguistic principle for *pradeshic (regional)* demarcations ignoring the provincial units of British India which it regarded as made for administrative convenience following the conquests of Indian territories during last two centuries. This linguistic principle side-tracked the communal and religious division of the country as well. The British realising the dangers of the revolutionary spirit of Indian people had tacitly recognised the virtue of linguistic principle for their purpose also when in 1936 they created two new provinces, Orissa and Sindh, based on linguistic identity of people of the region.

3.40. Between the pre-Constitution era of 1947-50 of Independent India, the Government was more concerned with the success in the amalgamation of about 700 princely (Native) States. The Constituent Assembly kept in abeyance the linguistic principle on the advice of the (Justice) Dar Commission Report and accommodated the princely States as Part B and Part C States of India in the new Constitution. However, in early 1950s the Indian politicians fanned by propaganda from alien lands also, raised the need for implementing linguistic principle. In 1952 the demand for Telgu speaking Andhra Pradesh was forcefully made followed by demands for Marathi speaking Maharashtra to be free from Gujarati dominance in Bombay, for Punjabi Suba, Malayalee and Kannada States or for Assam State free from Bengali and Bihari languages.

3.41. The Union Government established in 1954 the States Reorganisation Commission composed of Fazl Ali, K.M. Panikkar and H.N. Kunzru as its members. The Commission met all sections of people all over India for two years including the linguistic minorities and accepted the linguistic demarcation for States as far as practicable. The Seventh Constitution Amendment in 1957 implemented the Report. Subsequently, Bombay was in 1960 split into Maharashtra and Gujarat, and Punjab was in 1967 divided into Punjab and Haryana for further reconciling of the Indian Federation with the linguistic base for units. The State of Nagaland and the North East Hill Area Council were also created in the same process.

3.42. *The Emerged Linguistic Pattern*: The linguistic base for the units of federal India was a redemption of promises made by the Indian National Congress leaders from time to time since 1920. The demand for this redemption was made by members of various existing political parties on individual thinking basis. The regional parties emerge on the basis of fulfilment of attitudes distinct from homogeneous whole for the Country but are not accompanied by any separatist tendencies. Normally, a State of the federation is autonomous within List II matters of the Seventh Schedule to the Constitution of India and it is expected that the government of the State will represent the special demands or needs of the particular State in the various inter-State bodies including the Finance Commission. The Members of Parliament from the States also participate in the proceedings of the Parliament and here represent the view points and the interests of the State.

3.42A. The reason for the growth and survival of the regional parties is elsewhere, that is there are some parties which want to or have the capacity and resources to operate only for the State Assemblies and so these take up the causes in which people of that region are interested; which in some cases may comprise one or more nearby States. Also, whenever there is stagnation in a National Party due to the persons controlling it not making way for new generation of politicians to rise, or they get the fear of being sacked or replaced by another set at the time of election, the breakaway form a State level party to begin with. This has generally happened to the Indian National Congress and also to Janata Dal. On leadership issue in Gujarat, the B.J.P. also had such a split in 1996.

3.42B. Such parties are now forming Governments, as in Kerala, Tamil Nadu, Orissa, Kashmir, Punjab or Assam and are able to control the membership of House of People also from their area. The regional parties Assom Gana Party, Akali Dal, D.M.K. and T.M.C., National Conference, Kerala Congress, Ganatantra Parishad (Orissa), A.P.H.L.C. (Assam), Jharkhand Mukti Morcha, Shiva Sena (Maharashtra), Telgu Desam Party

(Andhra Pradesh), Karnatak Congress Party or Forward Bloc (West Bengal) have made impact not only in their respective States but also in the Parliament. When there is coalition government at the Centre, the MPs of regional parties get into the Union Council of Ministers also.

3.42C. Now since late 1990s the regional parties are not strictly tied to linguistic ideals which were satisfied in 1956 or afterwards, but generally use the State politics as a platform for representation in Parliament, from where they believe the interests of their region can be better safeguarded or realised. It will be observed that the Election Commission does not recognise the term 'regional party' but the term nevertheless is popular with Indian journalists and media.

3.43. One notable result of the multiplicity of the State or 'regional' parties is that the evolution of 'National Parties' has been hampered since such parties require huge financial investment and expenditure. For the twelfth House of People election in 1998 only B.J.P. and the crippled Congress (I) and Janata Dal as 'National Parties' were in sight. The 'Hung Parliament' phenomenon has become a normal feature for the Union from 1989 onwards which the State Parties seem to enjoy and relish. It is possible that out of the impasse created by the malady of hung parliaments a mature system of two or three parties only at the Centre would emerge sooner or later.

3.43A. However, the twelfth general election of March 1998 for Lok Sabha produced a mixed result. It was interpreted as a verdict of people against United Front which stood for multitude of smaller regional parties as reality of future Indian politics. The United Front was a pre-election coalition and depended on leading another coalition of regional parties for forming the government after the elections. After the elections both BJP and the Congress Party which had approached the electorate for single party majority, improved their position emerging as the first and second largest parties but without clear majority. When the BJP formed the coalition government in March 1998 with inside support of nineteen parties and outside support of three parties, the regional parties particularly those which were constituents of United Front felt demoralised and this United Front has gone into a swing for disintegration. The general electorate and public opinion appeared to have realised that voting for small parties or independents for the Union Parliament does not bring political certainty and stability for the country. With more than forty parties represented in the twelfth Parliament, the parliamentary government in absence of one political party having a clear majority House of People, seems to be unworkable. Since 1989 the parliamentary democracy is operating in India on the 'default' settings of a computer, an intricate system of commands that the Constitution has provided for democratic political organisation of the country now operated mainly by the executive and in marginal situations by the judiciary or by the Ministers.

3.43B. The thirteenth general election of 1999 increased the number of small parties in the House of People (Lok Sabha) but the pre-election National Democratic Alliance under leadership of B.J.P. had an edge and produced a stable parliamentary system subject to avoidance of splits within the Alliance.

4

Law for Party Splits and Defections

4.01. The Constitution of India was framed by the Constituent Assembly (1947-49) as a complete document which laid down the fundamental liberties of the people, the organisation of governments and the political or economic ideals to be achieved by the future governments. The government was to be a representative democracy which was in fact to be dependent on the wishes of the people and had to justify itself before the people every five years at the time of general elections.

When we look into retrospect it is seen that the problems which the country faced during the first twenty years of freedom brought forth several imbalances in the working of the Constitution. One of them was that instead of a balanced multiparty democracy there was practically one political party, that is, the Congress Party (Indian National Congress) rule which was practically a government dictated by Prime Minister Nehru. The peculiarity of the situation was that Indian politics was Congress politics and Nehru was Congress.[1] There were no opposition parties capable of providing an alternative to Congress Party in Parliament and the State Legislatures. One can say that the democracy was operating in a jumbled up two tier manner, that is, democracy within Congress Party and the democracy in Parliament. Parliamentary democracy at the time

[1] The role of Indian National Congress in Indian polity, etc., discussed in detail in Chapter III, *Supra*.

of Independence in essence meant freedom to hold views contrary to the Congress Party ideology. The leaders of all political parties somehow believed that within the framework of the Constitution their status will only increase and will not decrease with passage of time, that the politics was to be the essence of Indian life.

4.01A. The situation envisaged by the framers of the Constitution and by the active politicians who as Ministers operate the government machinery took a plunge in other direction when the charm of ministerial status prompted professional politicians to shift their party loyalties for personal stability by the middle of 1970s in alarming proportions. Crisis was created for ruling as well as opposition parties by constant party splits and defections. In 1985, the Tenth Schedule added to the Constitution by amendment, laid down elaborate law for regulating the party splits and defections of elected representatives in Parliament and State Legislatures. This obviously makes an impact of freedom to hold and change to diverse and different political views as individuals who are also active politicians.

1. THE PARTY SPLIT ASSESSMENT

4.02. During the political monopoly of Indian National Congress in the first twenty years of freedom, the main question was whether a political minded person believed along with Congress ideology or not. If not, he had the option of leaving Congress and forming a new party or of retirement from politics. There was no question of defection, it was rather split from Congress. The Socialist Party, the Krishak Mazdoor Party, the Praja Socialist Party or the Swatantra Party in 1950s represented establishment of political parties by politicians who were members of Congress but had dissented from the Congress political thrust from time to time. The Congress itself was a platform from which patriots had made sacrifices for achieving the ideals of freedom.. One hangover of this from these first twenty years of freedom was that those who did not follow

Congress Party ideals were declared by the Congress Party leadership as not being true patriots, if not branded as outright traitors.

4.03. The Constituent Assembly which had become first Federal Legislature by British Indian Independence Act 1947 and later continued as such under the Constitution of India till first general elections were held in 1952, was dominated by Congress Party and Prime Minister Nehru. During this period the socialist group of J.P. Narayan or the rightist politicians, like, Shyama Prasad Mukerjee, had resigned from the pre-Constitution Nehru Cabinet[2] which had existed from 1946, on the principle that they had political ideology different from Congress to pursue. In March 1948, Acharya Narendra Dev along with 13 other members of Congress Socialist Party resigned both from Indian National Congress (INC) and the U.P. Legislative Assembly since after Independence the INC did not represent their political ideology. Shyama Prosad Mukerjee believed that partition of country was wrong, he left the Nehru Cabinet and formed a new political party Jan Sangh along with the supporters from Rashtriya Swayam Sevak Sangh (RSS), the non-political Hindu organisation, for bringing renaissance in India based on Hindu culture.

4.04. When at Nagpur session of Indian National Congress of 1959, it was decided to pursue a vigorous nationalisation and development of public sector programme which was politically possible to do with absolute Congress majority in Parliament and State Legislatures, a big section of Congressmen left the organisation and formed the Swatantra Party, a rightist organisation, with the objectives of protection of private property and of free private enterprise with least government interference.[3]

---

[2] Before Independence the Cabinet was advisory Council of Governor-General, its party-wise composition under Cabinet Mission Plan was prescribed by the British Government and it functioned as a sort of coalition Council.

[3] Discussed in the Chapter III, vide, 'Political Parties by Fragmentation of Congress', etc.

Politics in early tears of Independence, for those who left Congress and formed new parties, was a means for fulfilment of patriotic instincts for the development of Independent India through political philosophy different from that of Congress or Prime Minister Nehru. The loyalty of the politicians of 1950s was not to particular leader or to a political party but to a cause based on freedom of conscience and a different perception of good or bad for the Country. The departure of some politicians from Congress Party to form a new party was justified as recognition of the right of dissent in politics under the Constitution of India. More than often, the dissent from Congress Party ideals also meant political suicide by leaders.

2. THE RATIONALE OF DEFECTION

4.05. The word 'defection' etymologically includes two ideas, first, the idea of breach or shifting of loyalty and allegiance from one base to another, and secondly, the idea of fraud, breach of faith or cheating involving fiduciary relationship towards the base. In ultimate political relationship the crime of sedition is committed when a person shows or commits breach of loyalty to the State of which he is a citizen. The most severe punishment is meted out to such a person which extends to death penalty. The *Case of Danby* was earlier discussed[4] in which the House of Commons of England in 1679 impeached the Prime Minister Danby for secretly negotiating a treaty with France at the time when the Parliament wanted a war with France. However, the problem before the Indian polity and the Constitution is how to deal with the 'defection' when a person elected by the people leaves his political party and joins another. The question asked is as to against whom the breach of faith has been committed, will it be against the electorate who elected him to Parliament or the political party which sponsored him or against both or none of these.

4.06. On this matter, the practice of Britain or other polities

[4] Chapter II, f. n. 15., *supra.*

of the West has been to regard that the personal liberty and the freedom of expression of the elected person are to prevail. The right to election is the political liberty of the elected person while to vote for proper person is the right and duty of the people who are first to make the choice of their candidate in a responsible manner and thereafter vote. Perhaps, the political parties are convenient collection of individual politicians who have similar approach to the political issues, problems and their solutions related to a place or time. The betrayal of the trust reposed by the people in their elected representative is a common concern and fear in all democracies. The framers of the U.S. Constitution in 1780s took precaution against this by insisting on separation of powers and by written guarantee of fundamental liberties of the people against the elected legislature as well against the executive.

4.07. At the same time in eighteenth century England, King George III had excelled in having a cabinet of his choice subservient to him by distribution of riches earned from the colonial possessions. His cabinet endorsed his decisions and enacted laws as suited him for exploiting the territories of the Empire. The political philosopher Burke worked hard as Whig Party leader and later as Prime Minister to teach the people about their duties in electing right persons to Parliament who would act as true 'representatives of the people' and not as 'King's friends'. The loss of American Colonies (1776-83) enlightened the people of Britain of the risk involved in making a mistake when electing their representatives to the House of Commons of British Parliament. The representatives, according to Edmund Burke, owed allegiance to the people who elected them and whose wishes and aspirations they were to achieve through Parliament. Burke in his speech to the Electors of Bristol in 1774 exhorted the people particularly those who stood for election that[5]

---

[5] Cited, See J. Griffith and Michael Ryle, *Parliament: Functions, Practice and Procedure,* (1989) at p. 70.

"it ought to be the happiness and glory of a representative to live in strictest union, the closest correspondence, and the most unreserved communication with his constituents. Their wishes ought to have great weight with him; their opinion, high respect; their business, unremitted attention. It is his duty to sacrifice his repose, his pleasures, his satisfaction to theirs—and above all, ever, and in all cases to prefer their interest to his own But, his unbiased opinion, his mature judgment, his enlightened conscience, he ought not to sacrifice to you, to any man, or to any set of men living." At the same time, "your representative owes you, not his industry only, but his judgment; and he betrays, instead of serving you, if he sacrifices it to your opinion."

4.08. Under the concept of popular sovereignty of the rationalism of eighteenth century as propounded by Rousseau, Adkin, Tom Paine and other contemporary political thinkers who also led France to get rid of monarchy through the French Revolution of 1789, the people and 'national interest' were paramount and meant the same thing. In England since the end of eighteenth century, the elected members of the House of Commons have to be true to the national interest and the country. The change of political parties by promising politicians has been a normal feature in England though not noticeable in the later half of twentieth century. It can be remarked that in England no legal or moral injury is caused to a party or the voters when the elected member exercising his own rights changes his party. Famous British Prime Minister Gladstone had after election on Conservative Party ticket become 'Liberal' in 1846 along with his supporters. Joseph Chamberlain a follower of Gladstone had together with 93 MPs changed over to Conservative Party after the Liberal Party split in 1886 and later became Prime Minister. Winston Churchill left Conservative Party in 1904 to become a Liberal and again rejoined it in 1925 and became Prime Minister in 1939 heading a 'national government' during the Second World War, which was without parliamentary Opposition. Likewise, in India, Morarji Desai,

Charan Singh, V.P. Singh, Chandrashekhar, HD Gowda and I.K. Gujral who became Prime Ministers had been defectors from Indian National Congress or Congress (I). Possibly defection leads to eclipse or shooting up in political career to the erstwhile sidelined or back-bencher of a political party.

4.09. Sceptical approach to politics and promises made by politicians of England during 1770s which led to the War of Independence in thirteen British colonies in America, marked the attitude of the framers of U.S. Constitution also from the very beginning. Emphasising on the great sacrifices and efforts made by the ancestors of American people both for freedom of the colonies from oppressive British rule and in meticulously laying down the constitutional principles and institutions on one hand and the fears to the constitutional fabric from the elected representatives on the other, the American commentator Story has observed that the (U.S.) constitutional:

> "structure has been created by architects of consummate skill and fidelity; its foundations are solid; its compartments are beautiful, as well as useful; its arrangements are full of wisdom and order; and its defences are impregnable from without. It has been reared for immortality, if the work of man may justly aspire to such a title. *It may, nevertheless, perish in an hour by the folly, or corruption, or negligence of its only keepers, the people.* The Republics are created—these are words which I commend to you for your consideration—by the virtue, public spirit and intelligence of the citizens. They fall when the wise are banished from the public councils because they dare to be honest, *and the profligate are rewarded, because they flatter the people, in order to betray them*"[6] (Italics are added).

---

[6] Story: *Commentaries on the Constitution of United States.* (Quotation from books); Corruption among Indian politicians has been aptly emphasised by Seervai, H.M., *Constitutional Law of India*, Vol. II, 3 ed. at p. 2723.

4.10. The truism expressed above in the context of the U.S. Constitution about the danger from the elected representatives who can in no time demolish the entire constitutional structure, created and endowed with all the excellence and sacrifices made by the ancestors, is very much applicable to India and is fully pertinent now after the 50 years of freedom. The Constituent Assembly (1946-49) had been fully conscious of the dangers ahead from irresponsible or selfish voters or elected members of Parliament devoid of altruism and constitutional morality. For the success of the Constitution, B.R. Ambedkar, Chairman of the Constitution Drafting Committee, had wisely cautioned and observed:

> "...While everybody recognised the necessity of diffusion of *constitutional morality* for the peaceful working of a democratic Constitution, there are two things interconnected with it. One is that the form of administration has a close connection with the form of Constitution. The form of administration must be appropriate to and in the same sense as the form of the Constitution. The other is that it is perfectly possible to pervert the Constitution, without changing the form of administration and to make it inconsistent and opposed to the spirit of the Constitution. It follows that it is only where the people are saturated with constitutional morality such as the one described by Grote, the historian, that one can take the risk of omitting from the Constitution the details of the administration and leaving it for the legislature to prescribe them. The question is, can we presume the diffusion of constitutional morality? Constitutional morality is not a natural sentiment. It has to be cultivated. We must realise that our people have yet to learn it."[7]

4.11. The morality ends where the law begins. The conventions, traditions and morals are the forerunners of law.

[7] *Constituent Assembly Debates*, Vol. VII, pp. 37-38.

Since the Constitution of a country is the *grundnorm* which exists and survives in the grey areas of politics and law, much of the *grundnorm* has to be constitutional morality as in Britain or it should be highly flexible where the Constitution is written. Rigid Constitutions have always needed revolutions for changing or making adjustments according to the demands of the time. It can be now said with the 55 years of Indian freedom in retrospect, on the basis of last few lines of the statement of B.R. Ambedkar noted above, that the Constituent Assembly had taken a balanced view of Indian political scene where the democratic rule for the country was envisaged. The corrective to some extent for lack of political education for representative democracy was provided by laying down written provisions in the Constitution of India for representative government in place of leaving political norms on the 'conventions'. The 'conventions' had evolutionary growth in Britain but the development of these the Indian public and polity had not experienced. Obviously, the Indian population and electorate have never been educated by books or by experience in their rights, duties towards Constitution and obligations by way of making proper choice of representatives to Parliament or State Legislature at the time of elections. They should have better knowledge in this sphere as well as in the matter of constitutional morality for the political parties and the leaders which is beyond the written text of the Constitution.

4.12. After the Tenth House of People was dissolved in 1996, fusion of constitutional morality with the election process was attempted through a Model Code of Conduct for political parties by the Election Commission of India. This attempt has been quite successful and has been appreciated by people and commentators. In the general elections held in March 1998 and subsequently, apart from the Model Code of Conduct for political parties during the elections, the multimedia, *viz.*, the newspapers, private TV Channels, voluntarily and at the behest of Election Commission or non-government organisations, made sincere attempts to educate people also about their political rights and duty to be discrete in choice of their candidates for whom they caste their votes, and openly exhorted them not to vote for candidates having criminal records irrespective of their party affiliations. This has had positive results.

4.13. Looking at the way the relationship between the elected Members of Parliament or State Legislatures and the political parties has progressed since 1970 leading to almost a chaos and panic among the political parties due to defections since 1977, it seems natural that for permitting bona fide defections and preventing harmful defections an analysis of the relationship between elected members with political parties and with public or electorate be made. The 'split in political party' based on dissent from policies and performance of party is within constitutional morality but 'defection' involving breach of faith, corruption and infidelity is political immorality which is generally detested.[8] The Supreme Court in Kihoto Hollohan *versus* Zachillu in 1992 tended to regard that in case of defection the presumption will be that 'lure of office or money' has prevailed while in "floor crossing" involved in split the presumption will be that this happened 'on the basis of honest dissent.'[9]

4.13A. It may be mentioned that in the famous JMM Bribery Case, in which several Ministers including Prime Minister PV Narasimha Rao got implicated, it was alleged that some MPs of opposition were successfully bribed for voting in favour of the government during the vote on no-confidence motion, the Supreme Court laid down[10] the rule that in view of the special constitutional position of parliamentary proceedings, the

---

[8] Seervai, H.M. *Constitutional Law of India*, Vol. II. 3 ed., 2723.

[9] 1992 Supp (2) SCC 651 at 687

[10] *P.V.Narasimha Rao v. State*, (1998) 4 SCC 626: *The Hindustan Times, New Delhi*, dated 19-4-1998. The dictum of Blackstone from *Commentaries*, I, 91 *et seq*, was quoted with approval—"The whole of the Law and Custom of Parliament has its origin from this one maxim, 'that whatever matter arises concerning either House of Parliament ought to be examined, discussed and adjudged in that House to which it relates, and not elsewhere.'"

receiving of money for voting against a no-confidence motion which (voting) takes place in the House of People cannot be examined and taken cognisance of by the Courts leading to prosecution under the Prevention of Corruption Act since it is the privilege of the House to punish or admonish the members of the House for misbehaviour; but, for the same act, the act of giving of bribe to an MP outside the House of People will be an offence fit for prosecution of the *giver* of the bribe under the Act. However, this rule will not apply to a Member who abstained from voting and he can be prosecuted for taking bribe.

4.14. The Tenth Schedule on anti-defection inserted into the Constitution of India by Fifty-second Amendment of 1985 was a hasty measure taken in a kind of panic. The experience of all parties at the outset of 1998 after dissolution of eleventh House of People has been to say that the Tenth Schedule needs thorough rethinking.

4.14A. The basic question to be answered is as to whom the elected person owes obligation: (a) to the party, (b) to the electorate or (c) to the Constitution.

4.15. *Elected Member and Political Party*: By political theory and past experience of three hundred years of the working of parliamentary democracy of England, it is now believed that the system works best with two or three political parties which are nationally organised. It is a political dream for Indian democracy that we have two or three well organised political parties instead of around 25 political parties which represented the people of India in the eleventh (1996) and about 40 political parties in the twelfth (1998) Lok Sabha (House of People). In addition, there have always been independents supplemented by unattached Members in Lok Sabha. There are regional parties representing local interests in the House of People which have contested the seats from their regions or States. Further there are now a number of splinter groups of 'national parties' functioning from States but which aspire to become 'national parties' in course of time, like, Rashtriya Janata Dal (RJD) of Bihar, Lok Shakti of

Karnatak, Rashtriya Janata Party (RJP) of Gujarat, Samata Party of Bihar or CPI (M) led Left Front of West Bengal.

4.15A. *Parties and Coalition of Parties:* Political parties are no doubt essential for stability in politics and smooth operation of representative democracy in Parliament but these are medium for achievement of certain ideals and are not ends in themselves. One party majority government is normal feature of democracy but a coalition of several parties forming government has to be tolerated. Coalition government is the second best since the survival or maintenance of coalition gets the first priority or attention of the leaders in place of looking after the administration of the country. Moreover, a coalition government functions on a common minimum programme or agenda of many coalition partners instead of the election manifesto in case of single party government. The promises made by the political parties to the people through their election manifestos become irrelevant and the desire to rule becomes more apparent.

4.15B. The enigma is that under a coalition government the executive becomes more dominating. Even the President, normally a titular head, can dare to be active by returning for reconsideration by the Council of Ministers a recommendation for imposition of President's Rule in a State under Article 356 of the Constitution or else by asking the Prime Minister to seek a vote of confidence as it happened in April 1999 at a time when the majority could have been tested in the House of People during the ongoing budget session in the normal course. The latter kind of Presidential activism led to unnecessary or controversial fall of coalition ministry of Prime Minister Vajpayee. The President may prefer dismissal of a Ministry in pursuance of his action rather than by its defeat on rejection of a Bill in the House. Also, the legislative activity by a coalition government is reduced and the political ideology of the leading partner of the coalition gets eclipsed by consensus formulations among the political parties forming the coalition. The Ministers either attend to routine work or leave the problems of administration on the secretaries and postpone policy decisions which may alienate public sympathy. On the other hand, a single party having more than two-third majority in the Lok Sabha and in the majority of States tends to be dictatorial since it has a tendency to amend the Constitution and the laws rather than to function according to the constitutionally established norms, as was the case with Indian National Congress and the Congress (I)[11] which amended the Constitution forty two times between 1950-1976, that is, 26 years.

4.15C. *Single Party Government and Party Members*: Comparatively, the single party having comfortable majority in the House is usually indifferent to the voice of its members since the lower cadres of the party seek patronage of the leaders and often there is a waiting list of aspirants, both from inside and outside the party, for the party tickets for the next election. Such a party may be dominated by a caste, a group or few dominating personalities. The Indian National Congress during 1954-1962 was dominated by Prime Minister Jawahar Lal Nehru and his close advisors, during 1971-1977 by Prime Minister Indira Gandhi and her son Sanjay Gandhi and from 1985-1990 by Rajiv Gandhi who was Prime Minister during eighth Parliament from 1985-1988. A political leader of Congress during these periods had the right of dissent only in the form of leaving the Congress Party. It was a split when several politicians after leaving Congress formed a new party in anticipation of next election. It was called defection if leaving the party jeopardised the stability of the ruling party or meant fall of the Ministry. As when Charan Singh left Congress Ministry along with 17 M.L.A. in the State of U.P. in 1967 and formed a new party and became Chief Minister of coalition called S.V.D. (Samyukta Vidhayak Dal) Government; similarly, Govind Narain Singh in Madhya

---

[11] Congress (I) formed in 1969 separately from Congress (O) was in July 1981 recognised as legal successor to Indian National Congress by the Election Commission, in a dispute regarding allotment of the election symbols; it was also recognised as a 'national party', whereas Congress (U) successor of Congress(O) was derecognised.

Pradesh defected from Congress Ministry and became S.V.D. Chief Minister of the State, or again when Charan Singh as one of the Cabinet Minister in Janata Party Ministry of Prime Minister Morarji Desai broke the Ministry in 1979 by forming a new Janata (s) Party and became Prime Minister under the rider or condition placed by the President of proving his majority in Lok Sabha within fourteen days which he could not prove, since the earlier promised support of Congress, did not come after he assumed Prime Ministership with the rider.

3. THE RIGHTS OF DISSENT, DEFECTIONS AND SPLITS

4.16. *The Individuals' Rights of Dissent and Defection*: Normally after defection a politician either withdraws from politics altogether or after joining another party or forming a new party becomes a Minister, Chief Minister or Prime Minister. Several times mass defections have led to a collapse of a Cabinet when as a consequence the ruling party looses its majority, else the defections help another party in forming the Cabinet by the tilt of majority in House of People or State Legislative Assembly. Because of these accompanying consequences the defection becomes a situation of breach of faith or a case of political infidelity which causes embarrassment to the political party suffering the defection. Otherwise, it is explained away as a case of split when the splinter group forms another party.

4.16A. The suffering political party also has to take care that the electorate and the supporters of the party in the affected constituencies do not continue their support to the defectors and for this the term 'defection' carries a moral stigma which the voters or the common people are made to understand. The arguments that the defection is due to opportunism or is due to greed of office, money and the like, help the party and its next candidate in retaining the votes in the constituency for their next candidate as against the defector. Conversely, in this process split in the party is on reasons of principles or that there is dictatorship or incompetent leadership in the party or the that the performance of the party is disappointing, or corruption and nepotism have overtaken the party, are helpful to the outgoing individual politicians in retaining the sympathy of the voters of the constituency on which both the faithful and the defector of the Party would depend in future.

4.16B. There is a third side to the situation of defection also. Is a member of a party in a permanent bondage irrespective of the fact that the party has failed to work out its election manifesto or promises, it has failed in the perception of the expectations of the masses or it is functioning to fulfil the personal ambitions of few leaders at the top of the ladder or that corruption has overtaken the party? If the votes depend on mobile public opinion which as Dicey has significantly emphasised,[12] the people or the voters silently make an assessment both of the party in power and the party in opposition and if the voters can legitimately switch over their preference and patronage from one party to another, the question is why cannot a politician think otherwise and leave the party which gave him ticket for election. Splits 'do happen' and 'unless the leaders are to become dictators within their respective parties they *ought to happen* from time to time', observes Ivor Jennings and adds that the people 'do change their minds between the dissolution of Parliament and the ensuing general election'.[13]

4.17. A prohibition of split or defection will signify that the members of a party do not have a right of dissent which will be contrary to the personal freedoms and personal liberty of the people both as voter and as an elected member on the ticket of a political party. At the same time, the principle of collective responsibility of the Council of Ministers requires that all the Ministers should think alike, whether they have been privy to a decision or policy or not. A disagreement within the Council of Ministers which is made public requires that either the Council

---

12 Dicey, *Law and Public Opinion in England.*

13 W. Ivor Jennings, *The British Constitution,* Cambridge University Press ed. V., p. 67.

as a whole or the dissenting Minister should change the position. The Deputy Prime Minister Devi Lal made 'wild' charges against Cabinet colleagues in an interview with a weekly magazine in August 1990 and as a consequence he himself had to leave from the Union Cabinet of the minority government of Prime Minister V.P. Singh.

4.18. The right of dissent in the decisions of a political party is theoretically a desirable thing otherwise the party beaks or it loses public sympathy which have far reaching consequences.

(i) In 1983, the Congress Party under Prime Minister Indira Gandhi had expelled Maneka Gandhi[14] for speeches made in public about the way Congress Party and the Government were acting. Even though the expulsion could be justified on grounds of maintaining party discipline, the public did not appreciate the expulsion since it reminded them of the dreaded dictatorial Congress Party rule during 'internal emergency' of 1975-77. Subsequently, Maneka Gandhi became a Minister in National Front Cabinet in 1989.

(ii) In July 1987, the Congress President and Prime Minister Rajiv Gandhi expelled from Congress Party—V.C. Shukla, Arif Mohammed Khan and Arun Nehru. In the ensuing intra-party squabble V.P. Singh and Arun Singh also resigned from the Cabinet and were promptly expelled from Congress Party. This set into motion the process of dissipation of Congress Party and in the ninth Lok Sabha election of 1989 held prematurely the Congress Party lost it popularity with the masses and had only 193 seats as against 401 seats in 1984 election. Since then it has not been returned as a single majority party in the House of People.

---

[14] Maneka Gandhi regarded herself as next in line to Indira Gandhi as against Rajiv Gandhi whom Indira Gandhi had inducted in the party as her helper after the death of younger son Sanjay Gandhi, Maneka Gandhi's husband. Sanjay Gandhi had been political adviser and pillar of strength to Indira Gandhi during 1974-79 and afterwards till his death.

(iii) Following the party practice of not allowing intra-party dissent, in 1995 the ruling Congress Party expelled Minister Arjun Singh from the Party on the grounds of holding diverse opinions on various matters and so ouster from the Cabinet of the Congress Party minority government of Prime Minister P.V. Narasimha Rao also naturally followed. While the first part was in public assailed as undue curtailment of the right to dissent within the Congress Party, the automatic expulsion from the Cabinet was a constitutional matter.

(iv) When soon afterwards, P.R. Kumaramangalam, a Congress Party MP, in June 1995 tabled a cut motion against the Government appropriation bill in the House of People, it was not put to vote by the Speaker on technical grounds but no disciplinary action from the side of Party against the defiant Congress Party MP followed since the Council of Ministers of the minority government was numerically in a very precarious condition in the House of People and the Congress Party could not have afforded any further split in order to survive.

(v) After the dissolution of the House of People of the twelfth Parliament, in May 1999, three senior Congress Party MPs, *viz*, Sharad Pawar, P.A. Sangma and Tariq Anwar suggested, in a letter to be discussed by the Congress working Committee, that a proposal for constitutional amendment be adopted as part of Congress Party policy and Election manifesto that only natural born Indians should hold the constitutional offices of President, Vice-President and Prime Minister of India. This would have disabled the Congress Party President Ms. Sonia Gandhi, a naturalised Indian, from becoming Prime Minister. At this juncture of time the nation was keenly debating whether A.B. Vajpayee (BJP) or Sonia Gandhi (Congress Party) should be next Prime Minister after the thirteenth election to be held in September 1999. Instead of discussing the issue, the Congress Working Committee summarily expelled all the three from the party for indiscipline for six years. The three expelled leaders formed a new political party, Nationalist Congress Party. This intra-party conflict between right to dissent and discipline was noticed by people.

4.19. The Constituent Assembly had wisely followed the British tradition under which political liberty[15] means the right to change one's perception of the worth of any politician or political party which offers itself for public cause, and therefore, to the public criticism and scrutiny. Prime Minister Indira Gandhi was expelled from Indian National Congress in 1969 while in Office. She formed another Congress (I) Party and continued as Prime Minister on the support of Congress Legislative Party in the House of People (Lok Sabha) which collectively defied the Congress Party stand but continued to have majority. In the mid-term election held in 1971 for Fifth Lok Sabha, her Congress (I) secured 355 seats out of 540 while the parent Congress (O) got only 11 seats. Both the public and those who shifted to her party from Congress (O) had judged the situation from moral and national interest angles under the available political liberty.

4.20. Again, Prime Minister Indira Gandhi had emerged as a national hero after 1971-72 war with Pakistan, but (i) her attack on private property through three, the 24th, 25th and 26th constitutional amendments of 1971, (ii) superseding of Judges after the judgement in the Kasavananda Bharati Case,[16] (iii) suppression of J.P. Narayan led *Satyagrah for Democracy* movement in the Country, imposition of 'internal emergency' in June 1975 followed by enacting of MISA (Maintenance of Internal Security Act) for effecting preventive detention of people, (iv) enactment of Prevention of Objectionable Matters Publication Act 1976 for suppressing freedom of press and (v) the postponement of general elections due in 1976 by extension of the term of the House of People by one year in 1976, were noticed by the people. When elections were announced in 1977,

---

[15] Political liberty which includes participation in the political process, State of Madras *versus* Gopalan (1950) SCR 80, is assured to the people by the Preamble to the Constitution of India.

[16] Kesavananda Bharati *versus* State of Kerala (1973) 4 SCC 225.

a number of her staunch followers and members of the Council of Minister including H.N. Bahuguna and Jagjivan Ram left Congress (I) and formed their own party and thereafter had merged with Janata Party. In the election to the Sixth Lok Sabha, Janata Party without any campaigning and funds at its disposal secured 296 seats while the Congress (I) came down to 153 from earlier 355 seats.

4.20A. This unexpected change-over was the handiwork of vigilant but mobile public opinion which had scrutinised Prime Minister Indira Gandhi with negative marking for her highly arrogant or dictatorial performance during 1974—77. But the mobile public opinion did not spare the Janata Party government either, which instead of concentrating on good government for public welfare, busied itself in 'witch hunting' of Indira Gandhi and her followers. In the mid-term elections held in 1980, Indira Gandhi was returned with more than two-third majority with 354 seats in the House of People, the Janata Party was completely routed and dissolution process in the Party had immediately started.

4.21. *The Ultimate Public Opinion—Neither Law nor Politics:* The unpredictable swings in general elections are nothing else but evidences of the ultimate sovereignty of people which makes itself felt, against the amoral behaviour of politicians and wrong public administration conducted by the ruling party or Ministers, through the parliamentary democratic process. In the democratic set-up envisaged in Independent India, the freedom of press, the right to know, the right to criticise and praise those who engage themselves in public activities or deal with public funds and the right to have a good and efficient government and to participate in it, are basic features and are constitutional rights of the people though not Fundamental Rights which the Constitution of India by various provisions protects.

4.21A. When there is too much of floor crossing, defections and splitting of political parties the defect is to be found in the political parties which allow themselves to be dominated by inexperienced or highly selfish leaders. Latter have perhaps little or no knowledge of the difficulties, sacrifices and labour of two or three centuries which had gradually led to the development of constitutional principles for parliamentary democracy in England. The Indian politicians now play with this system rather than understand and function gracefully under this system, when they run for the positions of Ministers, of Chief Ministers and of Prime Minister and publicly display the spirit of remaining in position of power at all costs. The ambitious politicians with their eyes set on becoming Minister, Chief Minister or Prime Minister regard political parties as vehicles or means for personal career which they change for personal benefit without any scruples. The corrective of the situation arising out of defections and party-splits in the form of introduction of Tenth Schedule in the Constitution in 1985, has been because of severity of malaise, but mistakenly sought in the prohibition of defections rather than in purifying the political parties of politics of opportunism and upgrading of the political and constitutional morality.

4. THE PROCESS OF PROHIBITION OF DEFECTIONS AND SPLITS

4.22. The verdicts of the general elections held in 1971, 1977 and 1980 were contrary to the expectations of major political parties. Instead of making any introspection to find the cause of their failure, the losing parties found it convenient to place the blame for their defeat on deserters, by split or defection. Each time after the elections the victorious party thought that their standing with the people was permanent and not that it was a 'swing' of support from mobile public opinion only which was temporarily on their side which they could easily forfeit. Therefore, the need was not only to prevent party men from leaving the party but also for the party to justify itself to the electorate by working for public welfare and winning durable public support.

4.22A. After 1971 general election Prime Minister Indira

Gandhi in 1974-77 believed that she had successfully exterminated other political parties particularly after 'internal emergency' was imposed in 1975 and that the people had no other choice but to elect her party to power again. But, her own trusted party men deserted her after the House of People was dissolved in 1977 and next general elections were announced. The political leaders outside Congress (I) Party formed Janata Party, a pre-election coalition of parties with diverse political ideologies, with one common factor that the 'internal emergency' regime was to be hated. The unexpected defeat of Congress in 1977 with the swing of popular support in favour of Janata Party also led leaders of the latter to believe, like Indira Gandhi, in their infallibility with public opinion. For maintaining their existence the leaders of Janata Party also thought of preventing the split of the Party into its constituents or defection to the Congress (I) Party rather than on constructive programmes related to country and people.

4.23. Earlier, in 1967, the large scale defections in States from Congress and from the minor parties leading to formation of coalitions governments in various States under the name Samyukta Vidhayak Dal (S.V.D.) prompted the Congress Party led Parliament to devise means for preventing defections which were bringing into play non-seriousness and politics of opportunism in the country. A 'Committee on Defection' under Chairmanship of then Home Minister Y.B. Chavan with parliamentarians, public men and jurists as its members, *viz.*, J.P. Narayan, M.C. Setalvad, Ram Subhag Singh, Minoo Masani, Madhu Limaye and Balraj Madhok was appointed (on December 8, 1967) to undertake a study of all aspects of defection and to suggest methods to end the malady of defections. The Committee in its Report dated January 7, 1969 had observed that after the fourth general election of 1967, in the short period between March 1967 and February 1968, the

> "Indian political scene was characterised by numerous instances of change of party allegiance by legislators in

several States. Compared to roughly 542 cases in the entire period between the First and Fourth General Election, at least 438 defections occurred in these twelve months alone. Among independents, 157 out of total of 376 elected joined various parties in this period. That the lure of office played a dominant part in the decisions of the legislators to defect was obvious from the fact that out of 210 defecting legislators of the States of Bihar, Haryana, Madhya Pradesh, Punjab, Rajasthan, Uttar Pradesh and West Bengal, 116 were included in the Council of Ministers which they helped to bring into being by defections."

4.24. The Committee on Defections made two soft recommendations:

(a) One year embargo should be placed on the defector in which period no office of profit such as, membership of Council of Ministers, post of Speaker or Deputy Speaker or chairmanship of any corporation, be given to him;

(b) The size of the Council of Ministers should be fixed: 11% of Members for Union Parliament and bicameral State Legislatures and 10% for unicameral State Legislature.

4.24A. However, as all the parties hoped to gain by defections and the Congress was itself divided between 'Old Guards' and 'Young Turks', the recommendations of the Committee did not make any headway. A Constitution (Thirty-second Amendment) Bill was tabled in May 1973 in Parliament which was completely different from the recommendation in the Report of the Committee on Defections. The Bill provided for disqualification of an elected Member from membership of the House:

(1) on voluntarily giving up of his membership of the political party by which he was set up as a candidate for election from his constituency and

(2) for voting or abstaining from voting contrary to the directions or whip issued by political party for voting in the House on a particular matter.

The Bill remained open for adoption for about two years but it was not pursued after 'internal emergency' was proclaimed and the Bill lapsed after the House of People was dissolved in 1977 for election. The Janata Party Government revived the Bill of 1973 as the Constitution (Forty-eighth Amendment) Bill, 1979, but it also lapsed when shortly afterwards the House of People was dissolved for the seventh general election.

4.25. The experiences of the next ten years after 1973 were intolerable to the political parties and the public alike. During this period a number of mergers leading to Janata Party took place followed by its complete breaking up into various constituent and new political parties. There were defections from the Congress (I) on mass scale in 1977 and after 1979 individual politicians again defected and joined Congress (I) on Indira Gandhi again becoming Prime Minister in early 1980. The Congress (I)[17] wanted to preserve its fabulous majority obtained in Lok Sabha in the elections held in December 1984 of which it was not sure having suffered from defections in 1977, and, the State Assembly elections in eleven States were also due.

4.25A. It is assessed that in between 1967 and 1983 there were around 2,700 recorded cases of defection in Parliament and the State Assemblies. Of these more than 1,900 had defected into Congress (INC) and Congress (I); fifteen defections had resulted in the defectors becoming Chief Ministers; and of these, ten Chief Ministers were Congressmen after defection. Prime Minister Rajiv Gandhi leading the Eighth Parliament (December 1984-December 1988) had not much respect for traditions and the old values, he had no time for frivolities, he was a man of quick perception always impatient to act, he had decided to free India of all progress-retarding hangovers including political

[17] In July 1981, the Election Commission in the dispute between Congress(I) and Congress(U) successor of Congress(O) decided that Congress(I) was successor of Indian National Congress and the Election Commission on the basis of the performance of Congress(U) in previous elections, derecognised the Congress(U).

defections which he referred to as 'legislative anarchism', he had a surgeon's disposition, he thought of ushering India into twenty-first century as a highly developed and sophisticated nation without poverty but with plenty and stable democratic government; and for achieving his ideas he had absolute majority in Parliament after the election in December 1984 with 401 seats out of 540 in the House of People.

4A. THE CONSTITUTION (FIFTY-SECOND AMENDMENT) ACT, 1985

4.26. Immediately after the elections, anti-defection amendment to the Constitution was unanimously enacted as Fifty—second Constitution Amendment Act which introduced Tenth Schedule into the Constitution. The Statement of Objects and Reasons for the Bill pertinently stated:

> "the evil of political defections has been a matter of national concern. If not combated, it is likely to undermine the very foundations of our democracy and the principles which sustain it. With this object, an assurance was given in the Address by the President to Parliament that the government intended to introduce in the current session of Parliament an anti-defection Bill. This Bill is meant for outlawing defection and fulfilling the above assurance."

4.27. The opposition did not like the haste in getting through the amendment of the Constitution, it was debated in Lok Sabha on January 30, 1985 and in Rajya Sabha (Council of States) on January 31, 1985. The avowed purpose of Tenth Schedule was to 'cleanse the political life of this country of the dirt accumulated over the years' and was prompted by the then prevalent cases of dissidence within the Congress Party in which the party-men openly criticised the leadership while continuing to sit in Parliament or State Legislatures.[18] The opposition

---

[18] Reference is taken to point to Shyam Sunder Mohapatra and F.M. Khan, Members of Council of States and A.R. Antulay and Akbar Ahmad, MLAs of Maharashtra and Uttar Pradesh respectively.

characterised the Constitution Amendment as meant to 'muffle dissent in a party like the Congress (I) where no internal elections are held and there is no inner-party democracy',[19] and that this was "the new Governments' first step towards totalitarianism".[20] However, the measure was to be limited in its application to those who get elected to the Parliament or State Legislatures as a party candidate and not to the supporters, ordinary members or office bearers of a political party.

4.28. The Tenth Schedule introduced by the Constitution (Fifty-second Amendment) Act, 1985 applies to produce disqualification[21] for being member of either House of Parliament or the Legislature of a State when under paragraph 2 (1) of the this Schedule when:

(a) the elected Member voluntarily gives up his membership of the political party which had set him up as a candidate for election,

(b) the elected Member votes or abstains from voting in such House contrary to any direction issued by the political party to which he belongs, without taking prior permission of such political party and when such voting or abstention has not been condoned by such political party within fifteen days of the voting or abstention, in case a nominated member of a House joins a political party under explanation to paragraph (2), he can also be disqualified for voting or abstention,

(c) an independent member joins any political party after his election, or a nominated member joins a political party after six months of his taking seat in the House.

4.28A. The disqualification on ground of defection as mentioned in (a) and (b) above does not apply in two cases *viz.*, (1) *split* in a party (paragraph 3); split for the purposes of Tenth Schedule, means any faction or group consisting of not less than one-third of the members of original party in such House and

[19] L.K. Advani, General Secretary of B.J.P. and MP (Rajya Sabha).
[20] Madhu Dandavate, MP (Lok Sabha).
[21] It amends Articles 101, 102, 190 & 191 of the Constitution of India.

the faction or group takes separate identity from the time of such split. And, (2) *merger* of political parties (paragraph 4). Merger means two or more political parties amalgamating by assuming a separate identity from the original parties or taking the name of one of the merging parties. However, a merger shall be valid when not less than two-thirds of the members of each legislature parties concerned have agreed to the merger. In the case of merger the original members have two options, either to become members of the merger or not to accept the merger and to opt to function as a separate group.

4.28B. In both circumstances the provisions of paragraph 2 (1) of Tenth Schedule, that is points (a) and (b) above shall not apply to impose disqualification on any member. Further, the Speaker, Deputy Speaker, Chairman and Deputy Chairman of the Houses of Parliament and the State Legislature are to remain neutral and can voluntarily give up the membership of the political party and rejoin it after these discontinue to hold the mentioned offices. *So long* as they hold the office, the disqualification of Paragraph 2 (1) shall not apply to them. It may be mentioned here in parenthesis that in Parliament the original paragraph 2 (1) (c) of the Bill which provided for disqualification when a member was expelled from the party was dropped when the provision was vehemently opposed on the ground that it could be brazenly abused by the party leadership by stripping a person of his status as Member which he actually gets from the electorate directly.

4.29. The Tenth Schedule by paragraph 6 provides for the enforcement and decision making machinery for the paragraph 2 regulations for disqualification on ground of defection:

"(1) If any question arises as to whether a member of a House has become subject to disqualification under this Schedule, the question shall be referred for the chairman or, as the case may be, the Speaker of such House and his decision shall be final;

Provided that where the question which has arisen is as to the Chairman or the Speaker of a House has become subject to such disqualification, the question shall be referred for the decision of such member of the House as the house may elect in this behalf and his decision shall be final.

(2) All proceedings under sub-paragraph (1) of this paragraph in relation to any question of disqualification of a member of a House under this Schedule shall be deemed to be proceedings in Parliament within the meaning of Article 122 or, as the case may be, proceedings in the Legislature of a State within the meaning of Article 212."

4.30. Paragraph 7 of the Tenth Schedule which placed a bar on the jurisdiction of Courts in respect of any matter connected with the disqualification of a member under the Tenth Schedule was in the case Kihoto Hollohan *versus* Zachillhu.[22] declared to be inoperative till the Fifty-second Amendment of the Constitution was ratified by the States as required under Article 368(2) of the Constitution of India, The reason given by the Supreme Court was that its contents in effect 'curtail the operation' of Articles 136, 226, and 227 of the Constitution of India which lay down the powers of judicial review.

4.31. It is further important to note that Paragraph 8 of the Tenth Schedule gives plenary powers to the Chairman or the Speaker of the House and these powers vitally bring the political parties under the supervision of the Chairman or the Speaker. Without prejudice to the plenary powers the rules may provide for:

(a) the *maintenance of registers* or other records as to the political parties, if any, to which different members of the House belong;

(b) the report which the leader of a legislature party in relation to a member of the House shall furnish with regard to any *condoning* of action for voting or abstaining from voting contrary to the direction or whip

[22] 1992 Supp (2) SCC 651.

issued by the party; including the authority to whom his report shall be furnished;

(c) the report which a political party shall furnish with regard to admission to the party of other members of the House, including the authority to whom this report is to be furnished and

(d) The procedure for determining question of disqualification of any member of the House under paragraph 6 with reference to paragraph 2 of the Schedule.

4.31A. Though the rule making power is plenary but such rules as are framed by the Chairman or the Speaker of a House shall be placed before the House and unless sooner approved they shall come into operation after expiry of 30 days. The approval may be with modifications. The rules may be disapproved by the House in which case these will be framed again by the Chairman or the speaker and shall be submitted to the House. The paragraph 8 (3) lays down that any wilful contravention of the rules by any person shall be dealt with in the same manner as the breach of privilege of the House.

4B. JUDICIAL INTERPRETATIONS OF TENTH SCHEDULE

4.32. Paragraph 2 of Tenth Schedule has been often interpreted by the Supreme Court and now it has acquired a practical shape. The following important aspects may be placed here.

(1) Paragraph 2 (I) (a): The term 'voluntarily given up his membership' are not the same as 'resignation' and have a wider connotation.[23] A person may voluntarily give up his membership by his conduct without tendering a formal resignation to the party. If an elected member joins another party the presumption shall be that he has voluntarily given up his existing membership of a party.

---

[23] Ravi S. Naik *versus* Union of India, 1994 Supp (2) SCC 641 at 649.

(2) *Unattached Members:* It has been further held[24] that in view of the Explanation to Paragraph 2 (1) of the Tenth Schedule even if a member is thrown out or expelled from the party, for the purpose of the Tenth Schedule he will not cease to be a member of the political party that had set him up as a candidate for the election. He will retain his *status ante,* though he is treated as unattached by the Speaker, till he joins another party which he cannot do without attracting disqualification unless it is as a member of splinter group under the exception of Paragraph 3 of Tenth Schedule.

(3) In practice also, when a party expels an elected member from the party, the member shall not be disqualified from being a member of the House.

(i) In 1990 Janata Dal expelled 25 Members of its party who were Members of Lok Sabha. They continued to remain Members of Lok Sabha and subsequently joined the Janata Dal (S) of Chandrashekhar to cause the split in Janata Dal. The then Speaker of the Lok Sabha, Rabi Ray, had chosen not to make inquiry into 'legality of expulsions' which would have required scrutiny of the rules of particular party organisation and its internal procedures for taking decisions. He expressed doubts if this was within the functions of Speaker and he had pointed out several blank spots or lacunae under the Tenth Schedule.

(ii) Similarly, in 1995 Congress Party expelled Minister Arjun Singh for anti-party activities, he ceased to be a Cabinet Minister but continued to remain a Member of Lok Sabha. Such Members are generally designated as unattached members.

The Supreme Court has, however, made it clear[25] that this does not create a fourth category of members, *i.e.*, apart from members elected on party ticket, or independent members or

---

[24] G. Viswanathan *versus* Hon'ble Speaker T.N. Legislative Assembly, 1966 2 SCC 353.

[25] *Ibid.*

nominated members of the House and they legally continue as the members of 'the party to which they belong' till they expressly by resignation or by implication such as by joining other party, voluntarily give up their membership of the party.

4.33. Paragraph 2 (1) (b): The question was raised in the case Kihoto Hollohan *versus* Zachillhu,[26] that the party whip system for compulsory voting according to the direction issued to an elected member by the political party to which he belongs is restrictive of the 'democratic rights of the elected members of the Parliament and the Legislatures of the States' since Articles 105 and 194 of the Constitution promise freedom of speech and freedom of vote in the Houses. The Supreme Court held that the freedoms under these Articles are subject to the provisions of the Constitution and the rules and standing orders regulating the Procedure of the Houses and observed:

> "The disqualification imposed by Paragraph (2) (1) (b) must be so construed as not to unduly impinge on he said freedom of speech of a member. This would be possible if Paragraph 2 (1) (b) is confined in its scope by keeping in view the objects underlying the amendments contained in the Tenth Schedule, namely, to curb the evil or mischief of political defections motivated by the lure of office or other similar considerations. The said objective would be achieved if the disqualification incurred on the ground of voting or abstaining from voting by a member is confined to cases where a change of government is likely to be brought about or is prevented, as the case may be, as result of such voting or abstinence or when such voting or abstinence from voting is in a matter which was a major policy and programme on which the political party to which the member belongs went to polls."

[26] 1992 Supp (2) SCC 651 at 716.

The Supreme Court added,[27]

> "For this purpose, the direction given by the political party to a member belonging to it, the violation of which may entail disqualification under Paragraph 2 (1) (b), would have to be limited to a vote on motion of confidence or no confidence in the government or (to a vote or abstention) where the motion under consideration relates to a matter which was an integral policy and programme of the political party on the basis of which it approached the electorate."

4.34. Disobedience of the direction of the Party on any of such motions would amount to disapproval by the member of the 'programme on the basis of which he went before the electorate and got himself elected.'[28] It will also entail in such circumstance a breach of trust reposed in him by the electorate.

4.35. In the above case the Supreme Court also laid down the requirement for the political parties which issue the direction or whip which results in such disqualification under paragraph 2 (1) (b) "is so worded as to clearly indicate (that the action of any Member) contrary to the said direction would result in incurring the disqualification under Paragraph 2 (1) (b) of the Tenth Schedule".[29]

4.35A. The whip is to be issued by properly authorised person or authority of the original political party and not by legislative party. In a politically much discussed instance in a State, this provision was literally and strictly followed in 1998 like any penal law by the Speaker of U.P. Legislative Assembly while he considered the question of disqualification of 12 MLAs of Bahujan Samaj Party (BSP) who had crossed floor and had

---

[27] *Ibid.*, followed by Supreme Court in Mayawati *versus* Markandeya Chand, (1998) 7 SCC 517 confirming the action of the Speaker in the matter of the case. F.n. 30 below.

[28] *Ibid.*

[29] *Ibid.*

voted for Kalyan Singh Ministry in a vote on no-confidence motion by violating so-called party whip. The Speaker found that as laid down by the Supreme Court the political party had not formally authorised anybody to issue the whip and the leader of the Party in the House cannot assume this power *suo moto*. Moreover, it appeared to be a case of oral whip without mention of punitive consequences. As such when no valid whip was issued, the verdict of Speaker was that there was no violation of any Party code under paragraph 2 (1) (b).[30]

4.35B. Interestingly, when voting takes place (i) on a no-confidence motion moved by the opposition against the government which is carried out or (ii) on a confidence motion moved by the Prime Minister which is defeated as it happened on April 17, 1999, leading to the dissolution of Lok Sabha, the members of Lok Sabha who disregarded the whip of the Party, only suffered from the wrath of the political party and not the stigma of defection or disqualification under the Tenth Schedule. For example, after the voting in House of People on April 17, 1999 the National Conference promptly expelled Saifuddin Soz, one of its three MPs in Lok Sabha, and it also happened with Anand Mohan Singh, the lone MP of Rashtriya Janata Party, who disregarded the respective Party whips while casting their votes on the confidence motion. The two dissenters remained unattached Members of Parliament till the President dissolved the House of People on April 26, 1999.

4.36. Tenth Schedule Paragraph 3, *Split in Party*: When a member or group of members of a party which are not less than one-third of the total members of such party in the lower House split, form a separate group and give up membership of such party, the disqualification from the membership of the House

---

[30] Based on newspaper reports; *The Hindustan Times, New Delhi*: March 1998. On Appeal against the decision of the Speaker made in the Supreme Court, this part was confirmed by Supreme Court, Mayawati *versus* Markandeya Chand, (1998) 7 SCC 517, per Srinavasan, J.

vide Paragraph 2 (1) does not apply. This provision honours the freedom of dissent within the party but in the form that the number of dissenters should be one-third of the of the members in the legislature belonging to such political party. Various situations have arisen in the interpretation and implementation of this provision.

4.36A. First, whether the members expelled by the party to which they belong can combine with voluntary dissenters to become or form part of the one-third strength required for recognition of the splinter group. When in 1990 Chandra Shekhar split the Janata Dal Party and formed Janata Dal (S) with 70 members of the House of People elected on Janata Dal ticket in November 1989 election, 25 of these had been expelled by the Janata Dal one day earlier. Without these 25 members the party of Chandra Shekhar, who had become Prime Minister of a minority government with outside support of Congress(I) in the meantime, would not have qualified for a valid split and the exception under Paragraph 3 of the Tenth Schedule. The Speaker avoided a decision on the ground that Tenth Schedule did not authorise him to investigate the 'legality of expulsions' made by a party when the members do not accept the decision.

4.36A-1. However, now the position is clear after the Supreme Court decision in the case, G. Vishwanathan *versus* Speaker T.N. Legislative Assembly,[31] Which held that unless the expelled (by the Party) members join another party, an action on their part, they continue to be the members of the Party to which they belong though the Party does not accept them as members of the Party. In the case, Ravi S. Naik *versus* Union of India,[32] with a slightly different setting, two members of the original party were declared to be disqualified as Members of the House by the Speaker. The High Court stayed the operation of the Order of Speaker pending judicial review of the Speaker's Order. In the meantime till High Court made the review, the original party

[31] See f.n. 23 above, AIR 1996 SC 1060.
[32] AIR 1994 SC 1558.

suffered split and the two members became part of the splinter group which had more than one-third of the members of the original party in the House. The Supreme Court held that the split was valid since under the stay orders of the High Court the two disqualified members had their disqualification in abeyance while the writ was pending.

4.36B. The effect of the decision of the Supreme Court,[33] has been to make it difficult for the original party in suppressing dissent and in preventing the consequent split in the party. This is proper since the political corruption rampant in 1990s benefited top leadership which were in power and this kind of political corruption does not tolerate the right of dissent for the honest or the lower cadres in the party. The Supreme Court had in the earlier 1992 case[34] held that in case of split in a party the presumption is that it is caused by dissent which is to be valued while the defection is motivated by personal gain which is an evil to be prevented.

4.37. *When Do Splits Occur?*: Splits generally occur when

(1) in the ruling party there is stagnation, that is, there are more aspirants for Ministership and they do not see any future for them in the party, or

(2) the ruling party has gone into disrepute due to non achievement of promised results and it is anticipated that in the next election people will not support it, or

(3) the ruling party has marginal majority and other parties hope to form government if their number swells through defection from the ruling party or other parties.

The defectors are generally carefully slow or shy in giving out their intentions and those who engineer split in their party are highly secretive. The negotiations for this purpose are closed door matters as was witnessed when during internal emergency of 1975-77 almost dictatorial conditions were prevailing and open revolt against Congress (I) could have landed party

[33] F.n. 23, 28, above.

[34] Kihoto Hollohan *versus* Zachillu, 1992 SCC, Supp (2) 651.

dissidents in jails. The splits are also associated with fulfilment of personal ambitions for becoming Prime Minister, Chief Minister or a Minister instantly. It is in the interest of ruling majority that the defection should be as difficult as possible so that the majority of their party in the legislature, which is always necessary for their own existence, is maintained.

4.38. Under above conditions, sometimes the defection appears to have taken place in parts and not instantaneously or in one stroke. It means that the original party can say that since one-third number was not reached when one group had split, the exemption under Paragraph 3 shall not be available to such group since such members of the group had already suffered disqualification. Obviously this will be the attitude of those who resist the split. However, (i) the niceties of the procedures, (ii) public statements made, intra-party disciplinary proceedings, (iii) reports made to the Speaker, (iv) the condonation for mistakes by the dissenter from party sought and refused or granted, (v) explanations sought, orders issued by proper or authorised office bearers of the party, and a number of other inquiries have to made before the final situation clearly crystallises for others and the Speaker who may be called upon to give his verdict on the validity of the split. As such it is understandable that those members who split and form new party and want either to remain identified as a new party or merge with another existing party interpret the time lag between different stages till the split is perfected, to take the stand that the split took place only at the moment when it became perfect and that there were no distinct stages in between this period.

4.39. The Supreme Court in Kihoto Hollohan *versus* Zachillhu, on the above issue observed caution in the inquiry as to the exact import of the timing of the 'split',[35]

> "—whether it is to be understood an instantaneous, one time event or whether a 'split' can be said to occur over

[35] 1992 Supp (2) SCC 651 at 717. Followed in Lakshman J. Satpathy *versus* Union of India, 1992 Supp (2) SCC 744.

a period of time. The hypothetical poser was that if one-third of the members of a political party in the legislature broke away from it on a particular day and a few more members joined the splinter group a couple of days later, would the latter also be a part of the 'split' group. This question of construction cannot be in *vacuo*.... The meaning to be given to 'split' must necessarily be examined...in the context of its particular facts. No hypothetical predictions can or need be made".

4.40. Where a declaration was signed by some MLAs belonging to a party declaring that they had formed a separate group which was produced during the hearing before the Speaker, this fact established the facts of split as well as the date and the constitution of the separate group. It was not necessary that a prior notice of the split be given to the Speaker.[36]

4.41. *The Decision of Chairman or Speaker in Paragraph 6*: According to Paragraph 6 (1) if any question of the disqualification of a member of a House arises, the decision of the Chairman or the Speaker of the House shall be 'final'. Along with this the clause (2) of this paragraph also provides that the proceedings regarding disqualification as above, shall be deemed to be privileged as that of legislature are under Articles 122 or 212. The question raised, therefore, relates to the status of Chairman or the Speaker with respect to the judiciary under the Tenth Schedule. The process under Tenth Schedule is an extension of the proceedings in Parliament and it finally decides the 'question' of disqualification. Is it an advisory or legislative or internal matter in relation to the constitutional scheme? Perhaps the framers of the Constitution (Fifty-second Amendment) Act intended it to be an internal matter just like any ruling of the Chairman or the Speaker during the proceedings of the House since the emphasis was on quick decisions in the matter. The Supreme Court in P.V. Narasimha Rao *versus* State,[37]

[36] Ravi S. Naik *versus* Union of India, 1994 Supp (2) SCC 641 at 660.
[37] (1998) 4 SCC 626.

has clarified that a power has been conferred under the Tenth Schedule on the Chairman of the Rajya Sabha/the Speaker of the Lok Sabha to decide the question as to whether a Member of the Rajya Sabha/Lok Sabha has become disqualified from being a Member on the ground of defection. An affirmative decision of the Chairman/Speaker may result in such Member ceasing to be a Member but it would not mean that the Chairman of Rajya Sabha/Speaker of Lok Sabha is the *competent authority* to remove a Member of the Rajya Sabha/Lok Sabha. The result of the whole exercise is the consequence of application of constitutional provisions and not of decision of Speaker or political preferences.

4.42. The Supreme Court in Kihoto Hollohan *versus* Zachillu,[38] categorically rejected any similarity between the privileges of House of Commons of England and the Indian Parliament on the privilege of the Houses to determine their own constitution. It referred to the earlier judgements in Indira Nehru Gandhi *versus* Raj Narain[39] in which 'observations as to the imperative judicial nature of the power to resolve disputes' relating to elections were made:

> "The concept of democracy as visualised by the Constitution presupposes the representation of the people in Parliament and the State Legislatures by the method of election. And, before an election machinery can be brought into operation, there are three requisites which require to be attended to, namely, (1) there should be a set of laws and rules making provisions with respect to all matters relating to, or in connection with elections, and it should be decided as to how these laws and rules are to be made; (2) there should be an executive charged with the duty of securing the due conduct of election; and (3) there should be a judicial tribunal to deal with disputes arising out of or in connection with elections...."

---

[38] 1992 Supp (2) SCC 651 pp. 703 *et seq.*

[39] 1975 Supp SCC 1.

> "In whichever body or authority the jurisdiction is vested, the exercise of the jurisdiction must be judicial in character. This Court has held that in adjudicating an election dispute an authority is performing a judicial function and a petition for leave to appeal under Article 136 of the Constitution would lie against the decision notwithstanding the provisions Article 329(b)."[40]

4.43. On this aspect of paragraph 6 of Tenth Schedule, the Supreme Court finally held in the Kihoto Hollohan Case that

> "The very deeming provision implies that the proceedings of disqualification are, in fact, not before the House; but only before the Speaker as a specially designated authority, The decision under Paragraph 6 (1) is not the decision of the House; nor is it subject to the approval by the House. The decision operates independently of the House. A deeming provision cannot by its creation transcend its own power. There is, therefore, no immunity under Articles 122 and 212 from judicial scrutiny of the decision of the Chairman or Speaker exercising power under Paragraph 6 (1) of the Tenth Schedule".[41]

4.44. On the inquiry whether the role of Chairman or the Speaker is that of a Court or Tribunal under the Tenth Schedule, it is noted that in a dispute which comes to the Speaker under Paragraph 2 of the Tenth Schedule, there is a conflict between the parties, one asserts while the other denies, one claims rights under the Tenth Schedule and imposes the accusation of violation of the norms on the other, of course there is no pecuniary or criminal liability but there is a charge of the breach of statutory obligations which is contested by the other. The Chairman or the Speaker does not have the 'trappings' of a court but the process revolves around exercise of quasi-judicial

---

[40] Justice Mathew: *Ibid*, at p. 121; Other Judges quoted are JJ. Beg and Khanna.

[41] *Ibid.*, p. 706.

power and so he acts like a tribunal. The test "...is whether the adjudicating power which a particular authority is empowered to exercise, has been conferred on it by a statute and can be described as a part of State's inherent power exercised in discharging its judicial function."[42] It has also been observed that "Broadly speaking, certain special matters go before tribunals, and the residue goes before the ordinary courts of civil judicature. Their procedures may differ but the functions are not essentially different."[43] The Supreme Court has categorically held that

> "The Speakers/Chairmen while exercising powers and discharging functions under the Tenth Schedule *act as a Tribunal* adjudicating rights and obligations under the Tenth Schedule and their decisions in that capacity are amenable to judicial review."[44]

4.44A. *The Finality Clause in Paragraph 6*: The Paragraph 6 (1) of the Tenth Schedule declares that the decision of Chairman/ Speaker on the question of disqualification incurred or suffered by member shall be final. It is now well settled that the effect of this stipulation in any statute is to cut short the process of appeals. This does not prevent judicial review of the final order but rather hastens it; since, when there is right to appeal the judicial review is staggered because an alternative remedy by way of appeal is available to the petitioner. The Supreme Court has held, in a similar situation, that under Section 105 of the Representation of Peoples Act, 1951 the order of Election Tribunal has been made final and conclusive but that "cannot in any way cut down or effect the overriding powers which this Court can exercise in the matter of granting special leave under Article 136

---

[42] Associated Cement Companies Ltd. *versus* P.N. Sharma AIR 1965 SC 1595.

[43] H.S. Mills Ltd. *versus* S.S. Jhunjhunwala, AIR 1961 SC 1669.

[44] The Kihoto Hollohan Case, 1992 Supp (2) SCC 651 at 711. See, f.n. 49, below.

of the Constitution."[45] A finality clause only limits or rather redefines the scope of the jurisdiction of the High Court or the Supreme Court. It is, therefore, (a) always open to the Court to examine whether the action of the Speaker is *ultra vires* the Tenth Schedule, (b) an inquiry based on error of judgement will be precluded since it does not contest the jurisdiction of the Speaker, (c) an action taken mala fide by the Speaker/Chairman can be examined[46] and (d) a judicial review can take place when non-compliance with rules of natural justice and perversity or violation of any constitutional mandate is alleged.[47] However, "judicial review cannot be available at a stage prior to the making of a decision by the Speaker/Chairman and a *quia timet* action would not be possible."[48]

4.45. In Mayawati *versus* Markandeay Chand,[49] the Supreme Court on the question whether the findings arrived at by the Speaker on the issue of disqualification of a member of the House on the ground of defection can be subject to judicial review only on the ground of jurisdictional error or also on the grounds of perversity, that is, the decision of the Speaker arrived at in the present case was so unreasonable that no Tribunal could have arrived at it, referred the matter to a Constitution Bench of the Supreme court for decision.[50]

---

[45] D.S. Mehta *versus* Raghuraj Singh, AIR 1954 SC 520, p. 522; *Union of* India *versus* Tulsiram Patel, (1985) 3 SCC 398, p. 507: with reference to finality in Article 311 (3) of the Constitution; Union of India *versus* Jyoti P. Mitter, (1971) 1 SCC 396, p. 410: in the matter of determination of age of a Judge by the President of India; or, B. Nayak *versus* Election Commission of India AIR 1965 SC 1892: finality with reference to decision of Governor in matter of disqualification of a M.L.A. subsequent to election. See, footnote 36 above, also.

[46] State of Rajasthan *versus* Union of India, (1977) 3 SCC 592; Makhan Singh *versus* State of Punjab, AIR 1964 SC 381

[47] Ravi S. Naik *versus* Union of India 1994 Supp (2) SCC 641 at 652-53, f.n. 49, below

[48] Kihoto Hollohan *versus* Zachilhu, *op. cit.*, f.n. 34, at p. 711.

[49] Per Punchhi, C.J., (1998) 7 SCC 517: Kihoto Case, *supra*, followed.

[50] Reference is still pending for decision, that is, May 1999.

4.46. On the whole, the Tenth Schedule gives a pivotal role to the Speaker or the Chairman in the matter of implementing the law of defections. It is better to call it 'law for defections' in place of 'law of anti-defection' since, as mention earlier in the beginning of this lecture, the calculated lawful defections are now order of the day and the splinter groups incurring disqualification in 1998 under the Tenth Schedule have been rare. The result in the reversed use of the Tenth Schedule has led to its severe criticism since the dissolution of eleventh House of People in December 1997 and it also led to a political cry for its thorough revision.

5. AN ASSESSMENT ON TENTH SCHEDULE

4.47. It is now a fact of Indian political life that the Tenth Schedule enacted in 1985 has by the end of century earned a bad reputation for itself. Its avowed purpose was to prevent defections from and splits in parties in order to bring end to political opportunism. The political opportunism was the corrupting malady of Indian politics which had come to stay after the demise of Prime Minister Nehru in 1964 and Prime Minister L.B. Shastri in 1965. It presumed that the top leadership of parties was noble, altruistic and selfless but the leadership at the middle and bottom of the party hierarchy was guided more by lure of office. The need for success of democracy in India was felt to be that the Prime Minister and Chief Minister should be free from power games of their own party-men so that they may devote their time and energy for the development of the Country.

4.48. When in 1973, the infructuous Constitution (Thirty-second Amendment) Bill was brought before the Parliament, the idea was to keep the Congress (I) Party intact which was mainly a party of members elected in 1967 to Parliament and the State Legislatures, while the Congress (O) had under it the control of old organisational set up of Indian National Congress but had few elected members in legislatures. The Congress (I) was constantly in danger of breaking down since its ideological base was artificial, and, it had practically broken down in 1977.

4.48A. In 1977, the Janata Party formed the government at the Union, it was a coalition of political parties of different shades which had only two points in common, *viz.*, hatred for internal emergency which was withdrawn in 1977 and hatred for Indira Gandhi feared as a dictator but whom the people had already voted out. In 1979, Janata Party government revived the anti-defection move by the Constitution (Forty-eighth Amendment) Bill for its own preservation against impending split and dissipation, which it could not prevent and soon resigned. The Constitution Amendment Bill had lapsed thereafter.

4.48B. Prime Minister Rajiv Gandhi sensed the insecurity to himself and Congress (I) Party by splits and defection and in a hurry after election in December 1984, enacted the Tenth Schedule by the Constitution (Fifty-second Amendment) Act, 1985, he completed the term, but his Congress Party dissipated and fared badly in the next election held in 1989 and after which it has not yet regained majority in the House of People, that is, the Tenth Schedule failed to save the Congress (I) Party. However, in the reverse gear, during the minority Government of Prime Minister Narasimha Rao, the anti-defection law was used to appropriately augment numerical strength of the Congress Legislative Party in the House of People even by doubtful methods which later attracted the indictment of Corruption on the Prime Minister in the year 2000. Yet, during the years 1996-97 the Congress (I) Party suffered too much from defections and splits in States and by January 1998 it was on the brink of collapse.

4.48C. *Tenth Schedule of the Constitution does not apply to intra-party and intra-coalition splits and defections*: It required special efforts for the survival of Congress (I) Party as such in 1990s. As a last remedial dose for survival Mrs Sonia Gandhi, widow of former Prime Minister late Rajiv Gandhi and a naturalised Indian citizen, was inducted as supremo of the Congress (I) Party. She was viewed by the party-men as inheritor of charismatic force of Nehru-Indira Gandhi legacy who could save the party from dissipation. She succeeded in preventing the fast erosion of Indian National Congress by mending the party discipline and gave some hope of its rejuvenation in 1999, but could not contain the outspoken character and the obtrusive ambitions of forming government at the Union possessed by the too many mature leaders in the top cadres in the Party. The Congress (I) Party could cash on the failure of BJP State Governments in Rajasthan and Delhi in the State General Elections held in November 1998. However, her keenness in providing alternate government to BJP at the Union by forcing Bihar cast massacre and suspension of elected government under Article 356 of the Constitution issue in Parliament, brought the inner contradictions in Congress (I) Party and inept leadership to the fore. But, there was nothing to be split out of Congress Party as Bihar Congress was already a splinter body and did not side with Congress moves. Later in April 1999, the Congress Party declared that it was prepared for fresh elections and if necessary to provide alternative government to BJP coalition and projected Sonia Gandhi as Prime Minister incumbent. The BJP coalition moved a confidence motion on the advice of the President of India when one of the original constituents of the coalition split and withdrew support depriving the coalition of numerical absolute majority. The motion of confidence was defeated by one vote and the government resigned on 17th April. However, the Prime Minister incumbent from opposition Congress (I) Party could not muster a better numerical backing and the twelfth House of People was dissolved on 26th April, 1999, for fresh general elections. This miscalculation substantially tarnished the image of Congress (I) Party and its leaders in the urban intelligentsia and created another instalment of pre-election defections from the Congress (I) Party itself. In the sequence, after the thirteenth general election in October 1999, the Congress (I) Party had its lowest ever representation in the Lok Sabha.

4.48D. In none of the above situations of splits and defections within political parties or coalitions the Tenth Schedule which leads to disqualifications was attracted. These splits and defections are now important part of constitutional history of India.

4.49. After the Eleventh House of People was dissolved in December 1997, the general feeling among all the parties was that the Tenth Schedule had failed in its purpose and the politicians generally projected the view that defections and splits should be completely prohibited and the penalty of facing the electorate must be imposed on the elected representative of the people. All the political parties test the Tenth Schedule by its efficacy in preventing split in their party but at the same time these welcome increase in their own strength by defections. When gainer they even plead for abolition of Tenth Schedule since this influx is easier if there was no Tenth Amendment to make it difficult and risky. Opportunist politics by adopting contradictions is not considered as illegal but only immoral behaviour by political parties of India now after the close of the twentieth century.

4.50. *Reasons for Failure of Tenth Schedule*: The political parties have in general found three reasons for the failure of the anti-defection provisions:

First, that the arrangement was intended to be a deterrent by providing for a quick decision leading to disqualification from membership of the House; for this the decision resulting in disqualification was to be taken not by a multimember tribunal but by the Speaker. This aspect has been frustrated by bringing in the safeguards of natural justice and other procedures of the courts which delay the final decision.

Secondly, the lure of ministerial post is openly extended by the parties to the defectors which is immoral but not contrary to the Tenth Schedule. In several cases, the defectors have become the Chief Ministers.

Thirdly, the Tenth Schedule has inversely not banned the splits or defections of elected representatives but has legalised the political immorality with the result the politicians when they defect they do so in calculated numbers, one-third or more of the membership. This number is generally so large that the whole party is shaken by the split or defections and also suffers in public estimation. The defection from Congress in Uttar Pradesh Legislative Assembly by formation of Lok Tantrik Congress and in West Bengal by the formation of Trinamul Congress had put the Congress in 1997 in its death throes. Similarly, the formation of Rashtriya Janata Dal in Bihar and Lok Shakti by splits in Janata Dal Party placed the latter in a dissolution process. However, the B.J.P. withstood the shock of split in Gujarat when Rashtriya Janata Party was formed in 1996.

4.51. What sagacious people think of the constitutional situation is that the parties do not go for introspection of their own shortcomings which include (a) selection of wrong candidates for election, (b) surrender to criminals who instead of supporting parties from outside now seek to become members of Parliament and State Legislature themselves, (c) adherence to impracticable or outdated objectives for the party and (d) obvious suppression of young blood in the party in favour of spent-force personalities. Most of the political parties have become leadership oriented, so they disregard and suppress internal freedom of views and intra-party debates, and work with the idea that it is for the party to lay down the objectives and it is for the people to blindly follow them in the mistaken belief that the leaders are the torch bearers for the people.

4.51A. If one looks back, Mahatma Gandhi, Prime Minister Nehru and other old time public leaders had moulded the public opinion as well as had changed themselves to new circumstances, that is, they were neither rigid nor headstrong and they never underestimated the wisdom of people and of adopting values changing with time, be they of culture, of economics or of international politics.

4.52. The ideas of anti-defection and anti-split are based on a much sought after party hegemony over the constituents or of the elected members of the legislature over the leadership of their parties. Loyalty of constituents to the party should have a high degree of permanency. From traditional and practical points of view this is desirable for the continuation of common front provided by the party in the House against other parties and which is in common interest of party members as well. It has been observed that the norm of loyalty to party is based on shared beliefs and that:

> "a divided party is looked on with suspicion by the electorate. It is natural for Members to accept the opinion of their leaders and spokesmen on the wide variety of matters on which those Members have no specialist knowledge. Generally Members will accept majority decisions in the party even when they disagree".[51]

4.53. Since the loyalty to party is an essential norm of politics the Members accept the party direction or whip at the time of voting and present themselves compulsorily when the voting is to take place. After a whip has been issued, to vote against the whip or to abstain from voting is taken to mean disloyalty to the party, whether it also amounts to infidelity depends on the result of inquiry as to who benefits by this disregard of the whip. Whether such a Member is to be regarded as unreliable or hostile or a conspirator is a matter to be decided subsequently by the party and the electorate. In England the party reaction:

> "...will range (depending on the circumstances and whether the offence is repeated) from a quiet word from a Whip and appeals to future loyalty, to a ticking-off or a formal reprimand (perhaps from the Chief Whip himself), to any one of a number of threats. The armoury of intimidation includes the menaces that the Member will never get ministerial office or go on overseas trips sponsored by the party, or be nominated by his party for Commons committee memberships, or that he might be

---

[51] Giffith & Ryle, *Parliament: Functions, Practice and Procedure,* (1989 ed.) at p. 119.

deprived of his party's whip in the House, or that he might be reported to his constituency which might wish to reconsider his behaviour when reselection comes round again."[52]

4.54. Before the Tenth Schedule was enacted in 1985, the position of dissenter in India was same as in England. It was an intra-party matter which did not attract constitutional attention. The party had all the opportunities of patching up the situation without making any prestige issue. However, now after the Tenth Schedule has come into operation, if a Member votes or abstains from voting in the House contrary to any direction issued by the political party, called 'whip' in parliamentary slang, he stands disqualified unless his action has been condoned by his party within fifteen days. The burden of proving that he has been condoned is on the Member. Of course the implementing authority Speaker under Paragraph 6 of Tenth Schedule whose decision on disqualification shall be final, requires that somebody, an authority of the parent party, should complain to him, that is, the Speaker will not *suo moto* act in the situation.

4.55. Obviously, now under Tenth Schedule the dissent of a Member or a split in party becomes a constitutional matter and does not remain a simple political lapse and this immediately attracts national attention. It becomes (a) a prestige matter for the dissenter, (b) an embarrassing matter for the party and (c) a situation to be exploited by other parties. There is rarely a chance for peaceful patch up between the party and the dissenter becomes a defector ultimately.

4.56. *People and Anti-Defection Law*: The Tenth Schedule has brought about a legal and not only a political change in the concepts of relationship of the elected Member with the party and the electorate or constituency which elected the Member as representative in Parliament. Qualitatively it is a downgrade

---

52 Rodney Brazier, *Constitutional Reform—Reshaping the British Political System* (1991) at p. 48.

development. Now it is not a debatable point in India whether the elected Members are representatives of people in Parliament or that they are nominees of a political party approved by the people constituency-wise. The splits include defection and voluntarily giving up of the membership of the party to which the Members involved belonged. At the same time the Tenth Schedule does not expressly make the split and defections any prohibited activity or offence committed against the electorate under the political concept of the 'right to recall'. The split is at present under the Tenth Schedule rather treated as a punishment for an offence of disloyalty committed against the party.

4.57. In England, the parties take care that the elected Member honours the constituency and his behaviour and disposition is in consonance with the standards acceptable to the views of the people of his constituency. To an elected Member the threat to face the constituency in the next election by resigning his seat without the support of his party or after having been dropped as the party's candidate, has a lot of deterrence on the Member since in such a case the image of the Member in public falls if he does not resign from the House while the support to the party from the constituency continues. Of course, there is no legal compulsion on the Member to resign. From a political party call for a recall election is made when a Member has misused his status for personal financial interests, has changed his political views while he continues as Member from his original party or has joined another party without seeking re-election from the constituency. However, the aggrieved political party has no immediate remedy in case of defiance since the Member continues to sit in the House and the party takes action by representing the situation of misbehaviour to the constituency.[53] In other Commonwealth Countries also the moral force of the party is regarded to be sufficient for maintaining party discipline and defection takes place only when a Member has finally decided to change the party on vital public issues.

---

[53] Rodney Brazier, *op. cit.*, pp. 52-53.

4.57A. It was rather hasty in India in 1985 to have thought of implanting a constitutional impediment on the elected Members in place of developing party discipline and upgrading party integrity for saving the democratic process.

4.58. The Tenth Schedule has clearly erred by making the numerical proportion of defectors to the elected strength of the party in the House as a test of legality for defection by way of split. This has neither the principle of loyalty to party nor loyalty to people as its basis. Somehow, as the constitutional scene has turned out, since the split of Congress in 1969, the elected Members of a party are taken to represent the party and the party programme on the basis of which the members get elected goes into background. It is in practice regarded as a matter of intra-party arrangement that the party is a means for winning representation in Parliament. As a practical proposition, the cream or the brain of the party are nominated for elections. When they get elected they become the substance of the party and represent the party particularly in the matter of programmes of the party and for what the party stands for. The constitutional scheme does not provide any regulation of political parties on this score apart from organisational democracy enforced indirectly by the Election Commission of India as its residuary power.[54]

4.59. It is obvious that the role of politics under the constitutional set-up in India has undergone tremendous change in basic values and now since late 1980s it is limited to grabbing the opportunity to form the government at the Union or in the States. This kind of political game valid under constitutional framework has little or no element of loyalty to the party or its election manifesto and it will be misleading to say that the elected members always have a sense of loyalty to the party or latter's promises to the electorate. This practical game or real politics has been played in a spate of the splits and defections

---

[54] Discussed in Chapter VII, infra.

which have taken place in States. Many instances of this political game can be given:

(i) In 1988 the politics of splits and mergers to forge National Front was successfully experimented by V.P. Singh who soon became Prime Minister.

(ii) In 1990 split in National Front created Janata Dal (S) and provided opportunity to Chandra Shekhar to become Prime Minister.

(iii) In 1991 Chief Minister Mulayam Singh Yadav defected from Janata Dal and formed his Samajwadi Party and continued to remain Chief Minister of U.P. with different alignments.

(iv) Soon one out of three CPI Members of U.P. Legislative Assembly constituted for himself Samatavadi Party and merged with Samajwadi Party without attracting disqualification under Tenth Schedule.

(v) So was done by the lone CPI member in Vidhan Parishad who left CPI Party and joined Samajvadi Party.

(vi) In September 1996, Arunachal Pradesh Chief Minister Gegong Apang split from Congress, formed Arunachal Congress Party which was immediately recognised by the Speaker under the Tenth Schedule and with the support of 51 out of 58 Members of the Assembly again formed the government as Chief Minister.

(vii) In Manipur in December 1997, 36 Members of Congress Party in the Legislative Assembly resigned alongwith the Speaker Nipamacha Singh, formed a new party Manipur Congress Party of the existing M.L.As and Nipamacha Singh became Chief Minister.

(viii) In Uttar Pradesh in February 1998, 24 Members of the minority government of Kalyan Singh belonging to U.P. Lok Tantrik Congress and Janata Dal withdrew from the Cabinet and formed a short-lived coalition government with Jagdambika Pal as Chief Minister with the outside support of Congress, BSP and Samajvadi Party in a House of 426 Members. Interestingly in the episode, there was no split and the matters moved within the umbrella of Tenth Schedule. Those MLAs who had already split in 1997 and 12 MLAs against whom defection cases were pending for decision of Speaker but who had been appointed Ministers in Kalyan Singh coalition government, were involved in the constitutional game of becoming Chief Minister as alluded to.

4.60. *Anti-Dote for the Vice of Splits and Defections*: Keeping in view the non-seriousness which is now associated with valid splits in political parties under the umbrella of Tenth Schedule of the Constitution, it has now become quite pertinent and essential to relate the validity of splits and defections in parties not to the 'party' but to the constituency or the 'electorate' by whose votes the Members find place in the Legislatures. Two conditions have to be, thus, incorporated in the Tenth Schedule and any law relating to splits and defections, *viz.*, in the Representation of People Act 1951. First, it should be incorporated that only those who stand for election and obtain a minimum of 15% of votes of the constituency shall be eligible to take oath and participate in the proceedings of the House. Secondly, a personal disqualification should be imposed on the defectors that unless a defector had obtained more than 25% of the cast votes of the constituency in the election, he cannot on defection or split hold any office under the Cabinet as unattached member of the House or as member of the other party which he has joined.

5

Formation of Government and Hung Parliament

1. THE CONSTITUTIONAL TASK

5.01. The pivot of parliamentary system of government is the Council of Ministers or the cabinet. Its formation is *sine qua non*, something which begins or sets in motion the new government after the elections are over. This follows as a natural consequence of the verdict of the election in the form of majority in the House of People of a party or of a coalition of parties. It may also involve exercise of discretions by the President and vote of confidence for the ruling junta expressed formally or informally by the new House.

5.02. At the close of twentieth century a general election to Lok Sabha (House of People), had been the most exciting public contest in India. The results of the polls extensively draw the attention and excitement of the urban population of the country. Depending on the nature of the role of a person or an observer, the general elections to the Lok Sabha provide a sad or hopeful commentary on political instability or maturity of the country. After the last phase of polling is over, the process of counting of votes starts, the results are declared in the media side by side and the whole counting takes hardly three to four days. Thanks to the electronic multimedia, the people all over India know the trend of the results of elections with reference to their favorite candidate or political parties as the counting proceeds. The excitement as well as the public reactions also reach their climax a little before the final results are announced.

5.02A. It is generally found that the election results for the Lok Sabha are unpredicted, uncertain and quite often the old gainers are losers. No one could have thought of defeat of Prime Minister Indira Gandhi and Congress (I) in 1977 general election to Lok Sabha and her thunderous revival victory in 1980. Similarly, the downfall or watershed in national politics reached by Congress Party in 1988-89 general election when it was returned only as single largest party without clear majority, or the eclipse of the United Front in March 1998 general elections to Lok Sabha, were equally unpredictable. This elements of excitement before the election and the unpredictability of results refer to the constitutional status of the Indian electorate in the process of the formation of Government after the elections are over.

5.03. Since 1990s the political spectrum of India has vitally changed with the emergence of regional parties and frequent splits in all-India spread parties. The splinted units of latter with the State units of the party become regional in character or become confined to respective particular States. These State or region based political parties not only contest State Legislative Assembly elections but also the seats for Parliament from their territories. Since the 1998 these parties are wielding considerable, if not majority representation, in the House of People as compared to the all-India political parties.

5.03A. Now, this phenomenon of regional parties is telling upon the installation of new governments, stability of the Union Government and also upon the nature of interests which Parliament has to protect or promote. The additional question that the country at the beginning of this twenty-first century faces is as to what should be done constitutionally, by making amendment in the Constitution if necessary, to give to the Union Government a stability, that is, a democracy which concentrates on governmental functions rather than on the art and science of manipulating majority for itself in the House of People (Lok Sabha). The problem of frequent elections also has financial implications both to the State and to the election candidates.

5.04. The Constitution was framed in 1950 with the presumption that generally all governments will complete full five year terms, However, the situation has changed since 1989. Now avoidance of fresh elections is a powerful political force which cuts across political ideologies and often combines politics of different shades at particular times. This new political adhesive force is fortified by the reality that elections are costly proposition for the country. In April 1999, it was stated by the Election Commission of India[1] that the mid-term election when held in September 1999, cost about Rs. 900 crores and that the minimum time required to gear up the election machinery comprising of 4.5 million officers and other cadres; and the minimum time required to hold the elections in about eight lakh polling stations spread all over the country was three months after the dissolution of the House of People.

5.05. While a popular government under the Constitution is mandatory for parliamentary democracy, the people's verdict is divided into more than forty parties which at the end of the millennium represent them in Parliament. This makes the political parties as well as the President of India and the people to desist from holding of frequent elections for Union Parliament. As remarked the elections are costly proposition both for the Government and the political parties apart from the results of no-management condition for the country's economy and prosperity. By popular conservative assessment the political parties and candidates normally had spent about Rs. 6,000 crores in 1999 for the 545 parliamentary constituencies. The minimum expense is Rs. 10 lakh per serious candidate and there

---

[1] *The Hindustan Times*, 'Crisis may Cost Country 900 Crores' Anil Anand, New Delhi, April 24, 1999.

are several serious candidates in each constituency. Most of the election funds come by way of donations from business houses who in due course compensate themselves by shifting the burden on public.

5.06. *Durability of Governments*: The Constitution by Article 83 provides a five year term for the House of People with the provision that elections can be held earlier if the House is dissolved by the President. The piquant situation is that while the eleventh Parliament elected in May 1996 lasted 18 months the twelfth Parliament elected in March 1998 lasted only 13 months. In both cases alternative government was not possible. The relativity between the people and the success of political parties is significant in this context. It is true that the electorate in India has been unpredictable and the political parties have somewhat failed to correctly assess and interpret the wishes of the people. At the same time the people who go to vote are not wholly carried away by the loyalty to individuals and look to the performance and promise-failures of those who have been in office. This latter anti-incumbency factor which generally goes against the ruling party has been steadily growing in the electorate. The five year term of the House of People in practice does not depend upon (i) the constitutional provision, or (ii) the professed promises of the contesting parties but on the choice and confidence of the people of each constituency at the time of election which depends on several factors.

5.06A. After fifty years of constitutionalism, the need is now felt and it is, therefore, suggested here that there should be a minimum duration, say two years, of each elected House, only after the expiry of which fresh elections should be held. The *vote of confidence* for a coalition or minority government should require a minimum, say, thirty percent vote only while the no-confidence motion in the Ministry should require a special seventy percent majority during these two years and not simple majority in the House of People. In situations of impasse a national government chosen out of members of Parliament by a constitutional process out of former members of Council of Ministers, based on seniority as Member of Parliament. This national government should function for the minimum duration of the House of People. During this period the U.S. constitutional system pattern under which the Congress can bloc legislative or policy decisions of the government but without censoring its existence should be followed. It may also be made mandatory that certain vital or sensitive issues, like imposition of President's Rule in States, should be taken up only after the assent of President has been taken by the national government. Of course, this will give an additional function to the President which he has by force of circumstances already acquired by now in case of the care-taker governments. The Council of States should also be given a better standing in the matter of financial matters during the tenure of a national government.

2. THE GOVERNMENT FORMATION: NORMAL PROCEDURES

5.07. As the results of the general election get consolidated the Ministry of Parliamentary Affairs[2] of the care-taker Government draws a tentative time-table for the constitution of next Lok Sabha which is followed by the installation of a new Prime Minister and a Council of Minister. For this the Election Commission issues a notification setting out the list of elected Members constituting the next Lok Sabha and this notification is formally presented to the President of India. The President

---

[2] The Ministry of Parliamentary Affairs usually manages the running of democratic processes on behalf of the Prime Minister with a view to strengthen the public and media relations of the government, the contacts with the constituents of a coalition in case of minority government, in the latter case it also functions as Chief Whip of the entire coalition. It also advises the Prime Minister and other Ministries in parliamentary strategies and procedures for consolidating the parliamentary functioning in the interest of the ruling party in normal times. After the election is over the Ministry of Parliamentary Affairs manages the first meeting of the new House of People.

makes a choice of the Prime Minister who recommends a list of his nominees for the Council of Ministers.[3]

5.08. A Presidential Notification follows the selection of Prime Minister, calling the assembly of the new Lok Sabha to which all elected members are formally invited for assuming membership. The President administers the oath to Prime Minister and the recommended members of the Council of Ministers. With the oath-taking of new Prime Minister the caretaker government comes to an end. The President also appoints a *pro-tem* Speaker who is by convention and generally the senior-most member in the new House. In the twelfth House of People, for example, in March 1998, Indrajit Gupta who had won the Lok Sabha election nine times, was appointed *pro-tem* Speaker to conduct the proceedings including the administration of oath to new Members of the House of People till the latter elected its Speaker. He became *pro-tem* Speaker for thirteenth Lok Sabha as well in October 1999. After the election of the Speaker, the President addresses the joint session of the new Parliament and the parliamentary functions are set rolling.

5.09. *Selection of Prime Minister*: The choice of Prime Minister though it rests on the President by Article 75 (1) yet in practice he has little or no option in the matter. In normal circumstances, when a political party has obtained a clear majority, the usual practice is that the party organization nominates its choice for Prime Minister which is thereafter confirmed or endorsed formally by the party's Parliamentary elected group since they have to show their loyalty to the Prime Minister. This name is forwarded to the President who has as yet never in practice rejected or objected to the nominee of such party which has a clear majority in the House. To reject the nomination will be creation of a constitutional crisis for which the Constitution as drafted in 1950 does not provide any solution. Therefore, the acceptance of the nomination is a 'Convention of

---

[3] See, F.N. 5, *infra*.

the Constitution'. However, it can be understood that when the President has been a senior leader of the party which has obtained clear majority, as it was with Indian National Congress till 1972, as well as during Prime Ministership of P.V. Narasimha Rao, he can exercise a behind the scene influence in the nomination at the party stage of the process. At one time or other, Presidents Radhakrishnan, V.V. Giri, Zail Singh or S.D. Sharma who were Congressmen, had exercised their personal influence in the selection of Prime Minister or Ministers of the Cabinet of the Congress Ministries of their period.

5.09. *Public Image of a Minister*: Should Prime Minister or Minister possess a clear and clean public image or record? It is not settled as to how much interference from the President will be forthcoming if a party goes on to select a Member of Parliament with a known criminal record to become the Prime Minister or a Minister. With changing sense of political morality in 1990s a new equation on the possible role of President for clean administration is becoming a popular expectation. In general, President S.D. Sharma was known to have pointed out to the Prime Minister in 1996 to take note of graft charges against the Governor of Himanchal Pradesh *while* earlier she was a Union Cabinet Minister and the Governor had thereafter resigned.[4] This was followed by resignation of two more Governors, of Kerala and of Uttar Pradesh for their earlier

---

[4] *Constitution of India*, Article 155: "The Governor of a State shall be appointed by the President by warrant under his hand and seal." Article 156:

(1) The Governor shall hold office during the pleasure of the President.

(2) The Governor may, by writing under his hand addressed to the President, resign his office.

(3) Subject to the foregoing provisions of this article, a Governor shall hold office for term of five years from the date on which he enters upon his office;

Provided that a Governor shall, notwithstanding the expiration of his term, continue to hold office until his successor enters upon his office.

alleged involvement in graft crimes as former Ministers. It may be mentioned that in 1990s the situation had become alarming when in place of pleasing politicians and MPs for their promotion of their crimes and for safety, the criminals prefer to get themselves elected as candidates of popular and successful parties particularly in States. It is also a sad feature now that a good number of Ministers and non-Minister MPs in India have become involved in pay-off and graft scams and are facing court proceedings.

5.09A. It may be noted here that it was good for the health of democracy in India that in absence of clear prohibition of criminals from contesting the elections to the Parliament or the State Legislatures, the Representation of Peoples Act, 1951, has placed a limited bar on convicted criminals for five years from the date of conviction from contesting the elections and this the Election Commission is now strictly enforcing. It will further improve the health of Indian democracy if the President as appointing authority of Ministers[5] recognizes a convention that those Ministers who have been charge sheeted for any cognizable crime and against whom the proceedings are pending shall not be recommended for appointment as Ministers. The President of India or the Governor of State should refer back for reconsideration such recommendations for their appointment as Ministers as and when made to him. A 'convention' depending on the Prime Minister has now grown that a Minister as soon as he is charge-sheeted before a Court for graft or other criminal charges resigns.[6]

---

[5] *Constitution of India,* Article 75: "(1) The Prime Minister shall be appointed by the President and other Ministers shall be appointed by the President on the advice of the Prime Minister.

(2) The Ministers shall hold office during the pleasure of the President.

(3) The Council of Ministers shall be collectively responsible to the House of People.

(4) Before...."

[6] Cabinet Ministers Buta Singh and Sadapatti R. Muthiah had to resign from Ministry of Prime Minister Atal Bihari Vajpayee in April 1998 when they were charge-sheeted for graft crimes committed earlier.

5.10. The principles discussed in this Lecture are generally applicable to the democratic process both at the Union and in the States since Indian Constitution is federal in character with two tier system of parliamentary democracy. Leading law-making or convention-creating examples can be drawn from both.

5.11. *Formation of Government—Absence of Clear Majority*: (1) Coming back to the process for the formation of Government in situations when no political party has obtained a clear majority, by 'convention' the pre-election coalitions of political parties with a coalition name are treated as single party. The National Peoples Front of Prime Minister V.P. Singh of 1988 and Left Front of Chief Minister Jyoti Basu in the State of West Bengal are such examples. The idea is that all the constituents of such alliance had decided to have one line of action in the matter of formation of ministry after the election. (2) The unified character of the alliance is demolished when any member of a party decides to withdraw from it after the election. The rest of the members of the coalition if they continue will be post-election coalition and will not get precedence over other parties or alliances having greater numerical strength of elected members in the House. As was mentioned in the earlier lecture, the coalition party differs from the single party in the matter of split under the Tenth Schedule of the Constitution of India. The splinter group is required for valid split to show more than one-third strength, of the original party and not of the coalition strength in the House. However, when there is a pre-election *merger* of parties as was the case with Janata Party in 1977 or Janata Dal in 1988 before elections the constituents lose their legal identity after the new party has been recognized by the Election Commission.

5.11. The constitutional aspect of the whole situation is that the President invites the leader of the single party in majority or a pre-election coalition in majority to form the government as Prime Minister. There is never any problem since only one party can have majority in the House and consequently the President has no discretion in this matter. The delay, if any, takes place in the internal process of the winning party in deciding upon their leader. Normally the parties declare the choice of their leader for Prime Ministership at the outset of the election, or else, as mentioned above after the election first at party level and thereafter at the party legislative group level they select their leader. The above procedure was also followed while selecting Atal Bihari Vajpayee (BJP) as the leader of the pre-election National Democratic Alliance (NDA) which obtained clear majority in the thirteenth general election in October 1999. The individual BJP score was 182 out of total 296 seats won by the NDA as against the required majority figure of 273 in the Lok Sabha. The pre-election coalition groups in States, however, in most cases postpone the selection of the leader of the coalition for the sake of maintaining coalition unity till the election is over.

5.12. The same process is followed when there is a vacancy due to death or resignation of Prime Minister. When there is a delay at the party level in selecting the leader of the party or coalition, the President appoints a (acting) Prime Minister for the interlude, as G.L. Nanda was appointed Prime Minister two times, each of 13 days duration after the death of Prime Minister Nehru in 1964 and Prime Minister Shastri in 1966. In both cases the delay was on the part of Congress Party. After the death of Prime Minister Indira Gandhi in 1984, President Zail Singh appointed her son Rajiv Gandhi as Prime Minister and his appointment was accepted by the Congress Party and the Congress Parliamentary Party.

5.13. After the House of People has been dissolved usually the last Prime Minister continues to head the care-taker Government. Under the Constitution there has always to be a Prime Minister and a Council of Ministers to aid and advise the President of India.[7]

5.13A. But, this matter is differently treated for democratic organisation of State machinery since it is not necessary that

---

[7] U.N. Rao *versus* Indira Gandhi, (1971) 2 SCC 63, 67.

there must at all times be a Chief Minister and a Council of Minister to aid and advise the Governor in a State. Under Article 356 of the Constitution[8] there can be a President's Rule under which the Governor as the delegate of powers by the President can have his own advisors and aides other than the personnel of the regular executive and members of legislature. Moreover, Article 163(1) enables the Governor to exercise all or any of such functions which by the Constitution he is required to exercise in his discretion, without the aid and advice of his Council of Ministers.[9] By combination of these two provisions, the

---

[8] *Article 356 (1)* provides:
"If the President, on the receipt of a report from the Governor of a State or otherwise, is satisfied that a situation has arisen in which the government of the State cannot be carried on in accordance with the provisions of this Constitution, the President may by Proclamation—

a) assume to himself all or any of the functions of the Government of the State and all or any of the powers vested in or exercisable by the Governor or any body or authority in the State other than the Legislature of the State;
b) declare that the powers of the Legislature of the State shall be exercisable by or under the authority of Parliament;
c) make such incidental and consequential provisions as appear to the President to be necessary or desirable for giving effect to the objects of the Proclamation, including provisions for suspending in whole or in part the operation of any provisions of this Constitution relating to any body or authority in the State;

Provided that nothing in this clause shall authorise the President to assume to himself any of the powers vested in or exercisable by a High Court, ..."

[9] *Article 163*: "(1) There shall be a Council of Ministers with the Chief Minister at the head to aid and advise the Governor in the exercise of his functions except in so far as he is by or under this Constitution required to exercise his functions or any of them in his discretion.

(2) If any question any matter is or is not a matter as respects which the Governor is by or under this Constitution required to act in his discretion, the decision of the Governor in his discretion shall be final, and the validity of anything done by the Governor shall not be called in question on the ground that he ought or ought not to have acted in his discretion.

(3) The question whether any, and if so what, advice was tendered by the Ministers to the Governor shall not be inquired into in any court."

Governors have often recommended imposition of President's Rule in their State on the ground that there is a failure of constitutional government in the State with or without further recommendation for dissolution of the State Legislative Assembly, the latter power can be independently exercised by them also under Article 174(2) of the Constitution. When the Union Government has a different political party and chances are that the State unit of this party will form the government, this recommendation of Governor for action under Article 356 is readily accepted. The President's Rule under Article 356 is a negation of the concept of parliamentary system of popular government.

5.13B. The position of Governors under the Constitution on the score of maintenance of due standards in maintaining a parliamentary system is occasionally under stress. The Governors being appointees at the pleasure of President do not have security of tenure and can be dismissed or transferred any time for any reason by the Union Government. The Governors have bungled or have earned displeasure of Union Government or disrespect and ridicule from the media and public when placed in tight corners of politics. Except for the brief periods between 1977-1979, 1989-1991 and 1996- to date, the Congress Party had been in power in Union and the Governors have had in these periods the tough task of finding good reasons for imposition of President's Rule under Article 356 of the Constitution in non-Congress ruled States or of preventing the other parties from forming the governments. Similar has also been the task of Governors in the United Front led coalition government at the Union during 1996-98. Similar charges were also voiced against Governor of Bihar in March 1999 during BJP led coalition government at the Union.

5.14. The following leading illustrations are typical and show the fusion of politics and exercise of constitutional powers all of which had the tendency of undermining the democratic parliamentary system in States during the years upto March

1998, when the elected majority party of a State had been deprived of its constitutional right to provide government in questionable circumstances.

First, after second general election Communist party assumed the power in State of Kerala in 1957. This was a development which alarmed all the non-communist parties of India and the opposition political parties of Kerala. The Congress Party, ruling at the Centre, led to a 'mass upsurge' movement led which paralysed the administration all over the State of Kerala. The Communist Party had working majority in the Legislative Assembly of Kerala State but on the recommendation of Governor on the ground that there was complete break down of law and order situation in the State, the President's Rule was imposed in the State in June 1959. Later, mid-term elections were held in Kerala and Congress ministry was formed in February 1960.

Second, in the case of Rajasthan in 1967 after fourth general election of 1967, Congress emerged as single largest party without clear majority. It was unable to form the government immediately while the opposition leader could show clear majority by parading his supporter before the President of India in Delhi. Governor Sampurnanand of Rajasthan who had been a veteran Congressman and also Chief Minister of Uttar Pradesh earlier, recommended President's Rule under Article 356 of the Constitution which was imposed. It lasted for about a month and was lifted when a Congress Ministry with Sukhadia as Chief Minister with the support of independent Members became feasible and was installed. In this whole process the Governor of Rajasthan was severely criticized for his pro-Congress partisan attitude.

Third, The Governor of Andhra Pradesh in August 1984 on change of Congress support from Andhra Pradesh Chief Minister N.T. Rama Rao to opposition leader Bhaskara Rao, over-night appointed Bhaskara Rao as Chief Minister. In this process he denied opportunity to N.T. Rama Rao of proving his majority on the floor of Assembly. Dramatically N.T. Rama Rao proved the support of majority members by parading his supporting members of Assembly in New Delhi before the President. The Prime Minister, Indira Gandhi admitted that the Governor had over-acted and had been hasty, and the Governor thereupon resigned. Subsequently, N.T. Rama Rao proved his majority on September 22 against the usurper and was re-instated as Chief Minister by the new Governor S.D. Sharma. The imposition of President's Rule was avoided by the Union Government by sacrificing the Governor.

Fourth, the composite use of Governor's discretion in appointment of Chief Minister and the powers under Article 356 for imposition or withdrawal of President's Rule for furthering the political interests of the ruling party at the Union in the States can be very disastrous. Uttar Pradesh came under President's Rule since October 18, 1995 and the Legislative Assembly was dissolved. After the general election held in Uttar Pradesh in early October 1996, it was a 'Hung Assembly'. The Governor did not formally call the Assembly and the result of election to the Legislative Assembly which had BJP as the largest single party was kept under abeyance. The Assembly was not called and constituted by the Governor on the ground that he was not satisfied on the stability of BJP Chief Minister. This was noted as a partisan move by the Governor since the United Front Government at the Union was keen that the second largest party, Samajvadi Party which was a dominating constituent of United front, should form the government with outside support. Further, the President's Rule was to expire on October 17, 1996 and could not have been extended. The Union Government revoked the President's Rule and re-imposed it afresh for six months on the night preceding expiry. Simultaneously, the notice for constituting of Assembly was also issued but BJP was not invited to form the government. Later when there was a political understanding between BJP and BSP for partnership under which for six months BSP was to provide Chief Minister and for next six months BJP was to provide Chief Minister and so on, the President's Rule was lifted on March 21, 1997, almost six months after the election had taken place.

Fifth, again, when BJP Government of Kalyan Singh with outside BSP support was 29 days old, the latter party withdrew support on October 19, 1997. The Governor asked Chief Minister to prove his majority on October 21 next. The Chief Minister could prove his majority by a confidence motion, 222 out of 413 members in his favour, with the help of defections from Congress and BSP but there was unprecedented violence initiated by Congress and BSP Members on the floor of the House during vote on confidence motion. The Governor dismissed the Ministry on the ground that it could not maintain law and order and recommended the imposition of Presidents Rule. The High Court stayed the dismissal. The Union Cabinet recommended to the President imposition of President's Rule in Uttar Pradesh on the report of Governor. In an unprecedented but historic action under Article 356 of the Constitution, the President K.R. Narayanan referred back the matter to the Union Cabinet for reconsideration with the note that in his opinion there was no breakdown of constitutional machinery in the State. The Union Cabinet relented and Kalyan Singh remained Chief Minister with the help of stay order of the High Court.[10] The whole episode brought forth the exposure and betrayal of constitutional trust when the Union Government and the Governor are hand in glove in the task of managing affairs of the State according to the plans of the Party ruling at the Union.

3. THE CARETAKER GOVERNMENT

5.15. Under the Constitution the President cannot be without a Council of Ministers and he has always to act on the aid and advice of the Ministers. In this regard Article 74 of the Constitution applies to normal majority government as well as to the care-taker or minority governments. But there may be situations of vacuum, as when a ministry resigns, or after the

---

[10] Paragraph 5.34 and Foot Note 21, *infra*.

elections time is required to form a Ministry. Additionally in the States there may be a constitutional failure of the existing government which necessitates a new Ministry but it may not be possible to do so expeditiously.

5.15A. The President[11] and the Governors[12] have the power to dissolve the House of People or the Legislative Assembly before the five year term is over. However, this power is to be exercised on the recommendation of the Prime Minister or the Chief Minister. By applying the convention of British House of Commons in India, whenever the Prime Minister having a majority and with the resolution of the Cabinet recommends dissolution of the House, the President of India is bound to dissolve the House of People. However, when the Prime Minister has been reduced to minority, the President is not *ipso facto* bound to dissolve the House and he must make an effort to find an alternative government. The opposition leader or leaders must have been approached for this purpose and must have shown inability to form the government or declined. Only when alternative government is not possible, that the President is to dissolve the House on the advice of the existing Council of Ministers.

5.16. The President should not in search of a government

---

[11] *Constitution of India*: Article 83 (2) The House of the People, unless sooner dissolved, shall continue for five years from the date appointed for its first meeting and no longer and the expiration of the said period of five years shall operate as a dissolution of the House;....
Article 85 (2) The President may from time to time—
(a) prorogue the House or either Houses;
(b) dissolve the House of People.
Article 172 (1) Every Legislative Assembly of every State, unless sooner dissolved, shall continue for five years from the date appointed for its first meeting and no loner and the expiration of the said period of five years shall operate as a dissolution of the Assembly;....
Article 174 (2) The Governor may from time to time —
(a) prorogue the House or either House;
(b) dissolve the Legislative Assembly.

[12] *Ibid.*

go in normal circumstances by considerations of stability which has an element of futurology. Many times the stability dogma has been used to prevent the legitimate claims to form he government and to play political games. Stability of a government after elections or on mid-term change over, has lately become a farcical proposition used for political ends and it shifts the burden, initiative and responsibility from the electorate and political parties to the President or the Governor. Of course it is neither prohibitory nor necessary to repeat the offer of forming the government to an aspirant or a party who has been once offered the opportunity of showing majority through a confidence motion and who had failed in the task of securing a majority on the floor of the House. But, when the equations have changed and fresh elections need to be averted the offers can be repeated.

5.17. Following the convention or practice of England, the President can also try for a national government instead of a caretaker government, when several parties with similar ideology or for the desire of avoiding election in near future agree to share the Council of Ministers. In such eventuality the President can take active part in the formation of Cabinet by nominating a Prime Minister, as he does in case of a care-taker government, when the parties are unable to agree on a common leader.

5.18. There is a need for some thoughts on the choice of Prime Minister or Chief Minister when a care-taker government becomes necessary. The need is imperative (a) when the time gap between the term or the failure of government and next election is substantial and (b) also when there is a confusing political maneuvering as to who should head the care-taker government.

5.18A. At present the prevailing practice or the developed precedent is that the President asks the last Prime Minister who has lost the majority, to head the care-taker government. This practice is correct and does not require consideration when the House of People of a State is dissolved on the completion of the five-year term or the ruling party while in majority advises the President to dissolve the House. But when the Prime Minister has lost his majority and mid-term elections have to be held as a result of this the better course for formation of care-taker government would have been to call the leader of the single largest party to head the care-taker government. To illustrate the proposition in practical terms, when Congress (I) withdrew outside support from the United Front government in December 1997 the party position in Lok Sabha was: B.J.P. and its pre-election Allies—187 MPs, Congress (INC) and its pre-election Allies—137 MPs, and United Front (NF and LF) pre-election Alliance—101 MPs. However, the President asked the Prime Minister I.K. Gujral leader of United Front which was the third largest group, to continue as head of caretaker government which functioned for more than four months till mid-March 1998.[13]

5.18B. Though the above action of the President was correct conventionally, it would have been obviously more democratic if this had taken place after the refusal of BJP and Congress to head the caretaker government. Similar anomalies had taken place when Charan Singh in 1979 and Chandra Shekhar in 1991 had headed care-taker governments.

5.18C. In the democratic process in States the misuse of this anomalous constitutional convention has been often witnessed. Recently, in December 1997, the RJP Ministry in Gujarat State suffered set back when Congress withdrew outside support and there was intra-party split also. The Governor dissolved the House instead of asking BJP to form the government and he justified the dissolution on the ground that the Cabinet resolution recommending dissolution was of a date earlier to the withdrawal of Congress support and the party split which left RJP in minority. In this case RJP continued with the caretaker government till March 1998 while BJP had been claiming ostensible working majority in the Assembly and had been seeking opportunity to

[13] Foot note, 23, *Infra.* From December 4, 1997 to March 19, 1998.

form the government before dissolution. After the results of election BJP formed the Ministry in March 1998. In this case, it had been a political fact that the split in BJP Gujarat State Legislative Party had been prompted or blessed by the Congress backed by the United Front Government at the Union and they were politically interested in preventing re-emergence of BJP in Gujarat. This abuse of constitutional power would not have taken place if the caretaker government would have been formed by the single largest party in the State Legislature as suggested above.

5.18D. The point made here is fortified by that which could not take place with the formation of care-taker Union Government in April 1999. On rejection of confidence motion in favour of BJP led coalition government, the situation was that BJP led coalition had 270 members, the Congress Party had 139 members and the Third Front coalition had 133 members. All vied with each other for forming the government till next elections were held. The President appeared to be inclined in favour of the Congress Party which was given open-ended consultation opportunity for forming the coalition or minority government and which could claim only 239 supporters ultimately. But the President had ultimately to take into account adverse political and media reactions to his moves and had to compromise with BJP led coalition for the care-taker government when the twelfth House of People was dissolved on 26 April 1999 after 13 months of its life.

5.19. *The Relationship between Care-taker Government and the President:* This relationship is perceptibly deferent from the normal relationship of President with the Council of Ministers since the House of People is not in function. The caretaker Government is not supposed to take vital policy decisions which generally require approval of the Lok Sabha but if it has to take such decisions this must be done with the added approval of the President since the President of India is constitutionally a part of Indian Parliament, vide, Article 79 of the Constitution.

Such Government must not make important appointments like those of Governor or Ambassadors, or sign treaties or adopt vital new international policies. Where no alternative lies but to act, the consent of President seems to become necessary. For example, the caretaker Government of Prime Minister Vajpayee in May-June 1999, had to face Pakistani intrusion on the borders of India in Kargil Sector and India had to conduct almost a major war. The assent of President to the actions taken by the care-taker Government had become an integral constitutional procedure in this period.

5.20. It stands to reason that the Union Government must always be functional with full powers at all times in national interest otherwise the enemies of the nation whether internal or external will take advantage of the constitutional situation. This was again and again felt by the interim BJP coalition caretaker government. The opposition parties had never failed to criticize the caretaker government for the lapses in decision-making or administration during this period as strategy for the general elections by influencing the voters against the coalition parties forming the Union Government. This naturally meant that the opposition took for granted that there was not to be any line drawn between the powers of the caretaker government and regular government and good governance was always necessary.

5.21. The Tamed Presidency. The Constitution of India as mentioned earlier does not envisage a President's administration of any sort at the Union.[14] There must be a Council of Ministers with Prime Minister at its head at all times to aid and advise the President in all administrative matters. For this purpose, the status of a normal majority government, of a coalition government, of a caretaker government and of a minority government are the same. (a) After Janata Party Prime Minister, Morarji Desai had lost his majority in September 1979, the President invited Charan Singh, leader of breakaway Janata (S) Party to form the government with the condition to prove his

[14] U.N. Rao Case, f.n. 6, above.

majority in House of People within 15 days. Charan Singh had been promised support by Congress (I) before he had laid claim for forming the Government but after swearing-in-ceremony the Congress (I) confronted the Prime Minister with two conditions[15] which he did not accept. Since without the support of Congress(I) Charan Singh did not have required strength, the meeting of House of People was not called. In the meantime, the fresh claim of Morarji Desai of forming the government with support of independents and also of Jagjiwan Ram were rejected by the President. Prime Minister Charan Singh had never won a confidence vote of any kind in the House of People and his party had less Members in the House than Janata Party or Congress Party. He was appointed head of care-taker government in September 1979 by the President N. Sanjeeva Reddy. On the advice of the care-taker Prime Minister, the House of People was dissolved by the President for fresh elections which followed. (b) Similarly, the President sought the advice of Prime Minister Vajpayee for dissolution of the House of People on 25 April 1999 which the Prime Minister after Cabinet meeting rendered next day. The advice was accepted and in sequence the care-taker government under Prime Minister Vajpayee was appointed by the President.

5.22. The 'care-taker government' is a term which refers to the reason for continued existence of a Council of Ministers and the situation that the fresh elections are to be held; otherwise, the constitutional powers of normal government and the care-taker government are the same.

4. THE HUNG PARLIAMENT

5.23. The selection or choice of Prime Minister poses a dramatic situation for the President when there is a 'Hung

[15] The two conditions in general terms were, first, the former members of Congress Party who had turned hostile to Indira Gandhi were not to be included in the Cabinet, and second, on all major political issues regular consultations should be held with Congress Parliamentary Party, before any decision or action is taken.

Parliament', that is, no party has absolute majority after the election. 'Hung Parliament' may also come into existence subsequently when there is a split in the ruling party and as a result of which none of the factions has a clear majority in the House of People. After the election if there is a hung parliament the fault for the situation is no doubt with the parties but it is on the people collectively as well, that the latter failed to give a clear choice or verdict for the constitutional governance of the country.

5.24. *Alternative to Hung Parliament*: Naturally when the verdict of an election is indecisive, the best solution is to refer back the matters to the public. The public should resolve the situation by giving a clear verdict. For extraneous reasons, that is, general fatigue of the political parties after the election is over and economic strains, bankruptcy of parties or financial waste involved in immediately going for another election in a few days, the instinctive approach of public, constitutional administration and the political parties has been to let the parties themselves find a reason to postpone the next election as much as possible.

5.24A. The precedent for future rule in this direction was laid down in 1979, when Janata Party broke due to split, no one, neither the people nor any political party, was in a mood for fresh elections. It was not possible for Congress (I) to form the government and neither the President nor the people wanted elections. The specter of Congress (I) coming back with majority after the election was hateful to most since this reminded people of the troubles of the emergency period. Under these conditions the President invited leader of the breakaway second single largest party, Janata (Secular) Party Charan Singh to form the government on the basis of imperfectly promised support to his party by Congress (I) and the Prime Minister did not call the meeting of the House for confidence motion and tendered resignation but had continued till the elections were over for about six months (171 days) without facing the Parliament.

There was no public or political outburst against the state of stagnating constitutional snag.

5.25. The usual practice in such a case is (a) to let the interim care-taker government to continue, and (b) to begin with the single largest party in exploring the possibility of formation of government followed by other possibilities.

(i) The original precedent in this direction was set in the State of Madras by the then Governor of, Sri Prakasa, after the first general election of 1952. In a House of 351, the Congress had 155 seats, while the opposition parties and members joined, formed United Front with T. Prakasam as leader and approached the Governor with a claim of 166 members. The Governor called the leader of the single 'biggest party', Rajagopalachari though not a Member of either House of the State, to form the government, and asserted that only after the Congress ministry was defeated in the House, he will call the coalition group to form the government. However, some independents extended support to Chief Minister Rajagopalachari and he had won the vote of confidence.

(ii) In the State of Uttar Pradesh, the general election of 1967 provided a hung assembly and the Governor invited C.B. Gupta, leader of the single largest Congress Party with 198 members in the Assembly to form the government in the face of post-election alliance (*Samyukta Vidhayak Dal or SVD*) which claimed 188 seats and support of some independents. Only after Charan Singh defected with some Congress members and became leader of SVD and Congress lost its majority in the Assembly, the Governor invited Charan Singh to form the government as Chief Minister.

(iii) In 1968 in the State of Bihar after mid-term poll, in the elected hung Assembly, Congress, with 118 members out of total 318 members, was as single largest party asked to form the government.

5.26. The Governors' Committee appointed by the President V.V. Giri in November 1970, had been of the view that when no single party has the majority after the election, the Governor has to exercise his discretion keeping in view that the:

> "relevant test for the Governor is not the size of the party but its ability to command the support of the majority in the Legislature. The Governor has first and essentially to satisfy himself that the person whom he invites to form the government commands majority support in the Legislature."[16] For this reason the Committee stated that "the leader of the largest single party has no absolute right to claim that he should be entrusted with the task of forming a government to the exclusion of others" and that "the leader of the party which is in minority in the Assembly may also be invited to form a government without that party necessarily entering into a combination with other parties provided the Governor is satisfied that such a minority party leader would be able to command the support of the other parties in the Assembly for its policies."

It also recommended that:

> "if prior to a general election some parties combine on agreed programme or an electoral understanding that if such a combination gets a majority they will form the government, and if such a combination does secure a majority; the Governor may invite the commonly chosen leader of the combination to form the government, because the electorate in returning such a combination to the Legislature in a majority had already prior knowledge that it would be called upon to form the government. The Governor in inviting such a leader would be acting in accordance with the wishes of the electorate."[17]

5.27. That the claims of a pre-election coalition of parties can be preferred over the claims of single largest party in the matter of formation of Ministry in hung assembly was created

---

[16] *The Report of the Committee of Governors* (November 1971), p. 29.
[17] *Ibid.*

as a principle or precedent in Kerala after 1982 elections. The United Democratic Front (UDF) which was a pre-election coalition of non-communist parties was asked to form the government, while the Governor by-passed the claim of CPI (M), which had emerged as single largest party, to form the Government. This set the status of pre-election coalition on equal terms with political parties. The constituent parties of the pre-election alliance or coalition have two faces constitutionally.

5.28. In State of Haryana when after May 1982 elections 'hung assembly' came into existence, the precedent that single largest party should get preference over post-election alliance. This principle was applied by the Governor of Haryana G.D. Tapase. The Congress (I) could get support of defectors and independents and the Chief Minister Bhajan Lal formed the Ministry and later proved his majority on the floor of the Assembly while Devi Lal alongwith BJP and some Congress (I) fence sitters forming majority in a House of 90 members had paraded his supporters before the Governor one day earlier.

5.29. In the Case of S.R. Bommai, the Supreme Court[18] also recognized that the "Constitution does not create an obligation that the political party forming the ministry should necessarily have a majority in the Legislature. Minority Governments are not unknown. What is necessary is that Government should enjoy the confidence of the House." At the Union, Prime Minister P.V. Narasimha Rao headed a government of this nature from 1991 to 1996. The opposition party confuse the working majority that is, members present and voting in favour, which sustains a government, from absolute majority which is one half of the elected members of the House at any time.

5.30. However, the exercise of the discretion either by President or the Governor in such situation invites severe public controversies. These controversies are at times enigmatic when counter-claims are made by different leaders who often claim

---

[18] Jeevan Reddy, J.: (1994) 3 SCC 1, at p. 276.

the support of same members who are on the fence. Following illustrations are put on record here:

5.30A. (1) In August 1979 Charan Singh with his followers formed Janata (S) Party out of the majority Janata Party, thereafter a hung parliament had come into existence. President Sanjeeva Reddy invited Charan Singh to form the government with outside support of Congress (I), but after assuming office the Prime Minister could not show majority in House of People. Thereafter the President did not invite Morarji Desai again to form the Government. Simultaneously, Jagjiwan Ram also made claim for forming Government. However, the President ordered dissolution of the Lok Sabha under Article 84 of the Constitution on the recommendation of caretaker Prime Minister. This decision has created a precedent but this decision of President in the circumstances of the existing situation was never appreciated.

(2) In November 1989, after ninth general election hung parliament came into existence. President Vankataraman invited second largest coalition National Front to form the government after the Congress leader Rajiv Gandhi had expressly refused the offer.

(3) The National Front forming the Government in December 1990 was reduced to minority on withdrawal of support by BJP alongwith internal split in the Janata Dal which was the main constituent of National Front. The President explored the possibility of alternative Prime Minister instead of dissolving the House and allowed Chandrashekhar, the leader of next single largest party, Janata Dal (S) to form government with the outside support of Congress. After few months this outside support of Congress was withdrawn in March 1991 and on the advice of Prime Minister tenth general election to Lok Sabha was announced by the President.

(4) After the tenth Parliament Assembled in May 1991 it was a hung parliament and the precedent or convention of inviting the leader of single largest party was applied and P.V. Narasimha Rao formed the minority Government for Congress (I) Party.

5.31. President S.D. Sharma had, however, to face a lot of unjustifiable political criticism when he followed the same convention after the eleventh hung parliament elected in May-June 1996. Congress (I) Party was heading the caretaker government The President invited the single largest party BJP to form the government in preference to the claim of post election coalition of National Front and Left Front (NF and LF) as United Front. The United Front and Congress combined as against BJP Ministry which was required by the President to prove its majority by a confidence motion within 15 days in the House of People. The BJP failed and the United Front formed the government under the leadership of H.D. Deve Gowda, a non-MP and Chief Minister of Karnatak State, with the outside support of Congress.

5.31A. The interaction of party politics with constitutional requirements for caretaker Government exemplified by the above episode of eleventh Parliament is highly significant. The action of the President in first inviting single largest party to explore the possibility of forming the Government in May 1998 immediately dislodged the care taker Congress (I) Party Government of Prime Minister P. V. Narasimha Rao. The Ministers of this government had become infamous for the corruption charges against them and the Party had fared badly in the elections. Congress (I) Party was happy for heading caretaker government but it was third largest party after eleventh election. It wanted the stalemate to continue, being capable of playing with the art of surviving as a minority Government. The Congress(I) Party combined with United Front in preventing a BJP led Government but it gave outside help to United Front Government. Soon the Congress (I) Party showed dissatisfaction with Prime Minister Gowda and withdrew its outside support from United Front in April 1997 but later agreed to restore the outside support for United Front if I.K. Gujral was to be compromise Prime Minister, in order to avoid a general election. On this point the President in his own rights significantly intervened.

5.31B. It became a constitutional precedent when President S.D. Sharma invited I.K. Gujral to form the government only with the condition that the United Front and Congress agreed in writing apart from the time limit for proving required strength on the floor of the House. The document of agreement was officially conveyed by the convener of United Front to the President. Under the agreement a two tier co-ordination mechanism was created in order to ensure stability of I.K. Gujral Ministry. There was to be, first, a committee of Prime Minister and the President of Congress for direct consultations, and secondly, a parliamentary coordination committee constituted of 10 members each of Congress and United Front drawn from the MPs. This mechanism which was prompted by the President was viewed by commentators as a constitutional innovation in itself.[19] However, from the newspaper reports of the events, it appeared to be a political face saving device by which President, who had been a stalwart Congressman himself, bailed out particularly the Congress from the mess created by the then Congress President. Inspite of this coordination mechanism, the Congress withdrew support and the I.K. Gujral Ministry fell in December 1997.

5.32. The innovation was not repeated during the search and identification of ruling party after the hung parliament again came into being after twelfth general election held in March 1998, but it may be kept in shelf and applied subsequently in the formation of coalition government by minority groups. Nevertheless it emerges and signifies an element of 'pleasure' of President under Article 75 (1) and (2) of the Constitution. In the appointment of Prime Minister A.B. Vajpayee after twelfth general election of May 1998, the question mark of stability was very cautiously and tangentially applied by the President when he asked BJP nominee to supply in written form the support from its alliance parties, irrespective of consideration whether

---

[19] S. Muralidharan & J. Cherian, "A Constitutional Innovation", *Frontline*, May 16, 1997, 27; *The Hindustan Times*, April 22, 1997.

the latter would join the Cabinet or not. The idea was that only that government could be stable which had absolute majority, but after a few days the BJP, even though short of absolute majority in the written form, as the single largest party was invited to form the government.[20]

5.33. This kind of search, as earlier stated, in State politics and the process for formation of coalition governments was generally referred to as 'stability' factor in the choice of Chief Minister. However, since 1990s it has become necessary that President and Governors should be at least empowered to prevent making of mockery of elected government. There has taken place (i) a lowering in the political morality, (ii) induction or forced entry of unconvicted criminals in significant numbers into the politics and the State legislatures through elections, (iii) lack of knowledge of constitutional principles or the rules and conventions of the parliamentary democracy in the MPs and MLAs and (iv) a development of the instinct in modern politicians of insisting on doing things which are prohibited by law without changing or amending the law.

5.33A. These maladies were the real issues before the public in the twelfth general election and the elector did succeed in cutting the feathers of localized or regional parties which were furthering the interests of social bullies. It may be recalled that calling of information on particular issues or referring back matters for reconsideration by cabinet or placing conditions for proper working of a coalition before a Prime Minister is appointed, are constitutional functions of the President which he can perform independently of the Council of Ministers. These principles also apply *mutatis mutandis* to the Governors when formation of Government in States is involved.

5.34. *Stability Qualification for a New Ministry in Hung State Legislature:* While at the Union the stability qualification for a Prime Minister has been a development from late 1970s, the

[20] Foot Note 23, *infra*.

stability qualification in the case of State Council of Ministers has had a brisk application rather from the inception of the Constitution. The Union Government and the Governors have combined to couple the State democratic process and the formation of State Ministries with the concept of stability. Such phenomenon has been possible more so because of the powers of Governor and of the Union Government under Article 356 of the Constitution. The concepts of Article 356 bring with them a considerable degree of discretion for the Governor and Union Government in mid-term dismissal of a Council of Ministers even though it may have a numerical majority in the State Legislature. The imposition of President's Rule in the State is only an extension of the administration by the ruling party of the Union Government in the State. This process is always in conflict with the collective responsibility of the Council of Ministers to the Legislative Assembly and the rights of the elected members to direct the Ministry and to pull it for non-performance or failure to give results as desired by the people in a democratic way. The Governor and the Union Government usurp the functions of the Legislative Assembly by the misuse of constitutional powers under Article 356 of the Constitution.

5.34A. During the last fifty years of freedom of the Country the frequent dismissal of State Ministries by the Union Government on the report of failure of constitutional government by the Governor has been felt to be the most abused part of the Constitution. The stability concept has been frequently used for denying to a political party the right to form the government in the State, where the Governor uses his anticipatory or future-knowing powers to say that since the ministry shall not be stable, therefore, President's Rule should be imposed or should be continued in the State. In a power hungry world this in effect means the Governor ruling with the help of his advisors in close collaboration with the Union Government. In the previous pages the height of ignominy reached by the United Front Government at the Union and the Governor of Uttar Pradesh was alluded to, when after the general election completed in the

State early in October 1996, the Legislative Assembly was not constituted and thereafter from October 18, 1996 to March 21, 1997, no Chief Minister was appointed, because the Union Government and the Samajvadi Party did not want BJP to form the Government in Uttar Pradesh and were happy with continuation of President's Rule which was in effect United Front rule in Uttar Pradesh.[21] The Samajvadi Party was an important constituent of United Front Ministry at the Union.

5.35. However, the President has steadily followed at the Union the principle of inviting the leader of single largest party and then the next (second) largest party and so on, in the matter of formation of Ministry in circumstances of Hung Parliament and has left it for the House of People to decide whether they accept or reject the government in minority. For this the Prime Minister is required to prove his majority by means of confidence motion or no confidence motion for which usually 15 days time has been prescribed but this time starts *after* and not *before* the swearing-in-ceremony of the Prime Minister. This practice was started before the Supreme Court decision in Bommai Case[22] of 1994 which laid down the principle with finality that where practicable the majority of a party should be tested on the floor of the House only. This was to be done in subversion of other processes, like 'head count' or deciding on the choice by looking into list of supporters provided by the leaders in waiting. Of course as mentioned earlier, the pre-election alliances are treated at par with single parties but not post-election alliances.

5.36. There are consistent precedents at the Union level consolidating above practice on the search for a Prime Minister in hung Parliament.

(i) When in 1979, Prime Minister Charan Singh failed to muster his majority after he was sworn-in as Prime Minister, even the House of People was not convened

[21] See, foot note 10 *supra*.

[22] S.R. Bommai *versus* Union of India, (1994) 3 SCC 1.

for proving the majority, it was dissolved on the advice of Prime Minister and the mid-term sixth election for House of People was announced by President N. Sanjeeva Reddy.

(ii) Again, in November 1989, after ninth general election the President invited Congress and on its refusal the National Front to form the Ministry and prove its majority in the House which it did by a confidence motion.

(iii) Similarly, after National Front Ministry was reduced to minority by defection and withdrawal of outside support by BJP, JD (S) Party leader Chandra Shekhar was invited to form the Government and prove his majority on the floor of the House of People, which he successfully did.

(iv) After tenth general election, Congress as single largest party was in May 1991 invited by the President Venkataraman, it formed the Government and completed the term with the help of outside support of United Front and abstention at the time of confidence motion or no-confidence motions of those members and parties which did not want fresh election.

(v) In 1996 same procedure was followed by President S.D. Sharma. First, within one hour of submission of list of elected members by the Election Commission he invited the leader of BJP the single largest party to form the government and to prove the majority within 15 days, the House of People was convened and after long debates Prime Minister A.B. Vajpayee sensed that he could not muster majority and resigned before voting for confidence motion. After that the President invited the leader of United Front to form the Ministry and prove the majority within 15 days. Prime Minister H.D. Deve Gowda could prove his majority with the outside support of Congress Party.

(vi) In March 1998, after the twelfth election the BJP was asked as a preliminary step by the President to supply a list of its supporters showing absolute majority, before A.B. Vajpayee was asked to form government. It could prove its majority by a confidence motion on the floor of the House within stipulated time and functioned for thirteen months.

(vii) When the AIADMK withdrew support on April 14, 1999 from BJP led 18 member post-election-coalition Ministry which had survived one majority test in the 1999 budget session in the meantime, the President K.R. Narayanan asked Prime Minister Vajpayee to seek a vote of confidence from the House. The Coalition Ministry immediately resigned when the confidence motion was lost in the House of People by one vote 3 days later, with 269 in favour and 270 against. The resignation sets a finest example of democratic spirit.

In all of the above cases of the formation of Ministry at the Union when there was 'hung parliament' the President did not apply the subjective principle of stability but followed the political theory principle of democracy, that is, it is for the elected representatives to be satisfied for the formation of a Ministry and to remain satisfied for the continuation of a Ministry.

5.37. However, an improvised form of stability criterion was attempted to be applied in favour of second largest party, Congress (I) Party in this case, by President K.R. Narayanan after the twelfth general election to the House of People in March 1998. In the new hung Parliament, the single largest party BJP was asked to provide written commitment of support from its political allies for proving its absolute majority in an outside-floor-of-the-House-process which would show absolute majority, that is 270 out of 539, before it was formally invited to form the government, unlike as had been done in June 1996. The BJP took time or failed apparently and in the meantime the President consulted Congress and also the third single largest coalition party United Front. Both showed their inability to show 270 supporters and refused to align into a coalition. In the meantime the BJP had submitted documentary evidence which showed less than the required absolute majority number, 270, but the number nevertheless maintained it as single largest alliance if nineteen parties and outside support of three parties, it was invited to form the government[23] and to prove majority within ten days.

5.36A. If the decision for fresh election for dispensation of a stillborn House of People or a situation of impossibility by the sovereign people of India by giving a reconsidered clear verdict was possible, it was observed by the people that the third largest coalition of parties, United Front, would have continued as a caretaker government, as a legacy. The alternative as suggested earlier would have been to invite the single largest party, BJP, by the President.[24] to form a caretaker government.

5.37. *Politics of Avoiding Elections:* However, as the politics of the time showed, the Congress Party was not in favour of another follow-up election and the new Congress President stated that the immediate priority of the party was to reorganize itself for survival as well as for increased inner stability. It is thus an independent-of-politics situation that political parties link elections with their own fatigue and future prospects rather than with the considerations as to who will form the government. In May 1996 to July 1998 political scenario, the Congress (I) Party even refrained from criticizing the policies of arch-rival BJP Union Government in a bid first to reorganize itself. However, in April 1999, it dared to form a government with 139 Members in Lok Sabha and led the opposition to a confidence motion moved by the Prime Minister in favour of BJP led nineteen member Coalition Government. After the defeat of confidence motion by one vote, Congress Party was invited to form the government as second largest party by the President but failed as it could muster support of 233 Members only as against 270 Members supporting BJP led existing Coalition. The House of

---

[23] Foot Note 13 and 20, *Supra*

[24] Foot Note 23, *Supra.*

People was dissolved and the Coalition Government continued as caretaker Government till the thirteenth House of People assembled in October 1999.